'Beautiful, entertaining diary of the writer's quest to turn a neglected allotment and a concrete urban wilderness into places of beauty'   *Daily Mail*

'[Elspeth Thompson's] canvas is restricted – a diminutive London garden and an allotment – but she delightfully recounts the splendours and miseries of her gardening life. She writes beautifully and hers is exactly the kind of book that makes happy converts to the most agreeable of all occupations'   *Sunday Telegraph*

'Elspeth Thompson's delightful little book is just the thing to slip into a gardener's muddy stocking if you see it hanging up to dry on Christmas Eve . . . A charming potted history of Elspeth's gardening life'   *The Lady*

'Her writing is pure delight – light-hearted and knowledgeable with a casual charm and style – and very much of today'   *Anthony Noel*

'A new voice in garden writing: unpretentious, witty and refreshingly unsnobbish'   *New Eden*

'Combining humour with practical advice and anecdotes, Elspeth's experiences will both encourage and entertain gardeners, whether novice or experienced . . . Illustrated throughout with beautiful and humorous line drawings'
                                        London Magazine

Urban Gardener

Elspeth Thompson

ORION

The Sunday Telegraph

An Orion paperback
First published in Great Britain by Orion in 1999
This paperback edition published in 2000 by
Orion Books Ltd,
Orion House, 5 Upper St Martin's Lane, London WC2H 9EA

A CIP catalogue record for this book is available
from the British Library.

ISBN: 0 75283 723 0

Printed in Great Britain by
The Guernsey Press Co. Ltd, Guernsey, C.I.

Acknowledgements

I shall always be grateful to those at the *Sunday Telegraph* who made the *Urban Gardener* column possible: Lucy Tuck, Rebecca Tyrrel, Giles Kime, Elfreda Pownall and Melissa Denes; to many others for their behind-the-scenes editing and layouts; and to Clare Melinsky for her beautiful illustrations.

On the ground, as it were, I owe huge thanks to my sister, Sarah Thompson, and to my dear friends Simon Steele and Michael Clark, whose enthusiasm, hard work and humour have been invaluable at the allotment. Thanks also to my other sister, Rebecca Edwards, to Jacque, Steve and Conor, and all the other friends who have lent a hand in return for a marrow and a few lettuces. To all my fellow plot holders, some of whom figure (lightly disguised) in this book, I owe enormous gratitude – for the advice, the spare seedlings and the sense of silent companionship.

I would like to thank all those in the gardening world whose encouragement and inspiration has meant a great deal, particularly Mirabel Osler, Valerie Finnis, Frances Lincoln and Melanie Eclare. Also Susannah Charlton at Telegraph Books and Caroline Oakley and Juliet Ewers at Orion, whose hard work has enabled the columns to come together as a book.

Finally, I must also thank my husband, Frank, who, though he prefers to appreciate gardens from a deckchair with a beer in his hand, has not only helped with the heavy construction work at the allotment, but also provided endless comfort and encouragement when the slugs and bindweed have got me down.

For my parents

Introduction

The travel writer Martha Gellhorn once remarked that no-one really wants to hear about the wonders and successes you have encountered abroad, and that 'the only aspect of our travels that is guaranteed to hold an audience is disaster.' In many ways, the same principle holds true when it comes to gardening: rave about your old roses and the stunning colour combinations in your borders and eyes will glaze over; mention a slug epidemic or that your dog has chewed your prize clematis and you get instant smiles and sympathy.

I have real reason to be grateful for this aspect of human nature. Three years ago, I was sitting in a pub garden despairing over how I was ever going to write this new column when the builders had wrecked my embryonic back garden and my new allotment looked like a rubbish tip. The wise advice of a long-suffering friend was that which has been handed out to writers since time immemorial: to tell it like it is. This I have tried to do – but it took me quite a while to realise that the mistakes, failures and frustrations, alongside my mini-triumphs, would be a major factor in the degree of success that this column has enjoyed.

For as long as I can remember, I have wanted to write about gardening. I was born just a few miles from Sissinghurst in Kent, and the idea of creating a garden and writing about its progress has been one of my few real ambitions in life. I had always assumed, however, that this would have to wait until I had a big garden in the country and knew a good deal more about gardening – simply because that's what proper garden writers did. I had always lived in flats in inner London, where my gardening – though passionate –

had been confined to pots and containers on cramped rooftop spaces. When, in 1996, I bought a house with a tiny garden and took on my first allotment, it was to provide myself with a training ground – the space to learn more and practise more in preparation for that move to the country where the big garden (and proper garden writing) could begin in earnest.

But, as any gardener knows, things don't always happen according to plan. I had only had the allotment for a few weeks, and had yet to move in to the new house, when the then editor of *The Sunday Telegraph Magazine*, for whom I was writing regularly about other subjects, asked me to write a column from the point of view of the gardening amateur. She had heard me telling stories about the allotment – about the contrast between the 'new gardeners' such as myself, with their packets of rocket, paranoia about pesticides, and pretensions towards fancy potagers, and the 'old timers' with their neat, weed-sprayed rows of onions and deep cynicism about organic methods – and thought it would be a good way to liven up the magazine's gardening page. The idea had dawned on me, too, as I strove to carve the back garden of my dreams out of twenty feet square of solid concrete, that this, rather than rolling rural acres, was what many newspaper readers had to deal with. No one seemed to be writing with city gardeners in mind. And so the *Urban Gardener* column was born – and with it my career as a gardening writer, a good twenty years ahead of schedule.

In the beginning, I was terrified – scared that *everything* I had sown at the allotment would die, leaving me with bare soil and a totally blank page. But as spring moved into late summer and my first crops flourished, my confidence and enjoyment grew with them. Three years on, reading through all the columns to edit them for this book, the excitement of that first summer does seem to leap off the page. And whenever disaster *has* struck – in the form of blackfly on my beans, cats in the back garden or slugs devouring all my lettuces – I can now see that it has often provided the best copy. The only solution seems to be to keep a sense of humour in adversity and the numerous letters of support and recognition from readers in response to my teething troubles have been both a solace and a source of valuable advice.

I now find it impossible to imagine living in the city without this constant contact with nature. Yes, I still dream of a large garden with a view of fields or even the sea beyond, with more than one small tree and space to grow vegetables closer than a ten minute bike ride away. But until that happens, I am content to keep toiling away here in town, where gardens and those little patches of municipal green here and there seem so vital, so cherished and so utterly necessary. I have become passionate about these urban oases – whether front or back gardens, parks, squares or allotments, even a far-up fringe of green on a scruffy tower-block. Somehow, flowers look even more beautiful against a backdrop of grey: a balcony spilling over with red pelargoniums in a grim council estate; billowing white cherry blossom above streets of parked cars. There is something almost heroic about daffodils pushing up through tarmac – and in the activities of some of the people I've met who achieve similarly unlikely feats in their passion to encourage nature to thrive in the most unprepossessing surroundings.

Happily, urban gardening does seem to be on the increase. Whether rooted in a desire for better flavour, concern about pesticides and genetically-modified crops, or a half-unconscious desire for closer contact with the earth, many more city dwellers are experimenting with growing their own food, either on allotments (where they can still find them) or in tubs and raised beds in their own back yards. Garden centres, garden designers and garden TV programme makers have never been so busy; estate agents cite outdoor space as one of the prime requests of property buyers. Talking to my own friends I've sensed a yearning for a closer connection with nature – when I started out at the allotment I felt like something of an oddity; now more and more people are coming down to help or doing it for themselves. For the first time in history, compost making is deemed an acceptable topic of conversation at a London dinner party.

Gardening in the city has been good for me in all sorts of ways. I definitely feel fitter and the physical activity is much more fun than going to the gym. The hours of quiet work in the open air – either alone in silence or chatting with a friend – provide a peaceful respite from the pace and pressures of urban life. It is good for my state of mind. I have often felt helpless in the face of the world's environmental crisis, the destruction of the rainforests and the extinction of so much fauna and flora. Somehow, doing what I can in my own little patch helps me feel more hopeful... We *can* all make a difference. The sight of birds outside my study window as I write is a real joy – there were none when we arrived here three years ago. It's worth remembering that, while, in the countryside, new roads and buildings and modern farming methods have been destroying habitats for wildlife, our urban back gardens are providing safe havens for some of the creatures and plants that have been displaced. When you consider that the total acreage of domestic gardens in the UK is greater than that covered by all our nature reserves, this is quite a resource to be reckoned with. The old Green Party tenet, 'Think Global, Act Local', is as true as ever.

Most of all, though, the gardening and the writing of this column have been great fun. In effect, I have been paid to learn and I shall always be grateful to those at *The Sunday Telegraph* who took a chance with the idea initially and who have encouraged me ever since.

Sitting at home now in April, looking out of the french windows at ropes of *Clematis montana* strung like bunting around the little back garden, and watching clumps of lavender come into fuzzy new bud, I can see how far this little garden has come since we first saw it, wall-to-wall red concrete with a fine crop of chickweed coming up through the cracks. We look set for a good year at the allotment, too, with a new wildlife pond (which I hope will soon be a home to slug-eating frogs and toads) and some smart new beds and paths. But there is a whole lot left to learn. As is so often the case in life, I feel the more I know, the more I know I don't know: how to prune roses properly, stop my lettuces bolting or get to grips with ground elder just for starters. There are times when I feel totally bewildered and don't know where to start. But then, right on cue, nature comes up with the goods: a shaft of sun on a line of late lettuces or the first datura bloom. And then I remember exactly why I do it, and put my dreams of an acre or two in the country on hold in the face of the beauty right here and now in the city.

Elspeth Thompson, April 1999

1996

28 April 1996 ~ The Allotment

It's a long time since I've been this tired and this dirty. I have not taken up mud wrestling (though to look at me two hours ago you might have thought I had), nor some other grubby hobby. No – I have just taken on an allotment. It happened quite suddenly, the way alarming new commitments sometimes do, but London allotments are like gold dust and previous vain attempts to secure one have taught me that you have to be on the ball. One minute I was at a party, chatting to my friend Sarah about her plot in the part of south London to which I'll be moving next month – she thought there might be one free. Next thing I knew I was down there myself, signing my agreement to a ferocious set of rules (plots to be kept cultivated and weed-free on pain of confiscation; pets under sufferance; visitors by strict permission only), and handing over the princely annual rent of £19.80 for – a pile of rubble.

It was our own fault. I'd gone along with my boyfriend, Frank, who had nobly volunteered his considerable manpower for what I think he then considered another of my foolhardy schemes, and my sister, who for a share of the harvest had agreed to lend a hand with the heavy work and with watering in high summer. We were shown

a perfectly good allotment that had recently become free and was in need only of a little light weeding. In the back of my mind I suppose it wasn't quite what I'd had in mind – no little shed, bordered by a busy road on one side and on the other three by intimidatingly professional-looking crops that made me and my *Organic Vegetables for Beginners* handbook suddenly feel shy and inadequate. But I was quite prepared to go for it until the man with the clipboard uttered the fateful words: 'There is another one I could show you, but you won't want it.' Says who?

Off we trekked across the little turf paths between embryonic onions and pubescent red rhubarb, past rickety cold frames and rusty water butts, until we reached the opposite corner of the site.

'That's it. Number 26,' he said, shaking his head.

The ground was uneven, and the few patches of soil visible under the mouldy red carpet, holey groundsheets and strewn plastic bottles were thick with couch grass and brambles. About a third of the plot seemed to have been used as a tip. But it was peaceful and private, away from the roar of the traffic, and bordered on the west side by a hawthorn hedge (imagine a little wooden bench there, to sit on in the shade on summer evenings), and, to the south, a tall fence (can't you just see it strung with runner beans, sunflowers and morning glory?). More importantly, the soil, under all the carpet and debris (which even I knew would have kept down the worst of the weeds), was dark, soft, slightly crumbly and full of fat pink worms.

'Let's take it,' I said.

The next weekend we all turned up for action, feeling rather conspicuous with our shiny new spades. Twelve hours, two bonfires and a turf war with our neighbour later (all quite amicable, and we won), and two-thirds of the plot was roughly dug over and clear of rubbish and weeds. We left just as the sun was going down over the hedge, and in the low orange light the neat little plots with their bamboo stakes and skip-timber sheds had a kind of make-shift, shanty-town beauty. I know I am going to love this place.

5 May 1996 ~ The Allotment

For a balcony gardener such as myself, one of the major challenges and fascinations of allotment gardening is the matter of soil. No longer is it something I buy from the garden centre in neat plastic sacks carrying an unwritten guarantee that anything planted in it will grow. Instead, it is just there, something to be coped with, adapted to and, perhaps most alarmingly to a novice, diagnosed. A childhood spent on a farm of Kentish clay led me to suspect the soil on my new plot to be a little on the clayish side. This was born out by an experiment in my current favourite reading matter, *Organic Gardening with Love* by Thelma Barlow (subtitle: *Coronation Street Star Shares the Secrets of Her Organic Garden*; jacket photo: smiling Thelma in what looks like spotty pyjamas, striding through her organic garden with mobile phone glued to one ear and carrying a basket of strawberries) (see p. 243). Thelma suggests taking a small handful of soil, moistening it and trying to roll it into a ball: if you can't the soil is sandy; if you can and the surface can be rubbed smooth, there's a high proportion of clay. You can then do various further experiments rolling the soil into sausages and seeing if they bend: the best soils bend a little and then break, which is what mine did, after a little encouragement.

I was in need of cheering up, my first one-to-one encounter with the new soil in my life having suggested it contained a high proportion of rubbish and not a lot else. I'd plunged in the spade with gusto only to meet a Marks & Spencer's carrier several inches beneath the surface. Moving the spade several feet to the right yielded another polythene bag; to the left a pair of plastic bottles. When we inspected further, the whole of this raised third of the site was, in fact, just layers of refuse thinly covered with soil. We'd been had! The allotment committee has promised to help us clear the area with a mechanical digger, but I doubt if the soil at the bottom will be up to much, so I have plans to try hay bale gardening there. You put down bales of hay, which must be kept very moist, add a layer of compost and plant on top: as your crops grow, the hay rots down gradually, improving the soil beneath.

Gardening books, particularly organic ones, are packed with such trendy ideas. One of the most tempting is the 'non-dig' garden, but that's not for me this year, as I missed out on improving the soil last autumn and need to dig in plenty of well-rotted organic matter right away. Actually, digging is great fun, and my boyfriend, my sister and I go great guns in a rotation system with the two spades: the person who's not digging grubs up the weeds and puts the less terrifying ones on the compost heap. On a previously abandoned patch like this, you never know exactly what you're unearthing – I recognised thistles, thrashing brambles with rope-like roots that were yards deep, lots of nice nettles for compost and an alarming amount of couch grass, whose severed white roots were as plentiful as the poor severed bodies of worms we'd decapitated; both will live to tell the tale. There were also some peculiar roots like knobbly brown hands, with little shoots poking out the top, which looked vaguely familiar. Friend or foe? There was nobody to ask. The only other person we saw all day was our left-hand neighbour, who turned up just as I was putting my coat on to give my sister a lift home in reward for her sterling day's work.

'Typical, innit?' he said, pointing to my boyfriend, who was still working up quite a sweat in the middle of the patch. 'Minute there's a bit of heavy work to be done, the women are off like a shot.'

Leafing through Thelma later that evening in the bath I realised why those brown, hand-like roots had looked familiar. They couldn't have been asparagus crowns, could they?

12 May 1996 ~ From Balcony to Garden

As I prepare to leave this central London shoe-box for a house south of the river, I realise it is the balcony that I shall miss most. This might seem odd, considering I am about to acquire my first ever proper urban garden, but a decade of fiddling about with pots above the rooftops has left its mark on me. Before this I lived in a flat above a busy row of shops which had a south-facing asphalt terrace that I filled with flowering shrubs and bright annuals in old tin baths and fire buckets. In summer we used to haul the furniture out through the windows and sit reading the papers while passengers on the double deckers waved at us through a screen of sunflowers.

Since then, things have got smaller but a little smarter. At ten by five foot, this balcony is less than a quarter of the size of the terrace, but it looks out over a tree-filled park, with a wall-to-wall view of green leaves in high summer. It is sheltered by the balcony of the flat above – a major advantage over a garden in bad weather – and some of the best memories I shall take away are of watching, safe and dry, as a summer storm thrashed around the sky and sheets of rain lashed a few feet from my face. The south-east aspect makes it a sunny spot for breakfast while the city kick-starts itself to life below. There's nothing like a quiet perch above it all for starting the day in a good mood.

Such is my love for this balcony that I have lavished on it the only major DIY operation I have undertaken since moving here three years ago. While kitchen shelves still languish unfixed, and I have learned to live with the avocado bathroom, the balcony got a completely new look last spring. It didn't start out as a huge project – just a lick of fresh paint on the floor. But in that sneaky way that DIY jobs have, it all got out of hand. First I had to move the twenty or so pots inside – earwigs and all. Then, once the floor of the balcony was repainted, the walls and ceiling looked a dingy grey by comparison so I had to do them too, balanced on top of a stepladder, gripping the paintbrush in one hand and a drainpipe in the other, trying hard not to look down. This was where I should have stopped, but suddenly the idea of painting black and white chequers on the floor seemed rather smart. I had forgotten that floor paint takes forever to dry. More than a week later, the novelty of sleeping surrounded by a jungle of pelargoniums had long worn off when two coats of yacht varnish solved the problem.

When it comes to plants, I have not been particularly adventurous, believing that a restricted range and colour scheme has more impact in small spaces than a little-bit-of-everything. In spring, there are different types of daffodil and white hyacinths in pots, some of which can be brought inside in succession as they come into bud; in summer, scarlet pelargoniums, sweet peas and nasturtiums; with morning glory, clematis and a rampant passion flower trained up the walls, and some crazy echeverias and succulents that thrive in full sun on the ledge. But my policy (basic to any form of container gardening) of frequent summer watering and a twice-yearly renewal of soil (just the top few inches if the tubs can't be emptied), together with liquid seaweed feeds throughout the growing season, has been well-rewarded. Last summer's triumph was a crowd of creamy *regale* lilies, grown from bulbs to nearly four feet tall, breathing their heady scent on June evenings beneath a string of candle lanterns. Yes, my new garden will be exciting. But it's the large flat roof, four floors up and with views from Telecom Tower to Crystal Palace, that I'm most looking forward to.

19 May 1996 ~ The Allotment

Going down to the allotment recently has been like playing a game of Grandmother's Footsteps. No matter how regular and industrious my own appearances, someone else always seems to have been doing something much more impressive while my back was turned: a smart new runner bean support has sprung up here; a row of newly-planted young globe artichokes there; and major earthworks are underway by the gate as a series of raised vegetable beds take shape. The warmer weather brings people out in droves – the recent bank holiday, when I was out of town, yielded all manner of new features, including several fruit-cages – like little rooms constructed entirely from skip timber and bird netting – and a nifty plastic polytunnel in which my right-hand neighbour is now raising exotic vegetables.

Seldom do I witness any of this activity myself: apart from a few hazy figures in the distance, my only regular contact is with the above neighbour, who kindly offered me his surplus 'Pink Fir Apple' seed potatoes to plant, and a friendly Indian gentleman who often breaks off from work on his immaculate patch to come over for an encouraging chat. 'I like you English women. You work hard!' he exclaimed to my sister and me, as we slogged away at the weed-encroached strip along the fence, where we have now planted beans to grow up strings attached to the stakes. (His own wife, sensible woman, makes a graceful guest appearance at the end of each day, when she parades up and down the rows in her sari, inspecting the crops and placing her order for supper.)

As is often the case with allotments, the plots are divided between the old guard, who tend to grow their crops in the traditional system of straight rows with narrow paths in between, and the 'raised bed' crew, usually younger and keen on organic methods, who construct beds of around three by six foot out of planks of wood and fill them with sacks of compost or manure. According to my books, this method is supposed to result in a higher yield and less of a battle with weeds, but it involves a lot more initial work. On our plot, I have decided to go for a mixture of the two, so that I can compare their effects. This is not purely in the interests of science: filling ten sacks of rotted manure from a dung heap at the local city farm (as much as you can dig out for a donation to funds) was such an exhausting and deeply smelly experience that I'm going to have to find another cheap source before embarking on making any more beds.

In the meantime, we have made a start sowing in old-fashioned rows, trying to keep to the basic crop rotation recommended in all the books. This has meant dividing the cleared half into three main areas, each of which will have root vegetables for one year; legumes and salad crops the next; and then brassicas (broccoli, cabbage, sprouts etc.), in succession, with another area for courgettes and sweet corn. So far we have sown one row each of radish, beetroot, lettuce (cos, lamb's and 'Year Round'), two types of spinach and a patch of rocket – the ultimate urban gardener crop and a gift from a friend – which are all looking encouraging. I have also put in some mangetout and broad beans, in shallow trenches lined with rotted manure, which seem to be doing all right, though I know I should probably be worrying about birds and slugs. The first sight of the beans, pushing their white, hump-backed shoots through the soil, made me feel like James Dean in *East of Eden* when he throws himself at the ground in sheer joy at seeing his crops begin to grow.

26 May 1996 ~ The Allotment

Thou shalt not covet thy neighbour's shed – but I do. Ever since we took on this allotment, I have been hankering after the ramshackle shed, built out of old window-frames and skip timber by one of our neighbours, that runs along its eastern boundary. Unlike many other allotment sites, where such sheds form part of the makeshift, make-do landscape, here they are few and far between. One of the many rules by which tenants must abide is that no structures taller than three foot can be erected – presumably because of the shade they might cast on adjoining plots.

Some people, somehow, seem to have found a loophole in these rules, one of whom is our neighbour – perhaps by virtue of the fact that he has a small, regular part as a market trader in a soap opera on the television. I imagine the glamour brought to the allotments by such association may have persuaded the committee to turn a blind eye. The powers-that-be show little lenience, however, in the matter of weeds, and I have already been told about several cases (usually involving youngish inexperienced types like myself), who have had to relinquish their plots because they let them go to seed. Over the last couple of months since I arrived, it has come to everybody's notice that the plot belonging to my soap-star neighbour has fallen into a sad state of neglect, and is bristling with thistles, bindweed and ground elder. Indeed, we have only seen the chap once, when he pottered in his shed for an hour and then went home. Apparently, his absence is due to a sudden increase in the soap's market scenes, but whether the Weed Police will be sympathetic, I do not know. Last weekend, two members of the committee were patrolling his plot and talking about official warnings. If the hatchet should fall, I am unashamedly ready to move in.

Shedless in the meantime, I have either to cart all my gardening gear around with me or leave it in the communal corrugated iron pre-fab between visits. Goodness knows how people with posh cars manage; my ancient VW camper van has turned into a garden shed on wheels, stacked to the gunwales with earth-encrusted tools, sacks of manure, and boxes of fish meal and calcified seaweed. I have grown accustomed to the smell, but my boyfriend says it is disgusting and is threatening to boycott the vehicle until the situation improves.

This is likely to be some time as – in for a penny, in for a pound – I have hit on the idea of using the van as a mobile greenhouse as well. During all those weeks when spring never sprang, I have been raising trays of basil, coriander, sweetcorn and sweet pea seedlings, as well as young tomato and courgette plants, along the ledges of the little kitchen in the back. Skylights in the roof mean the van gets maximum light, unlike the windows in my flat which receive direct sun for only a few hours a day. When the street where I'm parked falls into shadow, I just trundle the van round to the other side of the block. It's well worth the bemused looks from passers by at watering time.

My only concern is that the van's MOT is looming and that, to have even the slimmest chance of getting it through, I shall have to clear everything out. Still, if it fails, I suppose I could just drive the van right on to the allotment and use it as a shed for the rest of its rusty days. I bet its built-in fridge and cooker would make it the envy of the entire site.

2 June 1996 ~ The Land is Ours Campaign, Wandsworth, South London

'Just look at that. Beautiful!' says John Pendragon, pointing at a clump of blood-red aquilegias as proudly as if he'd grown them from seed in his own garden. Behind them, bluebells and wild geraniums nod in the shade of a gorse bush, and drifts of orange poppies and buddleia stretch down to the banks of the Thames, where a banner emblazoned 'Land and Freedom' flaps in the morning breeze. Sounds of laughing and singing carry from several hundred yards away, where a group of young people in bright ragbag clothes are drinking mugs of tea round an open fire. Mangy dogs weave a procession between tents and canvas benders.

John Pendragon could be anything between thirty-five and ninety. His battered brown face is beautiful, long and sad, and matted greying dreadlocks, well past his shoulders, give him the air of a Biblical sage or Indian yogi. A member of the self-styled 'Rainbow Tribe', he is a veteran of the Twyford Down, Solsbury Hill and Newbury road campaigns, and one of the founders of the 'Land is Ours' occupation of the former Guinness distillery in Wandsworth, south London (see p. 246).

Just one week after the protesters arrived, there is already evidence of the campaign's intention to transform the derelict thirteen-acre site into a 'sustainable village with gardens and public amenities'. Just past the entrance is a miniature Stonehenge made from old bricks and planted with pansies and petunias. An octagonal wooden meeting house and half-built geodesic dome dominate the main public area, and a series of impromptu gardens is taking shape around them. Raised vegetable beds have been constructed on the poor stony soil, filled with manure and compost and planted with sunflowers, sweetcorn, beans and lettuces; marigolds and violas brighten up the borders. Some have neatly lashed fences to keep the dogs off; others have low walls made from rocks and rough lumps of concrete daubed in bright colours. There are handpainted signs: 'Permaculture for the Planet'; 'All about companion planting'; 'This vegetable bed was prepared with love and a sense of humour and NO FUSSING'. A Heath Robinsonesque irrigation system, rigged up from plastic water bottles, old drainpipes and lengths of holey hose, dribbles water from the mains supply by the gate, and there's even a tepee greenhouse clad in clear polythene.

'It's great,' says Ben, an earnest-looking chap of about twenty, who is transplanting some young courgette seedlings donated by a well-wisher. 'I didn't even know what a daffodil was before I came here last week, but you learn a lot working with other people. Me and my mates are gonna do this outside an old closed-down factory in Manchester when we go back home.'

Perhaps such inspirations will be the project's most lasting legacy. Following a recent court hearing, it seems likely that the camp will be evicted before long, and that a branch of Safeway may eventually rise from its ashes. For John Pendragon, it's the wild area, designated a 'nature garden', with string barriers to discourage straying from the path, that will be the greatest loss. He leads me past compost lavatories and a painted 'healing tent' to a quiet corner where we find bearded irises, dog roses, laburnum, wild strawberries, and the clump of red aquilegias, which have self-seeded here, undisturbed, for decades. 'This is what we stand to lose with our build-build-build, buy-buy-buy culture,' he sighs. 'We can grow vegetables and make gardens in other places. But proper, wild nature like this takes years. In the end, I don't mind if we have to move on, but if this has to go...'

9 June 1996 ~ Home

Starting even a small garden from scratch is not a cheap business, and a recent thumb through the cheque stubs makes me think I might as well have buried our holiday money in the borders. My sister, who inherited an established garden with the house she recently bought, is revelling in that glorious series of surprises that comes with the first spring and summer in a new place – not a week goes by without some hidden shrub bursting unexpectedly into bloom, or bulbs pushing through where she'd assumed there was only bare earth. My own new garden – a classic urban back yard of about twenty square feet with high brick walls – is rather a different affair. The delights here will be of my own making, as the previous owner, perhaps more inclined to decorating than to gardening, did no more than whitewash the walls and lay a large, uneven slab of red concrete in the middle. When we arrived two weeks ago, the flower-beds around the sides were spilling over with a fine crop of chickweed and nothing else.

A blank canvas certainly has its advantages: no dodgy shrubs I wouldn't have chosen myself but would feel heartless grubbing up, and a real chance to experiment. But even a tiny space such as this can gobble up funds, especially in the hurry to get some plants in before too much of this summer slips by. My first idea was to stir together seeds of some of my favourite flowers – night-scented stocks, love-in-a-mist, sunflowers, white snapdragons, nasturtiums and sweet peas – sow them willy-nilly in the borders and see what happened. In the end I went for a more long-sighted approach, improving the soil by digging in ten sacks full of well-rotted horse manure, covering the walls with custom-built trellis (much sturdier and cheaper than ready-made stuff, but it took my father, my boyfriend and me the best part of a week to erect it and paint it white), and putting in as many climbers and tall border plants as I can afford. The long-term vision is that, when the french windows are opened from the kitchen/sitting room, it will be like looking out on to another decorative room, lit by lanterns and lined with scented plants that will waft in wonderful smells on sultry summer evenings.

I have tried to be economical. I have traipsed off to Columbia Road flower market at unearthly hours for basic climbers at half the garden centre prices (two *Clematis montana* and a couple of other clematis, a pair of well-established jasmine plants, a climbing hydrangea for the north wall and some evergreen honeysuckles). A rampant passion flower and some other clematis have transplanted well from my previous balcony, and there haven't been *too* many trips to the garden centre 'just for a packet of seeds' that got out of hand. My weakness, however, has been rare plant sales and nurseries. Egged on by an ingrained distaste for mean planting, I have allowed a sort of *folie de grandeur* to take root, and have bulk-bought white-spotted foxgloves, named delphiniums and other glories to plant in drifts of five, seven and nine in the borders. I have also splashed out on far too many pricey lilies (the last time I economised on lily bulbs they came up a garish yellow instead of the white I wanted). Provided they all do well it will be money well spent, but the problem with investing in plants – as those who suffered last summer know only too well – is that they can so easily shrivel up and leave you with nothing to show for your money. A week away on holiday and it could be out with the cheque book all over again. Perhaps it's just as well that, at this rate, we won't be able to afford to go away till winter.

16 June 1996 ~ The Allotment

Taking on an allotment in the spring, as I did, might seem like good timing, but it means that the first few months are terrifically hard work. All the clearance and ground preparation that established plotholders have carried out at their leisure over the winter, has to be done alongside sowing and planting and – in my case – frantically consulting the books to ascertain how, when and where things should be done.

After what seemed, at times, to be backbreaking effort, two-thirds of the plot is now in cultivation. The remaining patch, which backs on to the hawthorn hedge and is two foot deep in compacted rubbish, still awaits the attentions of the allotment committee Hedge Team, who are heroically working their way along the length of the hedge, collecting skip-loads of rusty tin cans and ancient shopping trolleys. Unfortunately for me, they began at the top of the site, and it looks as if it will be late summer or autumn before they reach our end. But perhaps that's not so much of a problem after all, as there's more than enough going on, even without the extra few yards.

Looking at the plot from my favourite perch by my neighbour's shed, it looks pretty encouraging, if slightly schizophrenic. The first sowings were made in traditional rows on the left hand side, but I have since become rather sold on the notion of a patchwork of small, square, raised beds on the right, with criss-crossing narrow paths in between. Keeping to the same basic crop rotation as on the other side, I have divided these into three sections of six squares each, with spring onions, more rocket, lamb's lettuce and baby spinach in the top section, and two squares of radishes that will make way for transplanted purple-sprouting broccoli seedlings; and in the second section, more broad beans, mangetout, peas and french beans, together with a patch of coriander and room for later sowings of lettuce.

The remaining area has been saved for courgettes and sweetcorn, raised in peat plugs and planted up in small pots in my van, then transplanted into well-manured soil when summer finally arrived. The sweetcorn seedlings, which look like small scrolls of green crepe paper, seem to be benefiting from Blue Peter-style cloches made from sawn-off plastic water bottles. I've also planted some seeds of both courgettes and corn straight into the soil, with a bottle over each sowing to aid germination. It will be interesting to see how the crops compare: my experience so far has been that things fare better if sown in the place where they are ultimately going to grow.

Quite early on, a mysterious chap a few plots down from me, who enters and leaves the site by vaulting over the hedge, leather cowboy hat pulled down over his eyes, knapsack on back and blue-eyed husky dog in tow, gruffly offered me enough spare lettuce and turnip seedlings to feed the entire population of Watership Down for a year. I painstakingly planted them in, trying not to disturb the fragile roots, and followed up with a weak seaweed feed, but the lettuces were soon overtaken by those I'd sown in situ, which will shortly be big enough to eat. Thinnings from the original rows were also held back, in spite of a dose of Dr Bach's Rescue Remedy (yes, you can even use it for plants). A perfect example of what the books call 'suffering a check'.

My latest passion is a sturdy young pumpkin plant grown by friends on their smallholding in Wales. I have been feeding and fussing over it, in the hope of raising a real giant and being added to the gallery of local paper stories on the walls of the communal allotment shed.

23 June 1996 ~ The Allotment

For the first couple of months, tending the allotment seemed all-consuming. In many ways it was like the early stages of a love affair. It took up all my time. Even when I wasn't with it, I thought about it incessantly, wondering what my peas and lettuces were up to without me. My social life suffered, as I cancelled weekends away to be with my new love, and bored all my friends with my wide-eyed enthusiasm. Even my sister (normally a very sane individual) with whom I share the plot, got the bug. Goodness knows what we used to talk about before we got the allotment – our recent communication has degenerated into endless answering machine messages about watering schedules and germination times. People thought we were going a bit mad. Sometimes, we wondered about it ourselves.

Now, however, I am pleased to report a return to normality. The spate of wet weather in late May helped. Light drizzle is one thing, but not even I was prepared to brave it to the plot in a thunderstorm. The rain also interrupted the obsessive need to water, though it's easy to forget to feed plants when they're getting a daily dowsing.

Basically, though, the period of frantic activity is over. Of course, there are all sorts of jobs to be done, including major projects such as constructing a lean-to shelter and a proper compost heap in the rubbishy, uncultivated end of the plot, making a cold frame out of old windows from our new house, and establishing a strawberry bed in a previously weed-filled border. But now that the first crops are in and growing, the main work is confined to watering, weeding (lots of nasty bindweed spears to nip the moment they poke through the soil), and picking out stones from the beds to line the paths.

Most importantly of all, the allotment has started to give something back for all our efforts. The other weekend we ate our first home-grown salad – silky, lime-green lettuce leaves, peppery rocket and spinach thinnings, with some rather impressive-looking radishes that were a fantastic glowing red and nearly three inches long. It has been a long-standing ambition of mine to be able to cut salad straight from the garden and eat it at its absolute freshest and best, secure in the knowledge that it has not been sprayed with pesticides thirteen times – the fate of most shop or market-bought lettuce. Unfortunately, we cancelled out any major vitamin gain by accompanying the salad with a large home-delivery pizza, but it was delicious all the same. I am already looking forward to the first peas.

By the way, an unexpected, but very welcome side-effect of having the allotment is a marked upturn in my health. Through no extra intentional effort, I have lost half the stone I put on after giving up smoking three years ago, and the fresh air seems to have given me a healthy glow. Everyone keeps remarking on how well I'm looking. They may still think I'm mad, but compared to what I used to do to keep fit – jump up and down to Madonna at seven-thirty in the morning and run like crazy on a treadmill to nowhere – it seems perfectly sensible to me.

30 June 1996 ~ Home

'It's most important that you should never be able to see all of the garden at once,' says Sarah Shurety, brightly. 'You want to create some mystery, some atmosphere, the feeling of being led from one area to another.' We are standing on the back steps of my new house. In front of us, the twenty square feet of my walled yard roll away majestically, with all the mystery of a mini municipal car park. Miss Shurety continues, unperturbed. 'The path out from the house should be curved, and must be wider as it leads into the garden,' she says. I look at the four cast concrete steps and scratch my head.

Sarah Shurety is not making these suggestions for mere aesthetic reasons. She is a practitioner of the ancient Chinese art of Feng Shui, which holds that the way we organise our living spaces – from the orientation of doors and windows right down to the positioning of our furniture – can have a dramatic effect on our energy levels, finances and general good fortune. Feng Shui for buildings and interiors is fast gaining in popularity in this country (Marks & Spencer and British Airways are among the companies said to employ consultants). But I had not known that the principles could also be applied to gardens until The Feng Shui Company (see p. 245) got in touch to suggest a visit.

I had secretly hoped for an Oriental-looking person in long flowing robes, so it was a bit of a surprise when Miss Shurety stepped over the threshold in her trim blue suit and matching briefcase, as brisk and efficient as a young bank manager. She wasted no time in setting about her task. The pond that I had planned to make in the left-hand corner was apparently a very good thing. 'That's the wealth area,' she explained, 'so flowing water will be very beneficial. Stagnant water equals stagnant finances, so have a little pump fountain, and make sure the pond is the right shape – curving towards the house.'

Curves are very much the thing with Feng Shui – creating much better energy than the straight lines in which my new garden abounds. Curved paths, curved ponds, curved flowerbeds – even the tops of the white wooden trellis I'd put up around the walls should ideally be cut at 'what we call a happy angle' – sweeping up and down between the posts. A mirror on the wall that faces the house (the area relating to fame) would be good for my career, thought Miss Shurety. If we want children, we should hang a windchime in the centre of the right-hand wall. And how about a love-seat in the 'relationships corner' (top right as you look out from the house)? Rather confusingly, the relationship area 'goes on holiday' every year and is now also to be found in the middle of the left-hand side of the garden, precisely at the point where the neighbourhood cats choose to scrabble over my wall. A statue was the ticket here, and I made the mental note that it could also serve as a springboard for the cats, limiting the damage to my climbing plants.

Apart from the fact that if I were to follow all her advice, my tiny garden would look like the crowded corner of a chi-chi garden centre, my yard apparently didn't present major problems in Feng Shui terms. Apart from one. According to Miss Shurety, the corner of a tall house diagonally opposite to the left is sending vicious 'cutting *chi*' (the Feng Shui equivalent of Darth Vader's light sabre) right through the garden and the rooms overlooking it. In China there have been court cases involving banks that position their offices precisely so as to send this zapping *chi* out to their neighbouring competitors, with a view to bringing on financial ruin and general misfortune. My first floor bedroom was said to be particularly badly affected, and anybody staying in it would be prone to illness and arguments. The remedy? (The nice thing about Feng Shui is that there is always a remedy, usually involving mirrors, crystals or wind chimes.) To place a series of silver balls on the tops of the trellis supports on that side. Over my dead body, I thought, with a shudder. But three days later, having had the mother of all arguments with a builder in precisely that bedroom, I'm not so sure...

7 July 1996 ~ The Allotment

Disaster has struck in the legumes patch. While the allotment is now yielding enough lettuce to supply at least a dozen restaurants, the peas and broad beans are hopelessly behind and host to a variety of

pests. My neighbours have been harvesting their peas for weeks – indeed, the park warden who cultivates the plot diagonally opposite mine has had to put up what looks like ancient goal post netting, about eight feet high, to provide extra support for his rampant plants. 'It's a French variety. Grows to at least six feet tall,' he says, kindly offering me some delicious crisp pods to chew as I poke a few sticks into the ground for my own miserable seedlings, which are struggling to make six inches.

Part of the problem is that I sowed them late. Many of the books suggest a first sowing on St Patrick's Day, at which time the allotment was just a pipe dream. We sowed peas, mangetout and broad beans towards the end of April, in blocks about a yard square, in soil that was well-dug and manured. Not only did they take several weeks to come up (on one occasion my sister caught me grubbing about to see what had become of them); of the few that eventually surfaced, at least half mysteriously vanished, seemingly overnight. Wondering if mice might be to blame – we see them from time to time, scampering around my neighbour's compost heap – I made a second sowing. By the time the new peas came up the weather was warmer, and my watering visits more frequent, so I was able to detect the culprit. The tiny folded leaves were notched all the way round with tiny bite marks – the work, so the books tell me, of the pea and bean weevil, which can demolish young seedlings in a matter of hours.

Traditional organic repellents include spraying with a nicotine mixture, which you have to make up yourself as it's now illegal to sell it. Apparently, a favourite pastime of a particular type of small boy is to pour droplets of the brew on to tiny insects and watch their immediate and agonising demise. Effective though the stuff sounds, the thought of boiling up fag ends scavenged from the local pub did not appeal, so I sent off to a mail order company for some organic plant-based pesticide which I thought might also help with the blackfly infestation threatening to obliterate the broad beans. Two weeks later, it has yet to turn up, but the peas, paltry in number though they are, seem to have cast off the dread weevil and recovered of their own accord.

The blackfly is another matter. At times, the urge to dig out the bottle of chemical zapper spray I kept as a last resort for use on the balcony in my old flat has been almost uncontrollable, but I can't fall at the first organic hurdle. Squirting with soap and water has helped (soft soap from hardware shops breaks down the aphids' protective covering but won't harm ladybirds), and I'm now pinching out the growing tips of the beans as soon as the tell-tale grey smudges appear. I've also tried a bit of companion planting and have set some young nasturtium seedlings among the beans. The idea is that black-fly like snacking on nasturtiums even better and will leave the broad beans alone. The trouble is that I am very fond of nasturtiums, and this seems rather like throwing them to the lions, so I've started to spray them as well. I'd better toughen up, or we won't have any beans at all.

14 July 96 ~ The Allotment

The atmosphere down at the allotment over the past couple of weeks has been almost party-like. The combination of sunny weather and crops that need harvesting has brought folk out in hordes, and there are often more people standing around chatting than there are working on their plots. Everyone has a different routine. Some like to make a day of it, sauntering about in a leisurely fashion and stopping for frequent breaks. An old Turkish gentleman who I'm told is a retired judge, manages to spin out his packed lunch and Thermos of tea all day, consuming them on a wooden bench near the main path, where he can exchange news and pleasantries with all who pass by. Others, like my right-hand neighbour, favour lightning strikes of devastating efficiency. He whizzes round watering his two plots in the space of half an hour, picking peas or strawberries and pulling out stray weeds as he goes, and then tears off again, leaving the plants quivering gently in his wake.

Not everybody uses the whole of their plot to grow vegetables. Some have little fenced off beds for flowers. A white-haired woman at the top of the site has had a wonderful show of roses, foxgloves and delphiniums all summer, while others, myself included, have sown a row of giant sunflowers in a sunny border. My friend Sue, who lives on the tenth floor of a tower block, has turned her plot into a surrogate back garden, with flowerbeds around the edge, a small vegetable patch at one end and the rest laid to lawn. She is most often to be seen sunbathing on a lounger with her nose in a book, oblivious to the hive of activity on all sides. But she still manages to leave with a bundle of rhubarb or a couple of lettuces under her arm.

Furniture comes in all shapes and sizes, from beautiful handmade benches to plastic sunloungers or old office chairs from skips. Everyone has something on which they can rest their weary limbs and watch the world go by. One couple have a matching set of table and chairs on which they lay out lunch with great ceremony – they must have the freshest salads in town. The chap with the husky dog who gave me the turnips has built a swing for his six children down by the hedge, while a Telecom engineer and his father have slung a hammock between two trees. The son says he likes it so much he used to come and sleep down here last summer when it got too hot in his house.

I try to time my own visits for the early evenings, when I come to water and pick some spinach or lettuce for supper. When all the work is done, I sit in the late sun and survey the patchwork of crops with quiet excitement. One of my neighbours might stroll over for a chat, and if they're the type who likes dishing out advice, I might throw out a question about my runner beans or courgettes. The sense of camaraderie among my fellow plot-holders has been an unexpected bonus of having the allotment, and I've surprised myself by the degree to which I've entered into it all. Though I don't know the names of many of them, still less the details of their day-to-day lives, for the few hours we're here, we are united by our odd enthusiasm, each engrossed in his or her little patch as the rest of London rushes by around us.

21 July 1996 ~ Continental Town Gardens

Landscape gardens and suburban lawns are all very well, but recent travels in France and Italy have left me thinking that we trail far behind our continental neighbours when it comes to urban gardening. What most European cities lack in comparison to our huge urban parks and back gardens, they more than make up for in the flamboyant use that flat-dwellers make of their own few square feet (sometimes even inches) of roof or balcony.

In Venice this spring, no roof was without its skyline fringe of green, and every balcony or window ledge was a cheerful jumble of potted plants. They were not just the ubiquitous red pelargoniums and trailing lobelia, either; I spotted blood-red snapdragons, feathery marguerites, ice-blue plumbago, and unusual-looking succulents that poked fat fingers through ornate metal grilles.

The gorgeous architecture helps, of course. There is no doubt that red pelargoniums are better set off against peeling amber stucco than sooty English brick or concrete. The sunnier climate must also encourage growth. But from Normandy to Naples, even the humbler back streets which get little or no sun are decked out with plants, all lovingly watered by hand at the end of each day, the colours fighting with bright lines of washing strung out to dry. In Paris and Milan, the darkest and dankest courtyards glimpsed through gates from the street, are crammed with pots of ivy, peace lilies and other shade-loving plants – with perhaps a trickling fountain to help dispel the gloom.

There is often something gloriously haphazard about these potted urban gardens. The containers themselves tend to be quite makeshift affairs – black plastic straight from the garden centre or old tin cans given a lick of bright paint every spring – a far cry from the tasteful terracotta that abounds in Chelsea or Edinburgh. In Greece empty olive oil cans, painted blue and filled with pink or red geraniums, sing out against the simple white angles of the houses; in Spanish towns the courtyard walls are dotted with pots like living flowery wallpaper. Throughout Europe, restaurants without a screen of plants round the street-side tables look somehow under-dressed – like a person who has forgotten to don a vital piece of clothing in the morning.

European town gardening tends to be outward-looking. Window boxes are most often planted to be viewed from the street, rather than from inside; some are particularly ambitious arrangements incorporating tiers of pots and songbirds in cages – while the plant-crammed courtyards give pleasure to passers by and neighbours alike. The British, on the other hand, never too hot on civic pride, still aspire to the 'home as castle' principle in our urban back gardens, clinging to an illusion of privacy as we sunbathe in full view of the entire street and try to screen out the racket made by our neighbours' children/radio/electric strimmer.

In this country, 'extrovert' town gardens tend to be the preserve of pub terraces or a few industrious eccentrics – such as the owners of the house at the top of Portobello Road in west London that is almost completely obscured by hundreds of pots and creepers, or of the flat in Percy Circus near King's Cross whose one window on to the square is decked out in an elaborate tiered arrangement of psychedelic annuals each summer. But what joy they bring. There is room for so much more.

28 July 1996 ~ The Allotment

For the past few weeks, the allotment has been a quiet refuge from the ravages of builders, who have taken over the whole of our new house. Its continuing productivity has provided me with cheerful consolation for the disasters going on at home. People who have gone through this sort of thing themselves will know how foolish it was for me to have even begun making a garden when major building work was about to start. The builders have used the yard as a rubbish tip and store for spare supplies – as I look out of the window now there are hundreds of lengths of uncut timber, copper pipes and architraves, all stacked up against the wall in an arrangement that almost totally screens my plants from sun – and from me. My attempts to weed and water do not help – the builders think I am crazy to be tinkering about with plants when there is so much work to be done inside. I asked them to put their stuff somewhere else – and my boyfriend even put up a discreet notice asking them to be careful of the garden, but builders seem to take great umbrage at such suggestions, and the practice soon resumed. Quite miraculously, few of the plants seem to have suffered too badly, though I fear many may be stunted.

So off I go to the allotment for an hour or two's peace, where the only things giving the plants a hard time are birds (the broccoli seedlings) and blackfly (the broad beans, though the situation is improving). My favourite jobs are watering the giant pumpkin plant, which is sending out curly tendrils in every direction, and encouraging the runner beans to get a grip on their wires. I had been feeling rather smug about my beans, having planted them out at the exact point when the weather turned warm (many of my neighbours sowed too early and lost their young crop). But now they have slowed up — overshadowed, I am afraid, by the giant sunflowers behind them, which I planted in the early days when I was still unsure whether I'd be able to get anything else to grow.

Inspired by Anna Pavord's brilliant book *The New Vegetable Garden* (see p. 243), I imagined a decorative bed filled with different varieties of lettuce, with the heads of the sunflowers poking between the strings of runner beans. The trouble is, I had banked on the beans getting a head start up the wires before the sunflowers got too tall, while the very cold spring meant that the sunflowers were already at waist height when it was safe for the beans to go in. Now they are almost eight feet high and look like something out of a child's illustration of *Jack and the Beanstalk*, their enormous leaves making great lozenges of shade directly over the beans. If they showed any signs of flowering at all, I wouldn't mind, but they just keep producing more and more leaves. Either they are heading for fifteen feet, with blooms the size of dinner plates, and will get me into the local paper, or they are destined to be flowerless sunflowers and a total waste of space. I must think positively, and look forward to the day when the builders in the back garden are no more, and a vase of giant blooms sits on the kitchen table, and the garden is growing away like mad outside the new french windows.

4 *August* 1996 ~ The Allotment

I have grown rather accustomed to solitude in our little patch at the bottom of the allotment site, so it was something of a shock to hear a voice just a foot away from mine on the other side of the fence from where my runner beans are planted. 'Better get a bit of weedkiller down here, mate,' it said, and there was a rustle in the brambles and undergrowth. I coughed and as I stood up, I came face to face with two of the squaddies from the Territorial Army centre next door. It's about time they carried out a clean-up: I've become rather fed up with the thistles and bindweed that creep in from the weedy patch beyond their tarmac parade ground. When I asked them not to encroach on my lettuces and beans with their weedkiller they saluted and clicked their heels.

The first round of crops I sowed back in April and May is just finishing and, like a mother hen saying goodbye to its chicks, I'm slightly possessive about letting them go. I've grown attached to the rows and patterns they make, and part of me wishes they could stay in the ground always. Like many first-time vegetable growers, and in spite of attempts at staggered sowings, we had far too many lettuces ready all at once. It almost broke my heart to pull up the ones that had gone to seed, even though they were towering above the rest like tottering lime green pagodas. The square yard of rocket that kept us in sharp, peppery salads all summer has had to go since it sprouted white flowers and became very bitter, but there's already more on the go. I think I'll keep a few heads of flower to collect seed: rocket is one of the few allotment crops that saves you considerable amounts of money for very little effort. £1.50p or so buys you a small bag of leaves in the supermarket, while a seventy-nine pence packet of seeds yields row upon row upon row of the stuff – thinning happens as you eat it, and the more you pick, the more you grow. Spinach is another good deal – the block of 'Perpetual Leaf Beet' we sowed back in May must have yielded ten pounds or more of leaves so far. As long as you don't take too much from each plant, it will have grown back by the next time you appear, two days later.

Surplus produce has come in very handy recently for taking round to local friends in return for a hot bath while the builders have been putting in the bathroom. Most popular have been the football-size bright purple turnips (though nobody seems quite to know what to do with them other than leave them on their kitchen tables looking beautiful) and the ruby chard, which I grew mainly for decorative purposes, its scarlet stems and veins glowing like stained glass in the sun. It won't be long till we can offer sweetcorn and courgettes.

However, now that the gaps between the lettuces and turnips are more frequent than the crops themselves, it will soon be time to transplant more seedlings from the far end of the plot, where I have a small seed bed among the potatoes. I've also been given endless packets of seed for winter crops – cauliflower, cabbages, Brussels sprouts – which could go in before too long.

So it's back to digging. The other night my sister and I were at the allotment till eight making space for new plantings in the sun-baked soil. As work drew to a close, the sound of a snare drum spattered across from the yard next door. It was the TA boys practising on parade. We slung our spades across our shoulders and marched to the gate.

11 *August* 1996 ~ The Allotment

The heatwave has turned the allotment into a real urban jungle. The lone pumpkin, ablaze with bright yellow flowers and swelling fruit, is romping through the back section of the plot and weaving its wild, tendrilled arms between the dozen or so sturdy sweetcorn stalks. The two lines of giant sunflowers, heading for twelve foot and still just about defying gravity, look like something out of a sci-fi film. As for the young courgette plants I put in six weeks or so ago, they have also suddenly taken on triffid-like proportions and are threatening to engulf everything else. I put in four seedlings raised in the back of my camper van, and sowed another eight *in situ*, which I reckoned would be a suitable number to see us through the summer. According to my neighbour, though, four is all it takes to feed a family, so we shall have something of a glut. Perhaps I might open up a market stall from the back of the van.

Watering has become a full-time occupation in the sweltering heat. Hoses are banned on this particular allotment site, which means endless trips to and from the nearest water-butt, arms swinging down like a chimpanzee under the weight of a pair of large watering cans. Luckily for me, this is only a hundred yards or so, and pleasantly bracing for the biceps, but those with plots a long way from water have been rigging up contraptions involving four watering cans, a wheelbarrow and lots of string. Every so often, intent on our rounds, we hear a thud, a slosh and a burst of swearing as another load falls short of its destination.

In hot weather, a daily watering trip is needed if we are not to find grave casualties on arrival, and the experience is often so exhausting that there's little energy left for weeding or other tasks. Latterly, I have taken to dragooning friends down to help, in return for as much spinach, lettuce and french beans as they can carry. This is all very well, but they tend to want to bring a few beers down and make an evening of it, which means that not a great deal gets done. One day the other week, I slogged up and down to the water-butt what seemed like a hundred times, while a small cocktail party gathered in the shade of the hedge and an over-enthusiastic dog skittered between the 'Lollo Rosso' lettuces, covering their frilly pink leaves with a fine layer of earth.

The alternatives to this chaotic and time-consuming state of affairs are perfectly illustrated by two of my neighbours. One has given up completely, letting his entire plot revert to thistles, dandelions and a rather attractive form of waist-high daisy. The other, a young chap of whom I am rather in awe, has built a sensible mulching system into his method of cultivation. At first I couldn't understand how he got away with so little watering. Then he explained that all his crops are planted into holes cut into sheets of black plastic that are tucked into the edges of his raised beds. All he has to do is water directly into the planting holes and the soil will retain the moisture for a good few days. 'That's what we'll do next year,' I say to my sister, as we enviously eye up his glossy aubergines and burgeoning leeks.

'If there is a next year,' she grumbles, rubbing her back with both hands.

18 *August* 1996 ~ The Allotment

It is almost impossible to be taken seriously on an allotment without a compost bin, so I am relieved and delighted to report the delivery of a very fine example of the genre, made for me by my boyfriend as a belated, if not madly romantic birthday present. Its design – two adjoining square bins with walls of slatted wood – is based on the rather ritzy one featured in *Terence Conran's Garden* DIY (see p. 244), but instead of the fresh new planks favoured by Sir Tel, we have used some ancient tongue-and-groove panelling that came down when we recently knocked two rooms in our house into one. Very smart it looks, too – though sufficiently home-brewed to win the approval of the 'makeshift and make-do' philosophy that is part of allotment life. Partly through circumstance (allotments are not usually the preserve of the well-off) and partly due to the thrifty resourcefulness that seems ingrained in most gardeners, whatever their income, nobody uses a length of new string where a sliced-off old sock or recycled bin-bag tie will do. To have won wholehearted approval, we should probably have tacked together four old builders' pallets with nails and crowned the heap with a square of festering old carpet, but I'm very glad we didn't.

I certainly wouldn't gain any Brownie points for the composting contraption I use at home: a spanking new wormery kit I ordered from one of the smarter garden mail order companies whose catalogues are full of luxury pine cold frames and novelty hose taps shaped like animals. It looks like a large grey dustbin with a tap in the side – in fact, it is a large grey dustbin with a tap in the side, and for the money (£54.99) (see page 246), it might have been more sensible to have bodged up a home-made version. The idea is that you fill the bin with all your unwanted kitchen waste and the worms (150 wriggling pink tiger worms that arrive in a plastic tub by separate post) will turn it into compost over nine or ten months, plus gallons of super-concentrated liquid plant food in the meantime.

As with all mail order products, the most complicated part of the whole procedure was orchestrating its arrival to coincide with a time when I'd be at home. Compared to that, putting the wormery together and starting the worms off with a meal of damp shredded

newspaper, a small bag of bedding compost and a couple of hand-fuls of vegetable peelings, was a doddle. It has been in the garden for six weeks now and it shouldn't be long before the first batch of liquid feed can be siphoned off.

In spite of the manufacturers' claims that the whole process is odourless and totally hygienic, I didn't expect my boyfriend to find the wormery a particularly appealing addition to our home. What surprised me, though, was his opinion that it was cruel to worms. Surely this is Worm Heaven – unlimited food twenty-four hours a day and not a hungry songthrush or blackbird in sight. A week later, though, it was a different story. The last of the fledgling blackbirds who had been nesting in our window box was refusing to follow its siblings into the great blue yonder and choosing instead to hop about the sitting room, ruffling its feathers and pretending it didn't want to fly *anyway*. Its mother's feeding visits had virtually petered out and we were afraid the poor thing would starve. It was my boyfriend's idea to feed it a worm from the wormery, but somehow it was me who ended up fishing one out and rinsing it under the tap, all the while thinking this was an a) mad and b) barbaric thing to be doing. In the event, when the tiny, pink worm was held out in front of the bird on a long fork, the bird flew off in sheer terror. I returned it to the wormery with the greatest relief. Fancy being scared of your lunch.

25 *August* 1996 ~ Stone Carving in South London

Compared to the centuries-old tradition of gardening as a whole, the history of the small urban garden is short and unprepossessing. Approaches to its design and upkeep tend to follow one of three predictable paths:

1 minimalist (the average bare back yard or bald lawn with a fringe of scraggy-looking plants)
2 Hampshire comes to Hackney with a crowd of cottage-y lupins and love-in-a-mist round the kitchen door
3 miniature Hidcotes – clipped hedges, ornamental urns and formal pathways all scaled down by the power of ten to slot behind the average city semi-detached.

The last category often works the best, but, curiously, one of the ideas that perhaps adapts most happily from large country house to small urban yard is seldom seen in practice – that of inscriptions in stone among the plants. The hey-day of inscriptions was the 18th century, when owners of early landscape gardens such as Stowe and The Leasowes set about leading visitors on a tour of the garden aimed at touching their hearts and imaginations by means of liter- ary, as well as horticultural associations. A grove of birches might have an urn carved with an ode to the spirit of the place; a view of the estate might be framed by an arch reminding one of the temporality of earthly possessions.

Recently, contemporary gardeners such as the Scottish artist and 'concrete poet' Ian Hamilton Finlay have continued the tradition in landscape gardens that are very much of the 20th century. Finlay's Little Sparta in Dunsyre in Scotland is as thick with beautiful and witty inscriptions as it is with plants – less a case of reading between the lines as of weeding between the poems. A plaque carved with Albrecht Dürer's initials is placed among a clump of grass arranged after his famous engraving; a wooden stile bears the epigraph 'thesis – fence; antithesis – gate; synthesis – stile'; while a bridge is simply carved with the legend, 'See Poussin, Hear Lorrain'. The effect is endlessly enriching – setting the mind off on travels that start and end in the sensual world of the garden but go everywhere else in the space of a few minutes.

Little Sparta, in spite of its name, is a large country garden. But it has long been my conviction that this sort of 'gardening with words' might be eminently suited to a small urban plot. Too much would look silly; too complex a message would be pretentious. The ideal would be two or three fragments, well-chosen, immaculately crafted and half-hidden in the leaves, to be happened upon by visitors and sought out by the owner in need of sustenance. I plan to start in my own back garden with a pond and trickling wall fountain in one corner – surely an excellent spot for an inscription. And I have found just the man to make it – John Pitt (see p. 246), who handcarves the most beautiful letters in slate and stone in a little pre-fab studio at the end of his long terraced garden in south-east London.

Mr Pitt's own garden is studded with plaques and pebbles

engraved in his very distinctive style. A sundial reads, 'Flowers talk; stones are silent'; a stone beneath two trees that almost meet reads, 'The trees embrace, our paths entwine'; a large round pebble is inscribed with a line of Yeats in particularly exuberant lettering – 'Dance like a wave of the sea'. He charges from £70 for a single word (customers often bring rocks or pebbles brought back from holidays) to £250 or more for a line of verse on slate, depending on the material and the precise amount of lettering. Mr Pitt says his aim is always 'to get through to the dynamic spirit of the letter' and bring the phrase or poem to life. All I now need to do is find a poem that will sit well with my pond, and south London's answer to Stowe will soon be underway. Hmmm.

1 *September* 1996~ Home

As the tide of builders' debris behind our house has gradually abated to reveal the uneven red concrete beneath, I have been weighing up the pros and cons of lawns for urban back gardens. On the plus side, they are lovely to sit out on in summer, kind to the knees of crawling kids and past-their-prime weeders, and just, somehow, the done thing in a garden, like candles on a birthday cake or hats at a wedding. They are also cheap – I have been quoted what seems a very reasonable price of eighty pounds to lay a turf lawn in our twenty by twenty foot patch, and if I were to be patient enough to sow one, the cost would be considerably lower (just twelve pounds for the seed and topsoil, once the concrete has been dug up and removed). We could even intersperse some plants of chamomile or creeping thyme (Thymus serpyllum 'Albus' with its white flowers, or the deep purply-red 'Coccineus' would look good) to release their scent when trodden on. And I have never thought there's anything wrong with a fine sprinkling of daisies.

But in such a tiny garden, is it really worth the bother? Sure, the initial effort involved in most of the alternatives – laying some form of paving, a pattern of old bricks (the current favourite) or even gravel would probably be greater than creating a lawn. But there the effort would stop, apart from a little light weeding between the cracks when I had nothing better to do. A lawn, on the other hand, would constitute a perpetual Job To Be Done. Like recycling the newspapers and cleaning round the bath, no sooner has the task been completed once but the next ordeal already looms. I have learned from friends and family that jobs such as this provide endless fuel in arguments ('I thought you said you were going to mow the lawn today instead of going to the football/playing the guitar/sitting about doing nothing') or as excuses ('Well, I would write that letter/go to the gym/bake bread/become a generally fantastic superbabe-earth-mother, but I'm afraid the lawn needs mowing and mowing NOW').

Such considerations aside, would I be able to bring myself to splash out on a new lawn mower for such a tiny space? I've always had trouble spending money on things I find intrinsically boring. (Shoes, painted ceramics, pictures that I have run out of wall-space for? No problem. Sensible nightwear, shower curtains, salad spinners – I suddenly feel so *poor*.) There is also, to me, something very sad and wrong about street upon street of houses where every individual battened-down little unit has its own battery of appliances – vacuum cleaner, Black & Decker Workmate, sewing machine and lawn mower – each of which gets used so infrequently they could easily be shared out. (My boyfriend says I should be living in a commune when I say such things, and he may have a point.) But if I were to borrow the neighbour's mower every month, might it not get a tad tiresome trundling it through the house each time?

Perhaps the best argument against a lawn, however, is what happens to them in August and September. Water bans or no, it seems near impossible to stop your sward turning into a depressing patchy brown expanse that crisps and rustles wherever you walk. The other day, I happened to be visiting that ultimate urban garden, the Queen's own at Buckingham Palace. Despite throngs of gardeners and more sprinklers than the Water Board would allow at Wimbledon, the rolling royal lawns were a subtle shade of straw, with scarcely a green blade in sight. She would no doubt blame the shifting, shuffling feet of all those garden party-goers, but if even Her Maj can't cope with a lawn in the city, what hope is there for me?

15 September 1996 ~ The Allotment

The long hot summer has taken its toll on the allotment, which I have to confess is looking rather raggedy about the edges. This wouldn't normally bother me: by the time I've watered everything and picked whatever crops need harvesting, the last thing on my mind is aesthetics. Besides, the patchwork of different coloured crops, with the tasselled blossoms of sweetcorn and towering sunflowers providing a backdrop, is, in many ways, quite an impressive sight. My mistake was to pick up one of the many books about ornamental vegetable gardens that seem to be around at the moment and to contrast the immaculate patterned beds in the photographs with my own novice achievements. In one picture, the purplish-blue bloom on a perfect triangle of cabbages (all with not so much as a single hole in their leaves, of course), was set against an edging of flame-red nasturtium flowers under a glowering, gunmetal sky. In another, different varieties of lettuce had been sown in decreasing concentric circles around a central wigwam of sweet peas; a courgette plant made a fan of leaves at each corner and the whole concoction was hemmed in by a hedge of flowering lavender.

It certainly looked beautiful. But the more I looked, the more questions formed in my mind. Where were the gaps in the rows where produce had been picked and eaten? Where were the new seedlings and their ugly covering of bird netting? Where were the inevitable brown leaves, bent stems and evidence of snacking by bugs and beetles? Not only must the pictures have been 'styled' and the vegetables subjected to the horticultural equivalent of hair and makeup, but the entire gardens must have been grown with photography in mind. As the last shot was clicked, one imagines the mad hurry to pick all those lettuces fast, before they went to seed, and to think of interesting recipes involving truckloads of savoy cabbage.

It is not as if I haven't tried to make my own plot look decorative. There was the idea to have sunflowers poking their heads through a wall of red and white runner bean flowers; in practice this failed because the sunflowers got off to too good a start and shaded out the beans. One square bed had a chequer-board effect of lime green endive interspersed with pink 'Lollo Rosso' lettuce, which looked good until I experimented with putting plates over the endive hearts to blanch them, and the Lollos bolted in the heat. (Actually, the latter have formed perfect geometric cones of purple leaves which look rather artistic among the lime, and I can always say I am doing it for the seed.) I grew a row of ruby chard purely for its scarlet stems (I still haven't bothered trying to cook it), and sowed squares of radishes and spring onions in alternating horizontal and vertical rows to make a basketweave pattern in the beds.

What fouls it all up are the weeds, which have slipped on the list of priorities due to extreme post-watering fatigue, and the wretched habit of everything to go to seed whenever the temperature soars. In this last respect, the allotment is not alone. Looking at my end-of-summer self in the mirror the other evening, on my return from a hefty watering stint, I could see the parallels in the common use of the term. Sweaty hair stuck to my skull, with a sunburnt nose, midge-bitten calves, and toe and fingernails ingrained with dirt through months of grubbing about in the soil, I was hardly looking my best either. For all the trendy books and glossy pictures, gardening itself is simply not a glamorous activity.

22 September 1996 ~ The Allotment

The first thing that anyone notices on entering the allotment site now is the crowd of giant sunflowers waving against the sky down in our little corner. Now that the triffid-like buds have finally opened, they look quite amazing, and we have a constant stream of visitors arriving to admire them. At eighteen feet high, they won't, sadly, get me into the *Guinness Book of Records* (the current record is twenty-three feet), but their two-inch thick stalks and their heads nearly two feet in diameter are almost twice the size of those grown by any of my fellow plot-holders. (It is a sad fact that gardening infects even the most laid-back with a keen sense of competition.)

I expect that the barrow loads of manure from the city farm are responsible, along with liberal feeds of liquid seaweed fertiliser. The sweetcorn, which I planted in a block alongside, is doing similarly well, with delicious cobs of corn of more than a foot long. The shelter provided by the fence and our neighbour's glass shed has also helped protect the sunflowers from the wind, and they haven't needed staking at all.

At first, the idea of cutting any of the sunflowers down seemed almost barbaric, but I finally decided that such fantastic feats of nature should be shared beyond the allotment gate. Pride apart, the magnificent heads are so high up it's impossible to see them properly from the ground, and what I want to do is stare into their mesmerising geometric patterns. A friend was having a house-warming in his new flat, which has a bright yellow carpet, and I thought that a giant sunflower would be the perfect gift, presiding over the party in a tall florist's bucket in the corner. My Swiss army knife proved completely inadequate for the purpose, so in the end we felled it with the garden shears, making a cut at an angle near the base of the stalk. Striding to the gate with the preposterous flower towering above me, I was suddenly reminded of my performance as one of the Three Kings in a Sunday school nativity play, when my top-heavy sceptre suddenly snapped and crashed to the floor. 'Are you going to use it as an umbrella?' quipped my Indian friend, Ahmed, as I passed by his plot. Sadly, though, the idea of the present misfired, as by the time I'd got it home the flower had wilted dramatically and was hanging its head at a less than jaunty angle – this in spite of having dunked it in a pot of water and plant food immediately it was cut. We decided my friend's flat could do without it and bought him a cactus instead.

Since then, my trusty neighbours at the allotment have come up with some tips to avoid the problem. 'Lemonade,' said the retired Turkish judge, when I told him what had happened. 'Fizzy lemonade. Use it instead of water and flowers will stay fresh for weeks.' Another veteran suggested inverting the stem immediately after cutting, and filling the hollow inside with water, making sure it doesn't escape when plunging into a vase. I've also been cutting the stems slightly shorter, which seems to help. The three blooms I've had on the kitchen mantelpiece have lasted for a full ten days now with no signs of distress.

The bulk of the crop remains in situ, however, and the huge heads are now beginning to turn into seeds, curling and curving at the edges like warped records. Someone on one of the other plots has picked out a smiling face on his, while mine have more random patterns where the birds have been snacking. I'm torn between saving the seed to toast and eat, or leaving nature to do its thing and heading for a sea of sunflowers next summer.

29 *September* 1996 ~ The Allotment

There has been a break-in down at the allotments. The other evening, as I walked to the shed at the top of the site, I passed one of the committee members applying what looked like coloured embroidery to the sides of her mesh fruit cage. It was only when I stopped to talk that I realised she was sewing up a gaping hole. Several other fruit cages in the vicinity had also been slashed, and it made me angry to see these careful, cared-for structures, lovingly maintained and patched together over the years, so thoughtlessly treated. Stealing the crops was not the motive, it seems, but the effect was the same, as the birds got into the cages and stripped the bushes in the early hours, before the crime was detected. Other plots had suffered mild vandalism – runner beans tugged down from their poles, marrows severed from the plant and smashed on the ground. My own patch was one of the few left unscathed.

The popular mythology of allotments abounds with revenge attacks. In the north of England, where they take vegetable growing far more seriously, the sabotaging of prize crops by jealous co-competitors is not uncommon, and men have been known to sit in overnight vigils beside a pumpkin – or even a row of onions – in the run-up to a show. Arthur Fowler's shed was burnt down on *EastEnders* – though whether he'd done anything to deserve it, I can't remember. And I've even heard of guns being toted on the allotments that back on to Brixton Prison. Here, though, the only aim in view seems to have been to annoy and inconvenience people. The culprits are thought to be a gang of young boys who hop over the new hawthorn hedge from the park, wreak their havoc and disappear. There's little that can be done until the hedge grows taller, so I hope they won't be back.

Teenagers are rarely keen on gardening. One needs a particular relationship with time – with the passing of the seasons – to get absorbed in it, and this seems to increase with age. Teenagers live for the present and think grubbing about in the soil a pointless pursuit favoured by the dull and dim and respectable. I can still remember being ticked off by my father for smirking when the Blue Peter Italian-style Sunken Garden was vandalised. But that was twenty years ago. I now find cruelty to plants surprisingly hard to stomach, whether it's the long, cold neglect of a pot plant crisping in the corner of a bachelor flat, or the wanton glee with which children pull the heads off flowers in front gardens on their way to school. When the waste of life is coupled with such disregard for the months of toil and quiet nurturing that are bound up in allotment gardening, it's doubly upsetting.

The committee has warned us all to be on the look out for ne'er-do-wells and to accost anyone seen behaving suspiciously. In an effort to increase security, the rickety old allotment gates have been replaced by new ones, seven feet high and more or less impenetrable, as I found last night when I forgot to bring my key. With the old door, I was able to squeeze round the side without too much difficulty. This time I was reduced to backing the camper van up to the fence, clambering up on top and vaulting over. Thank goodness nobody saw me coming back over with a clutch of marrows under my arm.

6 October 1996 ~ Home

Now that autumn is here and the trees in the local park are thick with berries, I've begun to think about providing for birds and wildlife in our little back yard. According to a new book, The Small Ecological Garden by Sue Stickland, (see p. 244), no garden is too small or too urban to become a wildlife haven. In fact, says the author, gardens have an important part to play, now that new roads, factories and modern farming methods are destroying traditional rural habitats. In Britain, the total area of domestic gardens is greater than that covered by our nature reserves, and even a tiny plot in the centre of the city can provide a safe haven for displaced creatures.

To date, the only wildlife that has availed itself of our garden has been the greater-spotted builder, sunning his lardy chest all summer long while attempting to destroy as many plants as possible in the course of a day's work, and a couple of neighbourhood cats who like to use the flowerbeds as a lavatory. The imaginatively named cat deterrent, 'Get Off My Garden', has seen off the latter (if only a handful of pungent-smelling granules could have dealt with the builders so effectively) and left me longing for other products in the range – 'Get Off My Computer', perhaps, or 'Get Off My Lunch' or 'Get Off My Nerves', for use indoors, and not just for cats.

According to Ms Stickland's book, our small walled garden, lined with wooden trellis, is ideal for creating a friendly urban micro-climate. The ideal barriers are those that filter, rather than block the wind, and the top of our trellis will eventually be rampant with passion flowers, clematis, honeysuckle and roses – the horticultural equivalent of a Woolworth's Pick'n' Mix counter for a hungry bird in winter. When it comes to trees, I'm inclined towards a hawthorn, whose bright red winter haws are as striking as its frothy white spring blossom, a spindle (*Euonymus europaeus*) for its deep purply-red leaves and earring-like fruit, and maybe a *Sorbus*, for its tight clusters of fruit and attractive leaves. These are all recommended for attracting birds and butterflies.

My pond, once it's finished, will have huge scope for wildlife – though I'll have to make sure the local cats don't get the fish. At the moment it's just a hole in the top left-hand corner of the garden, and it's never going to be bigger than three foot or so across, but even the smallest pond becomes host to thousands of tiny and not-so-tiny creatures almost overnight – the best way to encourage them will be to add a bucketful of water from the pond in the park.

I've even hatched a scheme for a wind-powered bubble fountain to trickle out of the wall and keep the water fresh. A small, brightly-coloured windmill on top of the wall would look jolly and might even help scare the cats away.

Ms Stickland's book is full of other ideas, from turning your garden over to a miniature wildflower meadow to advice on alternative pesticides, weedkillers and timber treatments. The text is straightforward enough for children to understand. Quite how her suggestions will work alongside another, rather different variety of wildlife that will shortly be sharing the garden, we shall have to see. My boyfriend has his heart set on a hairy grey lurcher puppy, who will be arriving some time over the next few months. Something tells me not to do too much more to the garden before the creature arrives.

13 October 1996 ~ The Allotment

I have become a potato bore. Diners at our house are force-fed huge piles of the things and cajoled into declaring how much tastier they are than shop-bought produce: how pleasantly earthy the flavour, how firm the flesh, how flawless the form. These are not just any old potatoes, you see. They are 'Pink Fir Apples' – the caviare of the potato world and much sought after for their pretty pink skins, waxy texture and new-potato freshness. My neighbour very kindly offered me some to plant in the spring, and I've awaited the first crop with excitement – and not a little trepidation.

People warned me not to expect too much; as befits their gourmet reputation, 'Pink Fir Apples' are reluctant to produce huge yields. I'd also never been really confident that I'd been doing the right thing with them. The cultivation of certain crops is shrouded with mystery for the beginner, as even the simplest and seemingly most straightforward books are peppered with confusing jargon. I wasn't even sure how 'seed potatoes' differ from your normal, run-of-the-mill spud, let alone how to 'chit' them. And as for 'earthing up round the haulm', forget it. If my neighbour hadn't offered translation services along with the seed I probably would have been too scared even to try. He had 'chitted' them (induced them to sprout small shoots) by setting them out in egg boxes in a light room for six weeks or so.

He'd then kept them in a cool dark place until it was time to plant them, in late April. I set the little potatoes (sometimes just a segment, with three sprouts on each one) in trenches in well-manured soil, covered them over and crossed my fingers.

I'm afraid I never did get the hang of earthing up the soil around the stem bases (this reduces the chance of light getting to the tubers and turning them green and poisonous), but it didn't seem to matter. Five months later, a fork plunged gently into the soil beneath the dying foliage came up jumbling with anything between ten or twenty pink potatoes – some small and round, some long and sausagey, some sprouting improbable protuberances like knobbly hands and feet. It was hard not to feel incredibly pleased with myself – although all I'd really done was water, weed and wait.

Perhaps I may have been lucky with my first year of allotment gardening, but one of the main lessons I have learned is that nature does more than half the work. Taking all the books and articles at face value can leave you convinced that absolutely nothing will grow unless you get it all absolutely right, and that getting it right is not only a duty, but a downright unpleasant and exhausting one at that.

I've already decided on an even more *laissez faire* system for next year: instead of digging in the manure as I did this year, I'll spread the surface with dung and seaweed next month, cover with black plastic sheeting (to keep the weeds down and nutrients in), and plant next year's spuds through crosses slit into the sheet. All I need now is some suitably obscure varieties to crow about.

20 October 1996 ~ The Allotment

Friends who have visited the allotment this year are usually politely enthusiastic about my new passion, mucking in with digging and weeding and looking convincingly pleased with the lifetime's supply of courgettes and runner beans thrust on them on their departure. But the other weekend I detected a familiar look on the face on one less outdoorsy acquaintance. It was the look I usually reserve for DIY obsessives whose idea of fun is spending days under the floorboards fiddling with electrics. 'Why bother?', 'Life's too short', is what the look says – or, in this case, more specifically, 'Why put yourself to

all this trouble when you could buy it all at Sainsbury's and you
wouldn't have to rinse the dirt off?'

'I suppose it saves money,' she said, when I challenged her to
share her thoughts. And I suppose it does, though I must admit that
economising wasn't my prime motive when I took on the allotment
this spring. While a neighbour manages to support his family of six
children with an impressive rotating crop of cabbages, turnips,
runner beans and potatoes, dilettantes such as myself are content to
have achieved self-sufficiency in baby spinach and rocket. When I
was choosing what to plant, however, the availability and shop-price
of organically-grown produce was certainly a consideration.
Radishes, rocket and speciality lettuces were the best bet to grow,
along with French and broad beans. My local health food shop has
been selling French beans at more than three pounds per kilo, compared to which eighty-nine pence for the packet of seeds and one
pound or so for the manure and seaweed necessary to produce
almost thirty pounds of beans is obviously a bargain. Tomatoes, at
fifteen pence per young plant, have also been good value, yielding at
least six to seven pounds per plant, despite my neglecting to pinch
out the side shoots and dust the flowers as diligently as I ought.

The real advantage, though, is in the freshness. Probably due to
the lack of preservatives, produce in the health food shop invariably
looks tired (to put it kindly), and even the local 'box system', which
delivers a box of assorted organic veg on your doorstep every Friday,
leaves you with wizened carrots and limp leaves by the middle of
the week.

One of the greatest pleasures of the summer was cycling back
across the park with freshly cut lettuce and spinach in the bike
basket, and eating it all when the flavour was still singing. Sweetcorn
reaches new heights of deliciousness with this straight-to-the-table
treatment – apparently the flavour (not to mention the nutrient
level) deteriorates within half an hour of the cob being cut.

Despite the rewards, though, if I didn't also enjoy the whole
process, I don't think I could have stuck all the early mornings, the
hours of digging and weeding, the copious watering sessions in
August. My visits are growing more infrequent now that autumn has
set in, which means that I treasure even more the smell of bonfires

and freshly dug soil, and the way the lazy sunlight slants through the rows of ruby chard, lighting up the plants like red and green lanterns.

27 October 1996 ~ Hallowe'en Pumpkins

This time last year I was travelling around America, where no porch or doorway, from New York to New Orleans, was without its collection of colourful, carved jack-o'-lanterns stacked up the steps to celebrate Hallowe'en. Huge piles of pumpkins were for sale on street corners, from bulbous monsters five feet across down to tiddlers for ranging along window sills. Punctuated by these enormous and improbable fruits, city life took on a jolly, festive feeling.

It hadn't initially occurred to me to grow pumpkins on my allotment, but when some friends in Wales offered me a sturdy seedling back in June, I jumped at the chance to have some of that autumn exuberance back home. Pumpkins and squashes are among the easiest vegetables to grow, provided the soil is well-manured and the position sunny and sheltered. Helped along by weekly doses of liquid seaweed, my little plant was soon romping cheerfully through the sweetcorn patch, and by early August small fruits had begun to swell. As instructed by the books, I restricted the plant to two fruits and slipped squares of hardboard underneath to protect against slugs. For a while I fussed and fretted over them in the childish hope of raising a championship-size pumpkin, but in spite of all my cosseting, the fruits stopped growing at about a foot across – perfectly respectable, but certainly nothing to write home about. I later found out that the plant was a smaller-fruiting variety, anyway.

For Hallowe'en, one pumpkin is to be made into a jack-o'-lantern and the other eaten – simply cut into slices, dotted with butter and roasted with lots of sausages. I can hardly wait. One thing I will most definitely not be doing with my pumpkins is covering them with gold leaf, cutting the tops off and scooping out the insides to make individual covered soup tureens, as recommended in Martha Stewart's Gardening, (see p. 243), a book I was sent recently. For those not familiar with Martha Stewart, imagine a prettier, less mumsy American version of Delia Smith, who knows as much about gardening and decorating as she does about cooking. Martha Stewart is a way of life to the American middle classes, who race to keep up with her relentless wonderwoman activity. Somehow, she manages to combine writing numerous 'how-to' books with running a large house and six-acre garden in Connecticut, creating a rose garden at her new home on Long Island, appearing on her own weekly television show and editing her own magazine, *Martha Stewart Living* which she intends to bring to Britain before too long. The magazine features Martha's monthly diary: on Tuesday she is cleaning and creosoting the boundary fences; Wednesday sees her transplanting 300 lettuce seedlings and constructing a pergola; on Thursday a dozen friends and relatives are coming to dinner. The books and magazines are full of jolly tips for how to use the twenty different types of basil she grows in her garden; how to make sugar leaves and rose-petals (home-grown, of course) and concoct elaborate table decorations involving ornamental cabbages, gingerbread men and baskets made from plaited purple ribbon.

I must confess to a certain admiration for Martha Stewart, but I wish she'd leave her pumpkins alone. This is America at its folksy worst. At least Shirley Conran in her Superwoman days, had the grace to concur that 'life is too short to stuff a mushroom'. Martha Stewart, one senses, would not only stuff the mushroom but gild it and make it into a piece of table art. And when it comes to pumpkin soup, call me old-fashioned, but what is wrong with a plain old soup plate?

3 *November* 1996 ~ Inspiration from a San Francisco Prison

Until three years ago, Frederick had been in and out of prison for much of his life, mostly for assaults on old people. Nowadays he picks flowers every Friday and takes them to San Francisco Farmers' Market, always keeping a bunch of white roses under the counter for a seventy-year-old woman who drops by the stall each week. He wouldn't disappoint her for the world. Rumaldo, a former heroin addict, has been a semi-permanent resident of one or another of California's state prisons for most of his fifty-three years. Now off parole for the first time in more than thirty years, he plants trees for a living, takes care of his family and leads a responsible life. His children are taking part in a project to transform their school playground from an asphalt yard into a garden planted with vegetables, herbs and flowers.

Behind this transformation of wasted lives and wasteland is a remarkable young black woman, Cathrine Sneed, who was in Britain for a rare visit last month. Cathrine knows what it is like to be down on luck herself: twenty years ago, as a pregnant teenage runaway, she hitch-hiked from New Jersey to California to start a new life. Somehow she got herself through school and, by now the mother of two young children, found a job as a counsellor in the San Franciso sheriff's department, where she spent years helping to rehabilitate ex-prisoners. It was a hard and dispiriting job, as eighty-five per cent of offenders were back in jail within ten years. A near-fatal kidney disease is what changed Cathrine Sneed's life – and that of so many others. One Christmas Eve in the late Eighties, a doctor offered her a choice: to remain in hospital and die, or go home and die. Cathrine did neither. Her boss, the sheriff, had brought her *The Grapes of Wrath* as a present; the book blew her mind and gave her the determination to get back to work and realise a new vision for working with prisoners. 'I became convinced that if people could reconnect with the land, they would feel hope and be more able to cope with life,' is how she puts it.

Still ill, she went back to work immediately, managed to convince the sheriff that her idea was worthwhile, and set about clearing eight acres of derelict land behind the prison and turning it into a vegetable garden. At the beginning, she worked with only women prisoners, who had to carry her out to the plot and work in their skimpy regulation pyjamas and flip-flops, even in cold weather. Then the men wanted to join in. Staff were amazed at the levels of commitment and co-operation; they had never seen the prisoners work so well together. Cathrine, who had no previous gardening experience, was given leave to take crash courses in biodynamic and market gardening. Within months, the prison garden was not only feeding the prison but also donating produce to soup kitchens for the homeless.

The crunch came when some prisoners demanded to be allowed

to stay on at the garden once their sentences had been spent. 'In one sense, it was fantastic, as it proved how much they got out of it,' says Cathrine. 'In another, it was just so sad that jail was a better place for them than the outside world.'

She raised money from local businesses for a post-release programme, and set about turning a donated patch of land behind a bakery into a garden project for ex-offenders. There, they grow organic vegetables and flowers to sell to local restaurants and at the San Francisco Farmers' Market. A Tree Planting Corps and a programme for 'greening' school playgrounds have also taken off. Fewer than half the workers have returned to jail. 'I see the guys' families and friends in the street and they all say, "I don't know what you did to him, but it's certainly working!"' says Cathrine. 'And I say, "I didn't do anything. It's the garden." It comes down to a connection with the land and making things grow with your own hands. When you have nothing else beautiful in your life, it gives you hope. I know. It saved my life when I had nothing at all.'

10 November 1996 ~ Home

I have always liked to have lots of potted bulbs around the house over the winter. This year, with the back garden of our new house yet to take shape, and much of the decorating still undone, they will be even more important than usual. With a little bit of planning, I've found it possible to have something in flower from Christmas right through the bleakest months of the new year.

The easiest bulbs to force for early blooming – and also among the prettiest and sweetest-smelling – are 'Paper White' narcissus. If you buy ready-prepared bulbs from a garden centre, all you have to do is plant them and wait four or five weeks for them to flower. I usually do five or six bowls full, often using gravel or pebbles in a glass container as an interesting alternative to compost. Other narcissi, hyacinths and crocuses also do well grown in this way. Arrange the bulbs among the stones, pour in enough water to just touch their bases and top up when needed.

Larger bulbs, such as traditional trumpet daffodils and tulips, I plant up in simple white or earthenware pots and place on a plate or saucer with a pretty rim; this year I have also used some of the gal-vanised tin buckets I bought for outside, remembering to bash some drainage holes in the bottom. Planting some of the tulip bulbs with the flattish side towards the outside of the container means that the lowest leaf will grow on that side and drape gracefully over the edge, rather than them all standing up straight like soldiers.

Rather than go for mixtures of flowers, which, apart from looking messy, cannot be guaranteed to bloom at the same time, it's best to restrict yourself to a single type per bowl or pot. In fact, just one white hyacinth in an old Italian painted cup that the handle came off is enough to make my work desk a far more cheerful place each winter. Similarly, keeping to one colour within an arrangement tends to look better than mixing – but make sure you buy your bulbs from a reliable source or you may get something different to what you'd intended. It's also important to get the planting depths right – just the barest cover-ing of compost is fine for most indoor bulbs, while some, like amaryllis, need to have at least half of the bulb exposed. There is something rather comical about tulips and daffodils that have been planted too deep and sport their top-heavy blooms on short stubby stems.

Most hardy bulbs (tulips, daffodils, hyacinths, grape-hyacinth and crocus) need a cold dark period (anywhere from eight to sixteen weeks) before they will bloom. In my old flat, I would leave them on the balcony under upturned cardboard boxes and bring them inside in stages. The sub-terranean passage outside the basement of the new house should be ideal. It's vital that you don't let the compost dry out. For extra-quick blooms from 'Paper Whites' and hyacinths, bulbs can be buried in damp peat moss inside a shoe box and stored in the bottom drawer of the fridge until roots develop.

Then put them in glass 'forcing' vases or pots of gravel or pebbles and move to a cool room with indirect light.

However you decide to do it, when the tips start to grow, set the bulbs on a sunny windowsill – light is essential to ensure strong, colourful blooms. When the flowers begin to open, the blooming period can be extended by moving the container to a cooler spot. It's an amazing thought that in just five weeks time, those bare, onion-like 'Paper-white' bulbs will be filling the whole house with their scent.

17 *November* 1996 ~ Home

I've realised why I've found it so hard to get settled in my study in our new house. It's the view – or, rather, the lack of one. My old flat, which was in the centre of town, had the miraculous advantage of a wall-to-wall view of trees – a row of elegant limes about fifty feet or so from my balcony. They provided a wonderful backdrop to my life – dusted with acid green buds in spring and maturing into a dense mass of foliage in summer, through which the sun cast a green-tinged underwater glow around the white walls. Even in the dead of winter they looked good, their slender branches etched with frost as the starlings squabbled over the food I'd put out on the window ledge.

My study in the new house looks out on to the street – a perfectly nice street, too, but sadly bereft of trees. When I look up from my second paragraph for a bit of a think, I am greeted not by a vision of leafy loveliness, but by one of my out-of-work neighbours, who, for whole hours at a time, performs strange stretching exercises on his

doorstep and then stands there with a grin on his face, watching the world go by. There is one tree – a small sycamore – diagonally opposite, but it's just out of my line of sight when I write. I miss my tree view so much I have begun to fantasise about galvanising the street into action and getting some more trees planted.

It may be the right time to put this dream into action, as next week is National Tree Week (or, strictly speaking, National Tree Twelve Days, as it runs from 20 November to 1 December, see p. 246). Among the many events planned throughout the country are mass tree-plantings at which, the organisers hope, more than a million saplings will be put into the ground, many in urban locations.

Trees are particularly important in cities. Street upon street of houses and parked cars look somehow harsh and unremitting without those free-hand shapes to soften the lines of the architecture. And it's not just a matter of aesthetics. Trees play a vital role in combating pollution – a seventy-foot tree releases enough oxygen to support ten people every day, so it's no wonder we instinctively feel better around them. Their impact penetrates deep into our psyche: recent research carried out in America suggests that office workers suffer less from stress and that hospital patients recover faster from operations if they have a view of trees. No doubt the effect on the work of a telecommuting journalist would be similarly beneficial.

I rang National Tree Week's organisers to sound out my chances of organising a tree-planting session in our road. 'Oh, no,' said a tired voice. 'You'll have to get on to the local council for that. Or, if you have a local residents' association you could apply to have a tree warden appointed in your area.'

Tree wardens are volunteers who are trained to plant and look after trees in their community. The keen ones apparently plan frequent plantings and try to use trees that are either indigenous to the area or tell a good story. One of National Tree Week's key events up in Seven Sisters, north London, will be the planting of seven lime trees (to replace the seven elms which gave the area its name, but were killed by Dutch Elm Disease). Apparently the local council is looking for seven sets of seven sisters to join in the celebrations.

When I pointed out that we didn't have a tree warden in our area, nor even a local residents' association, the Tree Week spokeswoman paused, and then said brightly, 'Well, you might want to think about training as a warden yourself.' For a second or two I was tempted – but with an allotment to tend, an empty garden to fill and a house to be decorated, I think I've got my hands full as it is.

24 November 1996 ~ The Allotment

Dark evenings have set in, fires have been lit, and the other weekend my sister and I finally put the allotment to bed for the winter. We spent an unexpectedly sunny afternoon digging over the soil, harvesting the few lingering potatoes and tomatoes and felling the giant dead sunflower stalks to cut up for compost. The bedraggled remains of the bean plants were left to rot down completely to release nitrogen into the soil (something that all legumes obligingly do) for next year's brassicas and lettuces, and a thick layer of farmyard manure (involving another smelly visit to the city farm) spread over the empty beds. One of our neighbours, who is a painter and decorator, is going to supply us with black plastic sheets that will keep the nutrients in and the weeds out and speed up the improvement of the soil. It may look rather grim and industrial, but it should mean we will have a lot less to do next spring than when we took over our patch this year.

Not everything is hibernating for winter, however. The spinach continues to sprout in our sheltered, south-facing plot, in spite of the first touch of frost, and the red cabbages and purple-sprouting broccoli are maturing nicely. We have planted garlic and an early sowing of broad beans. According to the books, broad beans put in now will gain a month on a spring sowing and beat the blackfly that were the bane of our lives last June. There is also a row of late leeks, as spindly as chives when they were donated (by one of the elderly men whose immaculate plots dominate the top end of the site), and now thickening well and putting out fan-shaped tails above the earthed-up soil line. It will soon be time to pull a few and boil up some vichyssoise.

By far the most exciting development this winter, though, is the rather fancy cold frame in which we hope to continue to raise salad crops for as long as we can. The system of using my VW camper van as a mobile greenhouse worked surprisingly well, apart from a few casualties – the result of taking corners too fast – but a friend of my parents, taking pity on such sorry deprivation, offered us their now-redundant cold frame. And extremely smart it turned out to be. Rather than the standard wood and glass job I'd expected, it's more like a mini-greenhouse, with adjustable glass panels that slide in and out of a green metal frame. It was bought at the Chelsea Flower Show in 1956, and is still looking dapper after four decades of use.

We've set it up in the sunniest, most sheltered spot, incorporated some well-rotted manure into the soil, and set some old slates round the perimeter in anticipation of wet and muddy weather. Inside, we hope to transplant home-grown seedlings of 'cut and come again' salad crops such as endive, 'Perpetual spinach' and rocket, which are supposed to be hardier than most. Winter lettuces are apparently rather tricky (prone to grey mould, downy mildew and sudden death), and I fear we may have left it all rather late. We'll just have to keep our fingers crossed and see what happens. If all else fails, this snazzy new addition to our plot will be ready and waiting for early crops next spring.

8 December 1996 ~ Avant Garde Gardens

'It was the perfect landscape material. It was easy to get hold of, it was cheap, it was biodegradable, anybody could plant it, it did well in the shade, you didn't need to water it.' The American landscape architect Martha Schwartz is not talking about some revolutionary new plant, nor even a paving material – she is talking about bagels. Yes, as in 'make mine one with smoked salmon and cream cheese'. In 1979, Ms Schwartz 'planted' a square of bagels, coated in yacht lacquer, in an urban front garden in Boston. This, according to the authors of *Paradise Transformed*, (see p. 243), an exciting new book on modern gardens, marked the beginning of an unlikely 'ironic' strain in modern American garden design.

Designing small, enclosed spaces, often with state-of-the-art modern architecture attached, Ms Schwartz became the champion of new urban gardens. One of her most extraordinary creations was for her mother's back yard in Philadelphia. It incorporated turquoise and green striped Astroturf, glitter-coated dustbins and shocking-pink net hammocks. When it was finished, a neighbour called the police to complain.

Following in Schwartz's footsteps came Topher Delaney and Andrea Cochran, who aim to 'personalise each garden from each client's personal narrative – their past, present, likes and dislikes, future obsessions, current occupation and family'. For one client, recovering from an acrimonious split with her husband, they created a Garden of Divorce, in which a stone table he had given her was ceremoniously upended and turned into a sculpture; the sun terrace he had spent many weekends laying was smashed to pieces, its jagged fragments half-buried in the turf like a concrete graveyard.

All of the above gardens are featured in *Paradise Transformed* by the Anglo-American garden designer team of Gordon Taylor (loud, witty West Coaster) and Guy Cooper (quiet, erudite Englishman). It is not often that one encounters gardens so uncompromisingly modernistic as these. Yet in a bizarre way, the designs are as much a continuation of gardening culture as the tempered versions of Jekyll and Repton that pass for modern gardens today. They are as comical as the water jokes that charmed visitors to Tudor gardens, or the references to both intensely personal and contemporary political events that weave their way around 18th-century landscape gardens such as Stowe.

There are only a few mentions of British gardens in this book. Ian Hamilton Finlay's poetic creation at Little Sparta in Scotland is praised for its carved inscriptions and concrete puns. Also featured is the Cosmological Garden recently designed by Charles Jencks and the late Maggie Keswick in Dumfries and Galloway, one of the most inspiring gardens to have been created anywhere this century. Here, ambitious earthworks have transformed the landscape into spiral mounds, sweeping dunes and crescent-shaped lakes – physical manifestations of Jencks' theories, inspired by the New Physics, about life, the universe and everything.

Paradise Transformed throws down a challenge to condense some of this new spirit into plans suitable for the average urban back garden. Peter Walker's roof garden on top of a townhouse in Boston shows what can be achieved in a space of twenty-two by sixty feet. The authors, too, are doing their bit: for a banker in north London they

have begun work on their own first truly modern garden – a con-
glomeration of elliptical metal pergolas, randomly smashed paving
and oversized urns set deep in a wall.

15 December 1996 ~ House Plants Against Pollution

It was presumptuous of me to assume Urban Gardener was the only
regular column for green-fingered townies. I have recently been sent
a copy of a rather impressive little magazine called BUG (Biological
Urban Gardening), (see p. 242), a bi-monthly which has been around
for almost three years. The issue I was sent included fascinating features about how to grow lemon-grass on a windowsill, gardening
using hay bales, and how to use pot plants to combat pollution in
the home. There was also a tantalising list of back issues with such
articles as How Injured Plants Communicate with Each Other, Possible Health
Problems from Summer Composting, and Do Parents who use Pesticides Cause
Leukaemia in their Children? I'm tempted to order the lot.

The pot plants against pollution article was riveting. I was alarmed
to read that the modern home is prone to all manner of insidious
toxins, such as formaldehyde (from carpets, plywood, flatpack furniture and insulation materials); benzene (from particleboard and
paint); propanol (from cleaning products) and dichloromethane
(from paint thinners and strippers), whose effects range from eye,
nose and throat irritations and nausea to nerve disorders and even
cancer. It might seem unlikely that a mere plant could provide a
defence against such a barrage, but it was a relief to learn that some
species have particularly efficient cleansing abilities.

The common spider plant is probably the best-known of these,
and is also effective against the harmful emissions that come from
the back of computer terminals. Another is the dragon tree
(Dracaena), which probably explains why its spiky variegated leaves
on a tall central stem are so frequently seen in offices. It's easy to care
for, reaching eight feet in ideal conditions (rich loam, warmth, light
shade and sparse watering). Syngonium (or the goosefoot plant) is also
effective against all forms of pollution – it needs a temperature of
15C (60F) and does best in bright, indirect light and a loam-based
soil which should be kept just moist.

However, almost any healthy houseplant will do the job, and a nice idea is to build up a staggered bank of plants on steps near a sunny window, where they will filter the sunlight and throw interesting shadows around the room. In bathrooms, or in large or bay windows that look on to the street, a flourishing collection of tall and bushy foliage plants can create an attractive living screen against prying eyes – altogether more desirable than blinds or net curtains, and good for you too. All this heroic hard work has no ill-effects on the plants whatsoever – all they need is to have their leaves occasionally sprayed with water and carefully wiped with a cloth to remove dust. What better excuse to create an urban jungle in your home?

29 December 1996 ~ On Christmas Trees

For me there is something rather wanton about chopping down a whole tree just for the sake of decorating the house for a few weeks at Christmas. I think it has something to do with my childhood, when we moved from the Kent countryside to the outskirts of London. Pine and spruce seedlings used to spring up in the patch of scrubby no-man's land where our long narrow back garden ended and the golf course began. My sisters and I would pretend that they were miniature Christmas trees for the various animals that made the area their home. 'That one's for the squirrels,' we'd say, on finding a perfectly proportioned specimen just over a foot tall, and we'd hang it with acorns and holly berries and strands of silver lichen. The fantasy was that on Christmas Eve the frost would come and cover it with silver stars so that, on Christmas morning, the squirrels would have a wonderful tree. Really small trees, some only the length of a childish finger, were for bugs and ants, while the larger ones would be for rabbits, stray cats and lost dogs.

Ever since then, I must confess to feeling slightly sentimental about Christmas trees. Even the recent introduction of 'farmed' trees (specially raised for the purpose on environmentally-sound reserves and so on) has yet to win me over – despite the fact that it is no more or less destructive than buying market-grown cut flowers, about which I have no such scruples.

Buying a potted, rooted tree that can live for the rest of the year in the garden seems a good compromise. Some people plant theirs out into the soil every year – but this takes a lot of time and trouble, and may encourage the tree to grow so fast that it will start crowding you out of the house. Besides, a half-grown spruce is not an easy tree to accommodate into the average urban garden. It's much more handy to keep your tree in a large pot or half-barrel that can be shunted in and out as required. This is the method my parents have been using for the last few years. Like a poor soul who only has one smart outing a year, the silvery blue spruce (£9 from the local hardware shop three years ago) makes the most of its two or three weeks of sitting-room splendour before resuming its habitual haunt in the shade of the garage wall each January. Naturally, a tree gulps down water when brought into a centrally heated room but, as with any container-grown plant, you also have to remember to carry on watering when the tree is back outside, to keep it at its best. Ours has a slightly bald inner section that dates back to a long hot summer of neglect, but this is easily disguised with lights and baubles.

If yours is a cut tree, or if you don't have room to keep it, or if you simply can't stand its needle-spitting ways any longer, you can still prolong its useful life in other ways. One option is to shred it for mulch to use on the garden – either borrow the shredder at your local city farm or club together with neighbours to rent one for a day. In America, big stores such as Ikea have schemes where they 'rent' customers a tree for twenty dollars; if the tree is returned the shop refunds ten dollars and turns the tree into mulch chippings which the customer can either keep or donate to a good cause. Sadly, Ikea has no immediate plans to bring the scheme to Britain, but it surely won't be long before someone follows suit. In the meantime, you can always clip off the branches yourself and lay them over beds and borders to protect favourite plants – a double layer is best as it lets air into the ground while keeping frost out. The trunk can be kept for next summer's bean poles or tomato stakes – or strung with nuts, leftover cranberries and dried sunflower heads to make a pretty New Year's treat for the birds.

1997

5 January 1997 ~ The Allotment

Three weeks have gone by since my last trip to the allotment. In the summer, such neglect would have been unthinkable. Even a gap of a few days would have seen lettuces bolting, beans wilting and slim dark courgettes becoming unwieldy striped torpedoes almost overnight. These days there is little change to mark the passage of time. The purple sprouting broccoli is rampant, though showing little sign of anything either purple or sprouting. The Savoy cabbages sown in September are filling out gradually, their pink-tinged, leathery leaves outlined in a white rime of frost, and a few brave lettuces are struggling along under the cold frame. But that sense of a life-force, of an amazing energy that seemed almost tangible amid the summer's jungly growth, has gone. The plot is almost asleep. All the while, though, beneath its unprepossessing blanket of manure and black bin liners, it is good to know that the soil is preparing itself for next year's crops.

Many gardeners love the winter. For some, it's the season for horticultural dreaming; for browsing through books and seed catalogues and cooking up plans for the summer. For others it brings on a bout of outdoor DIY. The few figures one sees down at the allotment these days, felty grey silhouettes in the early morning mist, are carrying out repairs to their sheds or cold frames, laying new paths from old cracked paving slabs or carting in old floorboards or lengths of skip timber for making raised beds. For me, it's a time for new year's resolutions – time to focus my thoughts and aims for the allotment in the year ahead.

Encouraged by this first year's success – everything germinated except for the sorrel, and most crops produced a respectable yield – I might try to be a little more ambitious. I'd like to try artichokes – globe and Jerusalem – and more decorative types of beans, and I would like to grow some fruit (raspberries, currants, strawberries, perhaps an apple tree or two, espaliered up the fence). If my absentee neighbour – whom I've seen only three times in the course of the entire year – should be forced by the committee to relinquish his plot, I might even consider expanding into his patch, though the waist-high weeds and thistles make me tired just to look at them. What I'm really interested in is his shed. My gardening tools – spanking new and shiny back in March – are shamefully rusty and rickety after months of being kept outside. I do try to keep them covered under plastic sheets, but the wind seems to blow the rain under all the same. One resolution for 1997 is to take better care of my tools.

Another will be to make some of my own organic feeds and fertilisers – this is surprisingly easy to do and can save substantial amounts of money. The liquid seaweed one I buy is perfectly good, and I'm not proposing to stink the car out by hauling great truck-loads of bladderwrack up from the coast. But it can be supplemented by home-made brews based on nettles and comfrey. Comfrey is the magic all-rounder of the vegetable garden. It can be used as a mulch, its leaves chopped and mixed with an equal amount of grass cuttings, or laid along potato trenches to enrich the soil. A liquid comfrey feed, impressively rich in vitamins and minerals, is made by simply chopping up leaves and immersing them in a large container of water for about three weeks, after which the dark and rather smelly concoction can be strained, diluted (between ten and twenty parts of water to one of comfrey liquid) and used as a fortnightly feed. Nettles can be prepared in the same way – and I'm lucky enough to have a fine supply over by the hawthorn hedge.

Another resolve is to finish clearing that area of all the rubbish that accumulated during the years our plot was being used as a communal dump. There's an old tin bath I've seen that should be perfect for making up my brews.

12 January 1997 ~ A Bit on the Side

Urban gardeners can be great complainers. If the problem isn't lack of space or light, it's noisy neighbours. But one of the biggest challenges for the average urban gardener is the layout of the average urban house. You'd have thought that one of the joys of the city garden would be the view from the house. Rooms facing the street may offer no more than parked cars and curtain-twitchers, but those at the rear should more than compensate with wall-to-wall greenery. Well, that's the theory. In practice, it is rarely the case. The culprit is the common custom of tacking kitchens and bathrooms on to the backs of houses to make a bottom-heavy L-shape. From the tiniest two-up-two-down to grand Georgian terraces, the principal view from the ground floor of a city home is often the 'side return' – that dark and gloomy corridor in which nothing will grow. Access to the garden is usually via this corridor – either from the rear reception room or a side door off the kitchen.

What can be done about this? The most dramatic solutions involve building work, which is never cheap and always disruptive. But it might be worth installing french windows at the far end of your kitchen, or glazing over the corridor to make a glass-roofed dining room on the side of the house that is neither inside or out. I've seen this work well, even in quite poky houses. Less self-conscious than a proper conservatory, the bright new space can make a delightful study, a summer sun room or just somewhere to keep the welly boots, barbecue and garden furniture.

But, unlike a glorified garden shed, it should be light and warm enough (depending on the direction your house faces and what heat you can provide) for growing and propagating a wide range of plants. If you fill it with as many as you can, you will now have a much more exciting view from both the back and the sides of the house. (In many houses the side kitchen window looks either on to a fence a few feet away or straight in on your neighbour's washing up.) If the space remains open, and particularly if it faces north or east, the best idea is to go for something simple. Rather than trying to fill borders with a sorry array of shade-lovers, why not plant a single evergreen bush, trimmed into a cone, ball or pyramid, in an unusual pot or container? If I had a house with this layout, I'd be tempted by a holly, trained as a standard ball, in a bright red pot which I could repaint if ever I became bored with it. You could even hang white fairy lights among the branches.

One of the things that attracted me to our house was its lack of a back extension – possibly because it may once have been a shop and appears never to have had a proper kitchen or bathroom. Access to our garden is via steps up from the basement and through a landing door on to a sunny raised terrace. Keen to bring views of the garden into the house as much as possible, we replaced a small sash window in the large kitchen-dining-sitting room with tall custom-built french windows. Alarmingly, these currently open on to a seven-foot drop down to the basement well, but the moment funds permit there may be a metalwork balcony crammed with pots of herbs and scented climbing plants. In the house of my dreams, one would be able to step directly through these french windows into the garden, so I've been racking my brains for schemes involving bridges and niftily designed walkways. But it all got far too complicated. In gardening, as in the rest of life, it's sometimes best to admit that you can't have everything.

26 January 1997 ~ Home

'Definitely dove grey and white chequers, with maybe just a dash of Schiaparelli pink to jazz things up!' declares Anthony Noel (see p. 246), cocking his head to one side as he surveys the twenty by twenty foot slab of concrete that is my back garden. 'Or what about some purple?' I try to look politely inspired but, frankly, I can't quite see it. In the hands of Mr Noel, a trendy and talented garden designer who created one of the most photographed small city gardens at his former flat in Fulham Park Gardens, bright stripes and shocking pink squares become something magical, even smart, complemented by his unusual planting. He is the master of topiary balls in striped pots, of mysterious black-and-white flowers, of furniture and trellis painted bright lime for one season, then turquoise, then pink with crazy black zigzags.

I shall never forget a visit I made to his garden one summer, when towering standard fuchsias in striped blue and white tubs gave the tiny space an air of being en fête – the swags of flowers like flags and bunting in the gathering dusk. 'You have to love the plants enough to dress them up, but not enough to make fools of them,' he is fond of saying.

Mr Noel, who I am delighted to say is now my new neighbour south of the river, had kindly come round on a rescue mission, to help reinspire me about our back garden, after its first fledgling plantings had been buried in builders' debris. 'This could be terrifically exciting' he said, suggesting a row of his beloved topiary balls along the top of the walls and a feature involving a mirror and some bits of broken fireplace that could be seen from the house. The garden chairs and table could be painted shocking pink, and house doors picked out in purple. I resolved to adapt some of his ideas but drop the over-the-top colour. It's been hard enough finding exactly the right shades of off-white for inside the house, without turning the garden into a horticultural Battenburg cake.

At the moment, the high brick walls are painted plain white, with sturdy white wooden trellis all the way round, up which is climbing – or, rather, crawling at a snail's pace – what will one day be a wall-to-wall tapestry of honeysuckle, ivies, clematis, jasmine and rambling roses. The trellis is to be hung with planters full of geraniums and trailing annuals, and my extensive collection of glass and metal lanterns. It should make a wonderful place to eat out on summer evenings. The important ingredient needed to accomplish all this is patience. However, I do need to decide what to do with the grim concrete slab left by the previous owner. Digging it up would not only be difficult, but also undesirable, as it might possibly result in an avalanche of mud into the basement.

Another designer whose opinion I consulted suggested covering it with timber decking, which is appealing, though expensive, and not something I could do very easily myself. Rather than the decking or the psychedelic squares, I think I might plump for a naturalistic mosaic of black, grey and white pebbles, set close together in concrete in a swirling pattern. It might take a while to complete, but it will be nice to have somewhere to put all those mementoes from walks and holidays, which end up in pockets or the glove compartment of the car. If I gathered them all together I'd have enough to lay a few square yards. And if it should look boring, I can always paint it pink.

2 *February* 1997 ~ Operation Cat

The past few weeks have been dedicated to Operation Cat. Since we moved here six months ago, six or seven cats have been patrolling our perimeter walls, frequently venturing down into the garden to use our trellis as a climbing frame or our flowerbeds as a lavatory. This has been mildly irritating at times, but my boyfriend and I are fond of cats, and a friendly feline presence on the sun terrace has more than compensated for occasional misdemeanours. Until now. The battle lines were drawn when, on returning from a week away at New Year, I found the ground floor window boxes had been commandeered as luxury litter trays. Daffodil and tulip bulbs carefully planted last autumn had been rooted up – some had rolled out on to the ground – and the surface of the soil was covered with droppings. A galvanised tin urn, filled with two rare clematis and a mass of white winter pansies, had met a similar fate.

We have sprinkled 'Get Off My Garden' cat deterrent all over the garden. We hiss at the sight of cats – I have even caught my boyfriend barking at them. But to little effect. Defeated by day, they have stepped up their nocturnal manoeuvres, fighting and scrapping into the early hours, and the ginger tom from next door has started spraying in the corridor by the basement door. Since we moved our bedroom to the back of the house, our sleep has been broken by their incessant caterwauling.

It has all got a bit much for my boyfriend. Normally possessed of an easy-going temperament, he has become obsessed by Operation Cat. To keep the creatures out of the basement corridor, he has constructed a laborious polythene lean-to, which may not look too smart but at least keeps our woodstack dry. The only trouble is, the cats, undeterred, have taken to skittering about on top and making even more noise. He now sleeps with one ear trained on the garden, and at the first pad of a paw, sits bolt upright and makes for the window, where a row of elaborately rigged-up spotlights are switched on and off in rapid succession. This certainly stops the cats in their tracks, but they are not the only ones to be alarmed. The other night I woke with a start, convinced I was in Colditz.

To protect our sanity, I wonder if any kind readers have ideas for repelling cats? The options so far dismissed include:

1 spreading tiger dung on the beds, which apparently freaks cats out (London zoo does not distribute it to the public and I am unaware of other suppliers)
2 using a nifty device advertised in Sad Person's *Innovations* catalogue, which emits a high-pitched sound deterring all cats within 2000 feet (this would include all the cats in the immediate neighbourhood, which seems a mite hard on their owners)
3 getting a cat of our own (we are shortly to get a puppy and one animal in the house is enough for me).

In the meantime, the ultimate irony is that the cold weather has brought a colony of mice into the kitchen. With unwanted cats outside and unwanted rodents inside, the logical conclusion would be to let the former in to fight it out. But I'm not quite sure where it would all end...

9 February 1997 ~ Town and Country

I have just spent a few days with friends who made the big move from Hackney to Hampshire last summer. Even in midwinter, sodden with rain and with nothing in flower, their 120 foot garden, surrounded by rolling green hills and fields full of cows, did induce a pang of jealousy. Their vegetable patch alone must be half the size of my allotment – not for them a bracing bike-ride whenever they fancy a lettuce – and I would kill for the romantic, rickety wooden bench beneath a pear tree at the top.

By way of consoling myself, I fell to wondering how much time my friends would actually be able to spend in their new garden, bearing in mind the long hours spent commuting and the weekends doing DIY, driving to the superstore and trotting townie friends like me down country lanes. A garden that big is quite a commitment.

Continuing in this bitter and twisted vein, I then began to question the *need* for such a large garden when rolling green hills, fields full of cows, etc., etc., are all at one's immediate disposal. A bigger garden is often cited as the reason for a de-camp to the country, but it's surely in the city, surrounded by wall-to-wall cars and concrete, that our efforts at gardening, however cramped and confined, have the most impact and give the greatest solace. To me, daffodils seldom look as beautiful as when springing from a window box in some dingy council estate.

Walking through Paris, Glasgow, New York or Rome, it is amazing how the spirits are lifted by a glimpse of a mossy courtyard, filled with ferns, through an iron gate off the pavement, or by a tiny balcony crammed with plants that brighten the street for everyone. And, for me, there are few more exciting triggers to the imagination than those rooftop fringes of green that signify someone's secret haven above the hubbub. It is one of my dreams to hire a helicopter to snoop a closer look at these private, chimney pot worlds.

Sure, I often dream of moving out of London, of setting up by the sea somewhere with a walled garden big enough for vegetables and a secret wooden seat from which to savour the view. But until I do, I won't waste time hankering for what I haven't got. I shall continue to cultivate plants on my window ledges, enjoying the cycle of their budding, flowering and ever-changing growth and the privacy their foliage affords from the street outside. I shall persevere in my efforts to turn our concrete bunker of a back yard into a plant-lined outdoor room. And, down at the allotment, I shall carry on wondering at the way a packet of seeds becomes a screen of flowering beans that not only feeds us all summer, but also softens the view of the high-rise flats beyond.

Why else does an urban gardener garden, I asked myself, as I hurtled back along the M3 to London. I can't find a better explanation than the one given by Rachel Carson, the pioneering American ecologist, in her book, *The Sense of Wonder* (see p. 244): 'Those who dwell... among the beauties and mysteries of the earth are never alone or weary of life. Whatever the vexations or concerns of their day-to-day lives, their thoughts can find paths that lead to inner contentment and to renewed excitement in living... There is symbolic as well as actual beauty in the migration of the birds, the ebb and flow of the tides, the folded bud ready for the spring. There is something infinitely healing in the repeated refrains of nature – the assurance that dawn comes after night, and spring after the winter.' You don't have to live in the country to experience that.

16 February 1997 ~ The Allotment

For most of last year I was secretly in awe of one of my neighbours down at the allotment. Not only are his two plots among the neatest and most productive on the whole site; he also grows by far the most interesting varieties. Where, I wondered, did he come across the deep purple and bright yellow french beans that were the envy of everyone who saw them? Not to mention his four varieties of cauliflower (one with florets like little green pyramids, that I've only ever seen for sale in markets in Italy), or his impressive crop of Chinese greens?

All was revealed when I recently plucked up courage to ask him. He orders his seeds from *The Organic Gardening Catalogue* (see p. 245) a company run jointly by the Henry Doubleday Research Association (HDRA) and Chase Organics – and one of very few specifically organic mail order services in the country. Like many first-time vegetable growers, I'd relied on the packets of seed available at the garden centre or in hardware shops – perfectly adequate, but nothing out of the ordinary. Not only had I been missing out on the vast choice of seeds available by post, my neighbour pointed out; neither had I been, strictly speaking, a true organic gardener. In spite of sticking faithfully to my seaweed, chicken- and horse-manure regime,

and resisting chemical pesticides even in the face of severe blackfly infestation, I was still raising plants from seeds that may have been produced using every wicked chemical under the sun.

Well, this year, all that is going to change. I have ordered all my seed from the *Organic Gardening Catalogue*, including french and broad beans (I couldn't resist the rather splendidly named 'Masterpiece Green Longpod'), four types of potato, some rather smart black radishes, and salad crops trendy enough to grace the shelves of Marks & Spencer. I'm also trying Jerusalem artichokes, as the soup is my favourite taste in the world (they send you fifteen of the knobbly tubers for £3.95), and some Pak Choi-Joi Choi, which looks like a Chinese version of Swiss chard (ninety-eight pence per packet). Not all the seed sold by the company is organically produced – but the selection available is increasing every year. Unlike organic vegetables in the shops, the price of organic seeds seems to compare favourably with the commercially produced competition.

The catalogue is packed with unusual things to grow – herbs and flowers as well as fruit and vegetables – and there are even handy cultivation tips among the entries and photographs. (Did you know, for instance, that growing buckwheat in clusters around the patch not only chokes weeds but attracts hover flies, whose larvae feed on aphids?) But it's at the back of the catalogue that I succumbed to the greatest temptation. There were all the snazzy accoutrements of my neighbour's that I'd envied for all those months last summer! There was the plastic polytunnel in which he grows enough fat juicy aubergines to feed the whole of Brixton (£21.60 for 4.5 metres), and there was the fleecy mesh with which he protects his crops from frost and birds (Envirofleece Plus, from £5.75). I filled out the order form straight away, before I got sidetracked by the pages of books and 'sundries' (wasp traps, bird feeders and hemp oil soap), benefiting from the ten per cent discount offered to those who join the HDRA. (The £20 annual fee contributes to research and education projects about organic growing methods throughout the world and allows free visits to the Association's show gardens at Ryton near Birmingham and Yalding in Kent.) So now I'm all set for a truly organic year ahead.

23 February 1997 ~ A Garden in Waiting

Gardens, like cities, are palimpsests – store-houses of personal myth and memory. A tree, just like that particular chair in that particular courtyard café, has its place in many other stories besides your own. Who knows now who planted it, and why; who stole a first kiss under it a hundred years ago; who sat beneath its branches looking up at the sky the evening war was declared, or paced up and down around it while his children were born upstairs? We think of gardens as 'ours', when really, all we are doing is adding our own chapter of experience and memory, along with the plants we plant or seeds we sow, to a long-existing story.

These thoughts were running round my mind the other morning, as my friend Matthew and I did some detective work in the garden of the house he's just bought. It is large by London standards – 100 feet long, wider than the usual urban strip, and pleasantly wilder than its more manicured neighbours. The enclosing walls are overgrown with roses and different sorts of ivy, and a trio of ancient metal arches is almost buried beneath the tangle of last year's Clematis montana.

As we rooted about in the watery winter sun, uncovering a clump of irises in the lee of an old summerhouse and thrilling at the pink nubs of peony buds pushing through the soil, I thought how appropriate it is to take possession of such a garden in winter. The winter garden is asleep – poised, like the year, between last summer and autumn, when it was still enjoyed by the previous owners, and the forthcoming spring, when my friend and his wife will finally move in. The plants themselves seem to reflect this transition: the shrivelled black leaves of phlox hanging limp like old washing while new growth bushes up from below; the faded heads of Chinese lanterns like party decorations left up for too long. Without their distinctive flowers and foliage, many plants are hard to identify: the clues are either brittle seed-heads, etched round with a white rime of frost, or tightly-folded buds that cling close to bare branches.

Very sensibly, my friend has decided to wait for a year before doing much to his new garden; to watch and see what comes up in the flowerbeds; what colours have been planted in the wide south-facing border. With a well-established garden, patience alone can be the best policy, and I have high hopes for this one. You can tell how much its previous owners loved it. They made a small pond in a sun-dappled corner, and planted drifts of daffodils and brilliant blue scillas through the borders and across the somewhat patchy lawn. A gnarled old wisteria, its trunk twisted, plump and plaited like rising dough, has been trained up the back of the house to the top bathroom, where one can imagine it poking welcome, fragrant fingers through the window in summer. A trellis loaded with jasmine, honeysuckle and a passionflower seems set to reach the first-floor balcony this year.

Who knows what else waits beneath the surface of the soil, roots even now responding, unseen, to the perceptibly longer days and (usually) milder nights? For a little while longer, that will remain the secret of the garden's former occupants, even though they're no longer there to see. But as spring moves into summer, and the newcomers familiarise themselves with the garden's rhythms, they, too, will be able to make their mark: to fill some of the gaps in the borders with their favourite perennials; to place a wooden seat where the evening sun slants against the house. Their little dog will find the warmest spot by the wall, or doze in the shade of the lime tree in mid-summer; their children will learn to walk on the lawn. And so, another layer of history will be added to the place. Till then, it remains a garden in waiting.

2 March 1997 ~ 'Earth Acupuncture'

'In my job you run a fine line between being useful and feeling like a madman poking sticks in the ground,' says Richard Creightmore, sliding what looks like a giant knitting needle into the gap between two paving stones outside my house. I know which the neighbours will think he is. Grabbing the end of the needle with both hands, he closes his eyes tight and jiggles it about in the soil. 'That should do the trick,' he says, with a toss of his ponytail.

Mr Creightmore is an earth acupuncturist. Just as a regular acupuncturist uses needles to heal the energy systems in the body, so

Richard claims to restore blocked energies beneath the earth's crust. This jiggery-pokery outside on the pavement was the culmination of a two-hour visit in which Richard dowsed my house and garden for the 'black streams' that represent blocked energy and can cause disease among people and plants nearby. To my alarm, he found three.

The scientific name for the phenomenon is geopathic stress – a build up of natural radioactivity in the underground streams along which it normally flows. Causes can include building work – in particular, the laying of electricity cables, sewers and tube train tunnels, which is why it is more prevalent in towns. The effects on humans can apparently run from mild depression and insomnia to ME and MS, malignant tumours, fertility problems and genetic mutations. Sleeping over the line of a black stream is apparently not a good idea.

In the garden it can be equally damaging. 'Have you ever seen a line of trees, all growing perfectly well except for one, which is sick and stunted? Or a gap in an otherwise healthy hedge or border?' asks Richard. 'Chances are there's a black stream running beneath it. That corner of the garden where nothing flourishes, in spite of all your efforts? Same problem.' Cankerous fruit trees, mossy patches on lawns and wasp and ant nests can also be signs.

Nature apparently has her own cure for geopathic stress: nettles. An ineradicable patch of nettles, docks or thistles can be both a sign of and long-term cure for the problem, according to Richard. If you wait long enough, the nettles should complete their work and die; but a spot of earth acupuncture may result in the disappearance of black streams immediately.

Wandering about with his metal dowsing rods, Richard found black streams running through our property. The rods swung together dramatically just inside the hall, indicating a strong line of stress running straight through the front door and out across the garden. The top right-hand corner would always be a problem, he said, in spite of its sunny aspect – and what should we see but the remains of a passion flower whose demise I had blamed on the builders.

The 'cure' was to stick a wand made from holly wood into the soil at an 'earth energy point' where two streams cross. Sometimes

Richard uses wooden wands, sometimes huge iron spikes like pokers, and they can remain in the ground 'anything from twenty minutes to a few years to a few centuries'. (One theory has it that stone henges were an early form of earth acupuncture.) Luckily, my garden needed only an hour and a half. Richard returned to test the spot every half an hour; the rods swung less vigorously to attention each time and, at the final reckoning, made not so much as a shiver.

The other lines had to be traced out to the street for treatment – a curtain-twitcher's dream. Was it coincidence that at the point one crossed the pavement there was a pile of glass from a car break-in? Richard didn't think so. One of the nice things about earth acupuncture is that it is supposed to benefit the surrounding area as well as your own little patch. So if our rather seedy street should suddenly sprout blossom trees and roses round the doors, I'll know what's behind it.

9 March 1997 ~ Home

Last month's plea for cat deterrents has resulted in a post-bag bulging with ingenious ideas. I am by no means the only gardener – urban or otherwise – who has been driven to distraction by unwelcome attentions of the feline kind. One reader was forced to give up gardening by the havoc wrought by thirteen cats in her Somerset garden; several have been reduced to tears; another resorts to moonlit border patrols in the early hours, armed with a water pistol in one hand and a child's spade as pooper-scooper in the other.

Many people suggested spraying the garden with a substance that cats find unpleasant. The only trouble is that ammonia and a tar-like substance called Renardine are not exactly fragrant to humans either. Olbas oil, cayenne pepper and curry powder, or a mixture of tea leaves and mothballs (shaken together in a glass jar for a month before use), definitely sound more palatable – but would have to be renewed with each rainfall. And in spite of the popularity of shredded citrus peel as a deterrent – and the assurance of Mrs Heap from Bury St Edmunds that 'it looks quite attractive' in her garden – I'm not sure I want my flowerbeds strewn with lime and orange peel.

Appearance is the fundamental flaw in many of the most inventive ideas. If, like Mrs Mason, whose roof terrace in Devizes was formerly plagued by cats, I were to address the problem with:

1 cut-off plastic bottles full of water, buried in the soil
2 chicken wire folded over the rims of earthenware pots
3 garden canes with three inch plastic pots on the ends placed between bulbs
4 zig-zags of black thread between the canes
5 balloons filled with water that the cats will explode with their claws

I think I might begin to question the appeal of a garden, no matter how gloriously cat-free, that looks like the fall-out from a *Blue Peter* 'build your own space ship' project.

Less obtrusive solutions include covering the soil surface with an annual spring layer of holly or rose clippings, which foliage would soon obscure, and growing rue or Russian comfrey – plants which most cats find offensive (many thanks to Sheila Willliams of Bath and Mrs Harrison of Deal in Kent). The most alarming suggestion goes to Monica Legget of Ipswich, who, after recommending Jeyes Fluid as her choice deterrent, talks darkly of 'keen and unscrupulous garden-ers who put *starfish* on their gardens, which kill the cat'. The most unlikely was the purchase of a rabbit – Mr and Mrs Wilkinson of Alnick report that since installing a white rabbit in a hutch in their garden they have 'no cats – but also not many plants, as he eats anything that grows an inch above the soil...'.

By far the most popular cat deterrent, however, is water – both for efficiency and for the additional sporting bonus it provides. A good-quality children's water pistol is the weapon of choice – 'One good squirt with my son's SuperSoaker 500 does the trick,' writes S.G. Wadsworth of Manchester – and seems capable of an accurate aim. Some readers take up sniper positions from an upper window; others lie in wait by the cat flap and fire through the opening. 'Although I am a cat owner,' says Philip Berkin of south London, voicing the opinions of many, 'I do find a direct hit on an enemy cat hugely gratifying – and only the dignity of the animal is affected.' Now you don't need to be an expert to know that, for cats, dignity is *everything*.

Though I'm immensely grateful for all the suggestions, many of which I have not been able to mention, I have to report one slightly disturbing side effect. I haven't seen my boyfriend for days. Forget the motor racing on television – or even regular meal times. He is upstairs at the bathroom window with the jet hose, practising his new hobby.

16 March 1997 ~ The Allotment

It has finally happened. After more than a year of total neglect, my neighbour at the allotment has had his membership withdrawn, and his plot has been offered to me. My new kingdom – a sixty-two by twenty-four foot patch of nettles, weeds and brambles, dotted with the ramshackle remains of cold frames made from scruffy skip-wood – may not look like much to crow about, but in allotment terms it is quite a coup. Adjoining plots, rather than two at opposite ends of a site, save the hassle of toing and froing with tools and watering cans in tow. But naturally, they are hard to come by. And not many have a south-facing ten foot high fence running right down one side – the closest thing to heaven for french and runner beans.

But the crowning glory, as far as I'm concerned, is the shed – a wonderfully rickety construction tacked together from old window frames and corrugated plastic, and the only such building on the entire site. I have coveted this shed for nearly a year, imagining myself pottering about inside on cloudy days, browsing through seed catalogues, propagating cuttings and raising tomato plants on the neat wooden staging. I could bring my own Thermos flask, like the retired Turkish judge three plots down, and sit with a cup of tea in the doorway, out of the wind. We could even store plates, cutlery and a calor-gas heater there for knocking up impromptu feasts on summer evenings.

The other weekend, my sister and I spent a sunny Sunday digging over the manured beds of our existing plot, planting broad beans and Jerusalem artichokes and preparing the soil for spring sowings of radishes, lettuce and beetroot. As a break from the hard work, we went for a prowl around our new property. We felt a bit like pioneers exploring an unsettled jungle. Wide-eyed enthusiasm for all we could do with this wild new frontier – a fruit cage, plastic polytunnels for raising cucumbers and aubergines, space to experiment with 'green manures' such as buckwheat and comfrey that are grown to dig back into the soil – alternated with pangs of despair at the amount of work it would entail.

We were buoyed up by last year's experience, which taught us just how quickly a virtual scrap heap can be transformed into a wannabe potager, and by the discovery of hidden treasure among the weeds and rubbish. We found an impressive-looking galvanised metal water butt over in the far corner, a well-built double compost bin (one can never have too many) and a long, low lockable chest which would be ideal for storing tools. Tall weeds obscure six or seven rectangular raised beds – the organic gardener's ideal growing medium – made from old scaffolding boards set deep in the soil. All that needs to be done is to lift off their thick fringe of grass and refill them with a mixture of well-rotted manure (from the city farm) and fresh top-soil (from a heap that's appeared after decades of rubbish was cleared from beneath a hedge). Most exciting of all, there is an old-fashioned flower bed with budding forsythia and pussy willows, clumps of oxeye daisies and daffodils and a couple of sturdy rose bushes. It has inspired me to turn a third of the plot into a cutting garden for flowers for the house.

As the first spots of rain plopped from a gunmetal sky, we retired to our glorious new shed to continue our plans. No sooner were we ensconced inside than the anoraked figure of Barbara, committee member with special responsibility for lettings, appeared at the door. She handed us this year's subscription invoice (a snip at £40.17 for the two plots). The committee is apparently delighted that such a keen team has taken over from our lazy ex-neighbour. It appears he was something of a maverick character and not at all popular with the powers-that-be. 'He got away with all sorts of things that are expressly forbidden in the bylaws,' grumbled Barbara, shaking her head. 'That shed will have to go for a start. No buildings higher than four feet on this site or we'll lose our right to be here.'

No amount of pleading – or promises of cups of piping hot tea on demand – could persuade her otherwise.

13 April 1997 ~ Home

Some might call me a glutton for punishment. Having finally freed our back garden from the ravages of builders and (thanks to a trusty water pistol) the neighbourhood cats, I have opened the door to potentially the most destructive force of all: Rolf the lurcher puppy. So far, he has confined himself to claiming the corner near the basement steps as his personal lavatory, and conducting an energetic game of hunt-the-ball across the concrete. Which is just as well, as the garden is looking surprisingly good for its first spring, and I intend to keep it that way.

The rambling roses, jasmine, ivies and several varieties of clematis have begun their long climb up the chunky wooden trellis – painted white to match the walls – which we erected on moving in last summer. Rosettes of new leaves, their fresh pale green contrasting with last year's glossy growth, have appeared on the evergreen honeysuckle (Lonicera japonica) – so much more preferable to the deciduous varieties which overwinter as an untidy brown tangle). And a white flowering quince (Chaenomeles speciosa 'Nivalis'), planted on the south-facing wall, is swelling into pink-tinged bud. Advice to train climbers horizontally seems to have paid off. When the aim is to clothe a large, high area as fast as possible, it can be tempting to send all the shoots upwards, but securing the side shoots sideways does, as the books say, encourage vertical growth all along each stem. I've tended to use green card-and-wire plant ties, rather than thread the growth through the trellis, as mature stems may become thick enough to buckle the wood.

At ground level, too, things are faring better than I'd feared. Foxgloves and delphiniums have defied the builders' worst intentions, pushing heroically through pools of dried-up plaster water (now scooped off). Teazles and acanthus (gifts from a friend who grows only spiky foliage plants in his rather scary garden) are also doing well. The only casualties appear to be a trio of silver-grey globe artichokes I'd been keen to cultivate in a corner, a drift of white lupins, a pretty viola and a clump of lime green Euphorbia x martinii.

The star of the show is my collection of hellebores, in various shades of dirty pink, white and milky green, which I planted in a large old fluted metal laundry tub. Hellebores are delicate creatures requiring moist but well-drained soil, so this tub, found in a junk-shop, quarter-filled with broken bricks and topped up with a mixture of compost, garden soil and well-rotted horse manure, seems ideal. Drilling drainage holes an inch or two up from the base, instead of on the bottom, avoids the need to stand the tub on chocks, and it looks very smart in one of the corners.

Although I didn't realise it at the time, planting hellebores in a high container means you are far better placed to appreciate their breathtaking blooms. The flowers hang down like bells, and are often half-hidden between large serrated leaves, so you have to cup a hand underneath to look into their faces. In public gardens, I've even seen keen plant-spotting types lie down on their backs in the mud to gaze at their ghostly beauty. Raising my hellebores four feet off the ground not only means no one will ever have to resort to such behaviour in my garden – which is just as well, given the habits of an untoilet-trained puppy – more importantly, the plants will be well out of Rolf's reach when his curiosity about the garden inevitably extends beyond the concrete.

20 April 1997 ~ Italian Balconies

In an old Italian movie – I think the title in English was *The Special Day* – a passionate affair between Sophia Loren and Marcello Mastroianni begins from their overlooking balconies in Rome. On the day of Hitler's visit to the capital, they are the only occupants of their block to have stayed away from the celebrations, and she, a mother and housewife, attracts his attention as she hangs out her laundry in the sun. It is hard to imagine such a romance taking root in Britain, where we guard our privacy to a point of obsession. On most balconies I know, a discreet trellis screen or sentry of clipped box trees would have put paid to any such dalliances before they'd got off the ground. Not so in Italy, where so much of life is traditionally lived out in public. If the stage is not the local bar or the evening *passeggiata* down the main drag of shops, it will be the balcony – which no apartment, however small or humble, seems to be without.

When I lived in Rome ten years ago, I spent a lot of time in a friend's flat in the southern suburbs of the city – one of Mussolini's *case popolari* and not unlike the apartment in the film. The little balcony, which must have been all of six by four feet, had an unimpeded view into the twenty or more similar balconies of the block opposite – and, thus, into twenty or more very different lives. Eating out on the balcony on summer evenings was like watching a bank of television screens, each tuned to a different channel. People had parties on their balconies – particularly during the football season when, throughout the city, the entire contents of the average sitting room – sofa, arm-chairs, drinks tables, televisions and all – would be hauled out through the windows so the match could be enjoyed *al fresco*. You'd never be in any doubt as to how the game was going. The roar that went up every time Juventus scored would ricochet round the walls like thunder.

People had arguments on their balconies – not cool, clenched-jaw, English-fashion arguments, but hot-blooded slanging matches in which faces were slapped and terracotta pots sent smashing to the ground below. We once considered calling the police when the man who lived directly opposite had his brother in a half-nelson over the railings.

In fact, people did everything out on their balconies, from cooking and eating to keeping pets (Great Danes, caged canaries and even a pot-bellied pig) and washing their dirty linen – both literally and metaphorically – in public. And on sweaty, sultry summer nights, they even made love on mattresses among the tubs of bougainvillaea, with little regard as to who might see or hear.

My friend's balcony must have seemed very dull by comparison. There was a week one summer, when I sat out there, night after night, nursing the insomnia born of a broken heart, with a pile of books, a stack of cigarettes and a bottle of grappa, till dawn broke over the stubble of television aerials. I'd watch, barely moving, as the level in the bottle dropped and the blooms on the blood-red hibiscus withered, closed and gave way to the new day's buds opening. There was, I seem to remember, a strange, self-indulgent solace in the thought that someone somewhere might be watching *me* out there among the chimney pots, hamming it up as the star of my own tragic movie.

4 May 1997 ~ The Allotment

Now that my second spring's sowings at the allotment are underway, I realise how much my confidence has grown over the past
twelve months. Last year, like many gardeners new to vegetables, I
feared that nothing would survive unless I followed the books and
seed packet instructions to the letter. I was meticulous about planting depths and spacings, and saw that the precise amounts of bonemeal, lime and calcified seaweed were added to particular parts of
the plot. And I sowed ridiculous amounts of radish and sunflowers
simply because I'd grown them before and knew I could bank on
them. The thought of an empty plot (not to mention a dearth of
subject matter for this column) was a constant fear.

As so often happens, however, experience has proved otherwise.
Either I've been lucky, or vegetable growing is by no means the
exact and obscure science that some specialists would have us
believe. As trial and error crept in, it slowly dawned on me that
nature is perfectly able to get on with things, given the right basic
ingredients and a modicum of human interference. Good soil is
definitely a must (all the effort, expense and smelly afternoons
acquiring large supplies of well-rotted horse manure were well
spent), as are good food (I've long sworn by an organic seaweed
liquid called Maxicrop), adequate sun and water and, of course,
good seed. But beyond that, my intentions this year are to worry less
and experiment more.

Apart from really tender stuff like tomatoes, peppers and basil, I
have not bothered to raise seedlings under glass. Last year's early
lettuce, courgettes, pumpkins, spinach and sweetcorn, fussed and
fretted over for weeks in my camper-van-cum-mobile-greenhouse,
did no better when planted out than much later sowings of seed
straight into the soil. Indeed, in some cases, they did worse.
Seedlings don't like being transplanted, no matter how and when
you do it (I followed an old country tip to do it in the early evening,
when the plant's life energy is concentrated in the roots, rather than
the leaves and flowers).

This year, I've decided to grow all my lettuce and salad crops in yard-square blocks, rather than traditional rows. Last year I had both, thinning out rows of lettuce to make further rows elsewhere. I got far better results from the blocks, where the seedlings were not disturbed: I sowed sparsely, and used any thinnings in salads, leaving room for the remaining plants to fatten up where they were sown. The main advantage of planting in rows is that weeding is easier in the early weeks, when you can use the hoe. But when the plants take off, a denser coverage of leaves helps keep the weeds down, as does a light mulch of grass clippings or compost. The spinach ('Perpetual Leaf Beet') and ruby chard I grew like this last year are still going great guns – and the patchwork of different coloured squares looks more interesting than rows.

In a long narrow strip next to the fence, I have sown a square yard each of rocket (seeds bought in Italy), 'Red Salad Bowl' lettuce, lambs' lettuce, mixed radishes and two ready-mixed selections of salad leaves including 'Saladini' (butterhead and cos lettuce, endive and chicory). As protection from frost and wind, I propped up six old sash windows on their ends to make a cloche. The first paper-fine leaves have already shot through and are growing fast.

11 May 1997 ~ Community Allotments in Dagenham

Move over Swampy and Sean Connery. I have just met my new hero. Barry Watson is a member of BOG – Becontree Organic Growers – a group of local people who are reclaiming three acres of previously derelict land in Dagenham, Essex, and converting it into community 'Permaculture' allotments (see p. 245). 'Be prepared for a culture shock,' Mr Watson had warned, when I'd telephoned to ask if I might visit. 'It's nothing like a traditional allotment site.'

At first glance the patch of ground, strewn with rusty shopping trolleys, plastic bags and cardboard, bordered on one side by storage yards and on the other by the further reaches of the District Line, looked a mess. But, as Mr Watson was only too keen to point out, everything was there for a purpose. 'The trolleys are for pushing heavy stuff about – no need to break your back,' he said, tucking his thumbs through the straps of a rather large pair of dungarees. The bags were full of dead leaves, pigeon droppings or smashed-up cockle shells. Along with the cardboard, these are all vital components in Mr Watson's primary passion: making soil.

Barry Watson is an advocate of Permaculture – short for permanent agriculture – a strain of organic gardening that originated in Australia but which is fast gaining ground over here. In a nutshell, its principles include the notion of minimum outlay and effort for maximum return, where returns are measured not only in economic terms, but also in environmental benefit, quality, convenience and – very important – enjoyment. Strict permaculturalists eschew such activities as double-digging and sowing annuals in rows in favour of the 'no-dig perennial garden'. And instead of transporting expensive materials from shops and faraway places, they see what can be obtained, for free if possible, on their doorstep.

According to Mr Watson, it would have taken five years of weed killing to reclaim this site by conventional methods. Instead, he did it the Permaculture way, jumping on the weeds to damage them, then covering them with a thick layer of old cardboard boxes. The cardboard is then watered well or left to catch the next rainfall. He adds six inches of horse manure (delivered free of charge by the local police stables), a layer of dead leaves, some twiggy clippings and grass cuttings, and covers the lot with an old carpet or more cardboard. 'Six months later, you've got beautiful fertile soil – and earthworms as big as pythons!' he laughs.

'A lot of this stuff can be had for free,' he continues. 'Local authorities are now having to pay someone to take away their clippings from the parks, and it's actually cheaper for them to dump them here. Ludicrous!'

Dagenham residents are beginning to join in the fun. Unlike a regular allotment, there are no proprietorial plots; people come along, put in a few hours' work and leave with a bag of produce. But it's a slow process. 'To lots of people round here, gardening still means buying a plant from Woolworth's for £1.99 and then £5 worth of chemicals to keep it alive,' says Mr Watson. 'So it's softly, softly.'

18 May 1997 ~ Home

Our young lurcher puppy has begun to work his worst in the back garden. The other day I found him gnawing at the stem of a *Clematis montana* that had just reached the top of the wall – the first of the climbers I put in last year to do so. My favourite brand of horticultural first aid – a poultice of cotton wool soaked in dilute seaweed feed and Dr Bach's Rescue Remedy, which has revived many a moribund plant in the past – failed to save it. The puppy's sharp little teeth had all but severed the stem. How long would it be until my other plants met the same gory fate?

I worried about the problem for a day or two. I don't want to turn into one of those dog owners whose gardens are so enmeshed in plastic-coated fencing that one can hardly see the plants. Then I remembered an old *World of Interiors* feature on the little courtyard gardens of Cordoba in Spain (see p. 241). Every spring, the locals whitewash their little gardens and cover the walls with dozens of potted pelargoniums. The splashes of red and pink, hung haphazardly up and down the walls, create the impression of a bright, flowery wallpaper. Sometimes the pots and paintwork are picked out in a contrasting colour, such as bright blue.

I decided to do the same with my garden. Not only would the plants be well out of the puppy's reach, but the eye would be attracted upwards while I waited for the other climbers, protected by a discreet fence of chicken wire, to make more progress. A trip to Columbia Road flower market early last Sunday yielded two large trays of scarlet pelargoniums for £8 apiece, and I supplemented these with a few pink striped trailing types – variety, rather than good taste, is the thing with this approach. There was no need to get out the whitewash (my garden walls are already white), and the trellis we put up on our arrival is more than strong enough to support thirty or forty small and medium-sized pots. (You need a lot to achieve the wallpaper effect.)

I spent a happy afternoon potting my pelargoniums and attaching the smart galvanised buckets to the strongest points in the trellis. You can buy terracotta pots specially designed for the purpose, with holes in one side, that can be hung from hooks in the wall, or collars that fit snugly round the pot and can be nailed to walls or fences (Habitat has stylish ones in white or galvanised metal). The pots do take a bit of watering. I'll follow the Cordoban example and clip the hose head to the end of a pole to reach the highest ones. But there's no question that the effort will be worth it. My garden now looks as jaunty and colourful as any Spanish courtyard and is attracting admiring attention from friends and neighbours. In fact, about the only creature not to take the slightest bit of interest in it all is Rolf, the lurcher puppy.

25 May 1997 ~ The Allotment

There's a big concrete slab on my new allotment where my next door neighbour's shed used to be. This is the shed that I coveted like mad for an entire year, only to be told, when I'd already taken on the extra plot on which it stood, that it had to come down. It was against the rules – something about not having planning permission for structures more than four feet high. We'd only had the new plot for two or three weeks when we were given an unofficial warning about it. So one windy Sunday, down it came – surprisingly easily, in fact, as I suspect it was falling down anyway. But it's a shame it had to go.

Sheds have always seemed to me a crucial component of the allotment landscape; as vital to the makeshift, make-do aesthetic as rows of peas and runner beans poles. Aesthetics aside, it would have been nice to have somewhere to keep our tools and seeds and to shelter when the weather turns bad. My boyfriend has had the inspired idea of 'burying' the shed – digging new foundations deep into the earth so that the height above ground would conform to the regulations, while its Tardis-like interior would be just as big as ever. It's an excellent idea – also suggested in a letter from a reader, Mrs Wilson from Carmarthenshire – but whether my boyfriend will be so keen when all that digging starts in earnest remains to be seen. Another reader, Miss Heap of Castle Cary, Somerset, sent in drawings of her ingenious idea to adapt the shed into a 'foldaway summerhouse like those foldaway caravan trailers'. Her illustration shows a hinged roof which can be raised or lowered, and a smart striped awning providing shade at the front.

Luckily, the new plot does provide some compensations for the loss of the shed. Having lain fallow for a year, the soil in the seven large raised beds (constructed by the previous owner) seems remarkably good. We have already allocated one bed for potatoes ('Pink Fir Apples' again); one for a further sowing of broad beans and peas, and two for cut flowers for the house. Another, which has high glass sides, should be good for encouraging early tomatoes or sweetcorn. Liberated from the ground elder that threatened to engulf it, a further bed is already spilling over with strawberry plants. And I think I may have spotted a few currant bushes.

Even more exciting are the flowers which we've stumbled across, growing wild among the dandelions and long grass: bluebells, oxeye daisies, deep purple bearded iris and a yellow dog rose. There's also a clump of apple mint, a fine crop of lemon balm and a large rosemary bush. This year, at least, we can afford to leave some of the new plot as it is. We can always call it a wildlife garden. And – who knows? – the concrete base of the shed would make a great spot for a barbecue. There's nothing nicer than corn on the cob, freshly picked and cooked where it grew. I'm looking forward to summer already.

1 June 1997 ~ Home

I'm a great believer in the power of flowers as a cure for the condition known as Terminal DIY. Ever since we moved in to our four-storey building site last summer, I've spent almost as much at the florists as I have at B&Q in an effort to divert attention from the large expanses of peeling paint work and crumbling plaster. It's now time for a floral remedy for the outside of the house. It looked fine in spring. But by the time I decided on my scheme for summer the hundred or so white and yellow daffodils that had looked so pretty in pots and troughs from February till May had long since faded. Until a few weeks ago the sole eye-catching feature was a heap of empty boxes and builders' rubble.

My idea was this: to combine an attractive, plant-covered façade with a sort of floral screen for the sitting room, whose wide bay window, only a yard or two from the street, is a magnet for Nosy Parkers. If I grew tall or climbing things in the window boxes, and trailing plants in the jumble of pots on the flat, asphalted roof of the bay, I should have a display which fulfilled many purposes at once. Morning glory and nasturtiums are the plants I chose – both for their ease of cultivation and for the glorious combination of the former's clear, bright, perfect-summer's-day blue with the latter's unpredictable rich tones of orange, red and saffron yellow. The climbing variety – the triffid of the nasturtium world, which I've known to reach twelve feet or more – is the one to go for. Last year's crop in our back garden covered a sunny wall with foliage and blooms right up to the first frosts just before Christmas.

The front of the house is less sheltered, but despite facing northeast, it gets a good morning's worth of sun, and the seeds planted a month ago are now well on their way. A dozen morning glory seeds raised in my camper-van-cum-greenhouse were carefully transplanted, and more seed sown in situ for good measure. I soaked the seeds overnight in a liquid seaweed solution to soften their hard casings (added by suppliers to prevent the hallucinogenic kernels from being eaten) and they all germinated within two days. Sawn-off plastic bottles upended over the seedlings protected early growth from the vicious and unpredictable late frosts. Around twenty plants are now snaking their way up the garden wire I trained around and in front of the windows (at intervals of about a foot), or even beginning to trail down from above. The nasturtiums have just produced their second sets of saucer-like leaves and are fast catching up. In the meantime, a few red pelargoniums left over from my efforts in the back garden will look cheerful while we wait to see if the scheme will work.

Ideally, the growth will be enough to provide some privacy in the sitting room and to filter, rather than shut out, the summer sun. It should make a good start to the day to come downstairs and count how many morning glory blooms have come out. Most importantly, the flowers will divert attention away from the scruffy exterior paint-work till we can afford to get it fixed next year.

8 June 1997 ~ Home

As spring turns into summer, it seems even more important to have a view from the window where I work. Since moving to this house last year, I have tried out three different rooms as a potential study, finally settling on a bedroom at the back of the house, where I have positioned my desk so I can see some trees. The average view from the back of a terraced London house such as ours is that familiar patchwork of next-door neighbours' gardens stretching into infinity on either side, with the rear extensions of the houses in parallel roads glimpsed (ideally) through greenery.

Nice though this can be, it has always had the effect of making me feel claustrophobic – all those little kingdoms, all those twitching curtains – so the fact that we look out over the flat asphalt roof of a single-storey warehouse has always seemed to be an advantage. I have the occasional mad fantasy about laying Astroturf on this roof, turning it into a tennis court or (best of all) a tropical garden with palm-fringed swimming pool. But most of the time I am content to gaze out at the trees beyond it and watch the neighbours' cats criss-cross the asphalt or sun themselves on the surrounding walls. I have sited my desk to include a small ash tree and two large elders in my line of vision – the progression of the latter from frilly white saucers of flowers to berries will be interesting to watch.

I was really rather pleased with this arrangement till I went to visit my friend Matthew, who also works from home – a rather larger house in a rather posher part of London. I wrote about Matthew's garden a couple of months ago – he and his wife had just bought the house and the 100-foot garden was wintry and bare, its secrets still locked in the freezing soil. Now, of course, it has come colourfully alive. From his first floor study window, Matthew looks out on a sea of ever-changing blossoms as first a *Clematis armandii* and then a *C. montana* 'Grandiflora' romp their way through the branches of a large pear tree. A deep red clematis has clothed a little arbour in improbably large flowers, and a clump of peonies has exploded into blowsy crimson bloom. There are hollyhocks, cranesbill geraniums and poppies still in bud – and lots of old roses scrambling up the walls among a tangle of honeysuckle, jasmine and climbing hydrangea. Lucky old Matthew. And, if he should ever tire of flowers, he can spy on his little dog burying bones in the flowerbeds or watch his wife walking their new baby up and down the garden path. I'm ashamed to say I felt slightly jealous of it all.

I returned home that evening to find a For Sale sign on the entrance to the warehouse behind our house. 'Development Potential' it read – and I rang the agents the next morning to find out more. Conversion of the warehouse into flats would be bad news for our little back yard, not to mention our light and privacy. Thinking on the bright side, though, if I could lay my hands on the £75,000 asking price, buy the building and knock it down, I, too could be the proud owner of a 100-foot garden.

22 June 1997 ~ Two London Roof Terraces

The other weekend I spent two glorious sunny evenings on two very different roof terraces. The first is a fashionable, almost minimalist affair on top of a tiny mews house near Holborn. It belongs to two friends, both architects, who have shown the same style and ingenuity on the roof of their house as they have in shoe-horning an open-plan living space and bedrooms for their three young children inside it. To reach the garden you have to step out of the first-floor sitting room window and on to a salvaged spiral staircase that twists in vertigo-inducing fashion up the side of the house. The scene that

greets you is surprisingly lush – wisteria and vines hang in leafy swags from thick chandlers' ropes slung around the periphery; a star-studded passion flower covers the south-facing wall, while a dark, variegated ivy stands out against the yellowish bare brick. A long bed made from weathered railway sleepers is planted with scented hedges of rosemary and lavender. Most of the other planting is in galvanised metal containers: not just the trendy elongated flower buckets that I bought from Ikea for my own garden, but good old utilitarian receptacles put to imaginative use. Shiny new dustbins provide homes for standard trees clipped into large lollipop balls – a box, a bay and a silvery weeping pear. A long tin bath, of the sort you can still pick up from old-fashioned hardware stores, has been made into an impromptu water garden, planted with reeds, bog irises and marsh marigolds – I imagine the frogs and toads that have made their home there will help keep the roof garden slug and snail-free. Smaller tin pots and buckets have been planted up with hebes, saxifrage and different types of grasses – the ideal plant for roofs as their spiky thin leaves loose less moisture in the sun than larger-leaved species. I particularly liked the smoky blue of *Festuca glauca* and made a note to include it in my own garden. All you need to do to convert metal receptacles into plant pots is to drill drainage holes in the bottom, fill the first six inches with broken bricks and rubble, and pour in a mixture of multi-purpose compost and well-rotted manure.

The second roof garden is in south London, just around the corner from our house – on top of a tenement block, high above the traffic among the chimney pots and water tanks. Unlike the Holborn garden, which was planned down to the last detail, this is a piece-meal, haphazard affair: a cheerful jumble of old Belfast sinks, black plastic builders' buckets, lengths of clay flue liner and old enamel bread bins spills over with marigolds and violas, mauve and white campanulas and the starry white flowers of rocket gone to seed. Height is provided by clouds of bronze fennel and bamboo, and even a few young trees planted in brightly coloured swing-bins among cushions of 'Mind-your-own-business'. I was intrigued by some shallow baskets planted with house-leeks and other small suc-culents that thrive in these rooftop conditions – they are old fruit baskets, used to bring mangoes and bananas over from the Caribbean and salvaged from the market on the streets below.

Everything in this little garden has had to be lugged up five flights of stairs – but the results are well worth the effort. The scenario is constantly changing; the containers are shunted about as different plants die or flourish of come into flower. Fellow occupants of flats in the block have started to follow suit, with other corners of the roof sprouting tomato plants or tubs of marigolds and nasturtiums. It's a real inspiration.

Our own flat roof is still bare while I concentrate on getting the garden going – but it's still one of my favourite places anywhere in the house. I like to sit up there in the early morning, drinking my coffee and watching the clouds clear as the town cranks into gear below. And where else in London can I get an unimpeded view of the sunset so close to home?

29 June 1997 ~ New Reading Matter

I was recently sent a copy of the second issue of The London Gardener (see p. 243), an elegantly old-fashioned publication subtitled The Gardener's Intelligencer for the Year 1996-7: Containing More in Quantity, and Greater Variety, than Any Book of the Kind and Price. Its slim red cover would not have looked out of place in the pocket of a famous 18th-century gentleman gardener such as William Kent – but seldom have I found such a scholarly-looking volume so hard to put down. Where else could one find witty, entertaining features on subjects as diverse and unlikely as The 'Mole Duke's' secret garden at Harcourt House, Cavendish Square (a horticultural Colditz complete with eighty-foot screens created for the reclusive 5th Duke of Portland, known as the Mole Duke on account of the extraordinary underground ballroom, hunting stables and tunnels he constructed at Welbeck Abbey), or The Model Traffic Recreation Area at Lordship Lane (a Toytown miniature road layout in Tottenham, still in existence today, in which Thirties children learned road safety in pedal cars hired out by the half-hour)?

This gem of a magazine is the annual journal of the London Historic Parks and Gardens Trust, an independent charitable trust founded in 1994 to 'promote education about historic parks and gardens in London and to seek to conserve and enhance these gardens for the education and enjoyment of the public'. Worthy aims indeed, but the Trust manages to combine a scholarly approach with a contemporary flair and sense of fun. Its headquarters are in the gingerbread-style Duck Island Cottage in the middle of the lake in St James's Park, rescued by the Trust from a sorry fate as a store for confiscated bicycles. A fascinating history of the Cottage appeared in the first issue of the journal in 1995.

Both Trust and journal are the brainchild of Todd Longstaffe-Gowan, a historic gardens advisor and landscape designer with an encyclopaedic knowledge of the capital's gardens. His inspiration was Thomas Fairchild's 'The City Gardener' (1722), the first ever publication by a celebrated London florist, nurseryman and botanist dedicated to the culture, treatment and improvement of 'little town gardens in London'. The magazine relies largely on charitable funding, and its impressive stable of contributors writes for free. Though the quaint design and typeface were adapted from 18th-century copies of the *Spectator* and *The Gentleman's Magazine*, the contents are by no means devoid of contemporary mischief. A piece on the public gardens of Bloomsbury, for instance, begins by quoting Virginia Woolf on the 'fat white slugs' that frequent her local tea rooms – one wonders what she would make of both the modern burger bar now named after her and, indeed, the expanses of office-worker flesh displayed in Russell Square on summer days. Also included is a rant entitled Public Parks and the Lottery Millions that calls for the renewal of the city's public gardens. The next issue, says Mr Longstaffe-Gowan, will include an impassioned plea to provide landscaped flamingo pools in modern day office blocks.

6 July 1997 ~ The Allotment

The allotments are looking at their most colourful and full of promise. Walking the 300 or 400 yards from the gate to our two plots in the far corner, I make frequent stops to admire the little flower borders that form an edging to many of the plots – leftovers from the days when few allotment holders had gardens at home.

In one bed, feather bronze fennel is interplanted with blue love-in-the-mist and old-fashioned marigolds; in another, raggedy white pinks and lemon aquilegias are dotted among different types of thyme. My favourite, for which I have to make a detour, belongs to an old couple right at the top of the site – even from the gate you can see the tall spires of thirty or forty delphiniums in every shade of blue, rising from bushes of dark red roses and jasmine.

Our own patch is looking pretty colourful, too. My ambitions for a cut-flower garden in our second, newer plot may have some way to go, as the seedlings are still quite small, but the vegetables are doing more than enough to compensate. The patchwork of square lettuce beds down one side looks particularly good in the early morning and evening when the low sun shines right through the leaves, turning Red Salad Bowl a deep ruby. The peas and mangetout have been flowering away like mad, the white butterfly blooms a cool contrast to the fleshy grey-green leaves. In an oblong bed, covered with netting to keep off the birds, is a chequer-board planting of brassicas and cos lettuce. The purplish-blue bloom on the young cauliflower and Brussels sprout leaves looks good against the bright lime of the lettuce, particularly when a shower has turned the earth a deep reddish-brown and left beads of rain among the leaves.

French and runner beans are beginning their long climb up the wires we strung from the boundary fence last year. I've chosen colourful varieties such as French bean 'Viola cornetti' (purple pods that turn green on cooking) and 'Marvel of Venice' (lovely deep pink and white flowers). A bed of dwarf French beans, which reach no more than two feet and are self-supporting, are already eight to ten inches high, with two rows of sunflowers double that height in their midst.

In the new patch, courgettes and marrows are doing well, planted on little mounds of compost and manure with a circular trough around each to retain water. We also have sweetcorn, aubergine and peppers in a raised bed with high glazed sides that we inherited from our former neighbour. The warm, wind-free conditions inside – like a mini-greenhouse without a roof – are what young sweetcorn plants love. I put some leftover seedlings in among the potatoes in an unprotected bed, so it will be interesting to see how their growth compares.

As far as colour goes, however, I have to confess that some of the most interesting effects are provided by weeds and by the odd plant I've allowed to go to seed. I've been slightly less strict this year – but just as ruthless with real offenders such as bindweed, couchgrass and thistles; some speedwells, ground nettles and clumps of a nice lime spurge have been left to flower away round the edges of the beds, where they shouldn't do much harm. Lettuces that have bolted rise like crazy pagodas above the red-veined leaves of young beetroot, while a ruby chard plant that carried on right through the winter is now putting its all into a last spurt of growth, and sending bright red shoots spiralling out in every direction.

Best of all though, is the one purple sprouting broccoli plant I left in order to collect its seed. The size of a small tree, with a thick woody trunk, its 'branches' have been a cloud of yellow blossom as the remaining straggly purple flowerheads opened. They are now forming spindly dark pods – the promise of next year's crop.

13 July 1997 ~ The Allotment

I don't know much about my fellow plot-holders. An unspoken tenet of allotment etiquette seems to dictate that all conversation be confined to the 'three w's': weather, weeds and weevils. You may be privy to your neighbours' secret recipe for successful compost, and know more than you would ever want to about their battles with slugs or cabbage root fly; you may even entrust one another to water during summer holidays. But as for whether or not these people are married, which films they like, or what they do for a living – all topics that might quickly come up if you were meeting at a party – forget it. Trivial concerns such as these are left behind at the allotment gates.

One can do a bit of detective work, of course, and that is all part of the fun. I know that my Indian neighbour is married, because his wife sometimes turns up in a beautiful sari to choose the vegetables for their supper. And the chap with the husky dog and leather cowboy hat has six young children to feed, all of whom have been trained to weed and water.

Clues to peoples' occupations can be found in the materials used for their beanpoles, cold frames and all the other ramshackle structures and supports that make up the typical allotment landscape. One of my neighbours – the young man whose impressive raised beds and plastic polytunnels are the source of constant awe and envy on my part – is a builder and decorator. His neat stone paths are made from leftover pavers from gardening jobs, and the timber for his beds is old scaffolding planks – sturdier than floorboards and not so prone to sagging. I know all this because he let it slip one day when he caught me comparing his smart pine tomato stakes to my flimsy bamboo canes. 'Perk of the job,' he said – and admitted to some fortunate over-ordering on a few commissions. This also explains the constant supplies of black plastic sheeting through which he grows his potatoes and strawberries – the plastic acts as a mulch so he hardly ever needs to weed or water. It may also explain why our own builders' bills were so astronomical; maybe they, too, were secret gardeners.

Another of my neighbours is a park ranger. He trains his peas up holey old council tennis nets and seems to have endless access to stakes and wooden fencing. Judging by the healthy state of his compost heap, he also deposits several local parks'-worth of grass mowings and hedge clippings there every week. And you can tell the ex-employee of British Telecom a mile off: that silly corporate imp with a trumpet blasts away all around the cold frames and glazed beds in which he raises tomatoes and sweetcorn.

I don't mind knowing so little about these people – in fact, I rather like the anonymity. It doesn't affect the camaraderie on a windy day, or the times when there's only two or three of us left, weeding and tying and staking till the sun goes down. What they all make of me – and of the two male friends who are helping me with the second plot while my sister is away working in America for six months – I can only guess. But one thing's for sure. Beyond the gates, dressed in anything other than filthy old shorts and without the statutory fine coating of soil on nose, knees and elbows, I doubt they would even recognise me.

20 July 1997 ~ Sculpture in Small Gardens

I had not thought of large-scale sculpture as an option for the small urban garden until a visit to the Barbara Hepworth Sculpture Garden in St Ives, Cornwall, last month. The cool contrast of her smooth white shapes against glossy green foliage suddenly struck me as perfect for town gardens, particularly those dark, dank corners in which few cheery things will grow. I'm not suggesting that everyone can afford to stick a Hepworth in their garden – indeed, judging by the recent increase in theft from gardens, it would be foolish for those who can to do so. But a well-chosen piece could add a whole new dimension to even the smallest garden.

I tend to think of modern sculpture in large grassy expanses, or placed to form a focal point at the end of a long vista. But there is no reason why it cannot inhabit an enclosed space. Rather like placing a huge bed or sofa in a small room, the effect can  actually end up making the area look larger and grander, rather than small and cramped. The secret is to keep it simple. Evergreen foliage plants make the best accompaniment; their leaves will shine in the rain to make a nice textural contrast, and cast constantly changing shadows in sunlight. Don't crowd a small garden with pieces or it will look like an upmarket garden centre.

Sculpture can enlarge a small garden not only by physical effects but by the power of association. The incorporation of a few words from a poem on to a slate standing stone can open up the garden to all sorts of outside thoughts and references. Abstract pieces can be the source of endless fascination – some of Simon Randall Page's work, for instance, can look like a fossil in one light, an oversized grain of wheat in another, or a mother cradling a child as the sun goes down. And pieces bought on holidays abroad bring memories, materials and the whole culture of that place back into your home.

If you're not convinced – or if the thought of sculpture outside seems impractical or downright pretentious, why not make your sculpture work for you? If you're considering a sundial, birdbath or fountain, a one-off piece by an artist may actually not cost any more than a cast-concrete monstrosity from a garden centre. At Wolseley Fine Arts, a small gallery in west London (see page 241), I saw kinetic water sculptures (or fountains, if you prefer) by Edinburgh-based Sam Wade for as little as £395. His sculptures have component parts that fill with water and empty repeatedly, creating a trickling noise like a mountain stream and a soothing visual effect – just the ticket for a leafy urban retreat. The owner of this gallery, a Dutch woman called Hanneke van der Werf, is a great enthusiast of sculpture in small spaces – when she lived in Utrecht, several large wooden figures fixed into planters on her 1 x 2.5m balcony earned her a certain local notoriety.

The tiny walled garden of her gallery is crammed with all sorts of sculpture, from bird baths with Latin inscriptions to beautiful nude torsos in cedar wood or stone. For most of the year, the interior space is devoted to modern and old master paintings and drawings, but she devotes the entire space to summer exhibitions of garden sculpture by contemporary artists. It would be a good place to start if the idea of sculpture in the garden appeals, as you can see what the pieces look like outside.

My favourite was a simple slate monolith beautifully inscribed by Richard Kindersley with the words 'Be Still and Know'. Or what about a series of three patinaed bronze reliefs of a female nude seen from the back. Cleverly lit and hung on a brick or rendered wall, they would be the perfect solution for that dark, uncultivable corridor at the back of the average urban terraced house.

27 July 1997 ~ Home

This time last year I was utterly despondent about our garden, which was all but buried beneath heaps of builders' debris. Even a few months back I often wondered whether the challenge of turning a twenty foot square of concrete into an urban oasis wasn't beyond me. So it is heartening to report that things are looking rather jolly out there.

The tin buckets of pelargoniums that I tied all over the white trellised walls have been flowering away like mad, the way they so obligingly do. Back in May, the walls looked rather bare between these blazes of deep red, but the gaps are fast filling up with climbers. The various types of ivy I planted on moving here did little the first year but are now making excellent progress, and a succession of different clematis, jasmines, passion flowers and evergreen honeysuckles are weaving among them, their blooms standing out against the glossy green backdrop.

In front of the climbers, also in the raised beds that I inherited (empty) from the previous owner, are lots of very tall plants. Delphiniums of every shade of blue, mauve and white, spotted white foxgloves and lupins have been blooming away amid a froth of lime green *Alchemilla mollis* and seedlings of *Nicotiana silvestris* (the taller, very fragrant tobacco plant) are coming into bud. Tallest of all are some teazels, ornamental thistles and hollyhocks which I was given last year and popped in wherever I could find space among the builders' rubbish. I'd planned to transplant them before they took off in the spring. Needless to say, I didn't, so they are now towering away right in the front of the border – but I like this rather eccentric effect. The thistles are especially beautiful – *Eryngium planum* has fine-toothed greyish leaves and spiky calyxes fanning out around the seedhead – and one of the hollyhocks, its buds still tight shut, has only a few inches to go before it reaches the top of the ten-foot wall. I'm very glad I left them where they were.

In front of the beds, hiding their rather ugly white concrete edges, is a jumble of pots and containers, some of which I brought with me from the balcony of the flat where I used to live. Old habits die hard, and although I'm delighted to have a proper garden, however small, I'm still very keen on containers. There are galvanised florists' pots filled with mounds of saxifrage and hebes, and lots of terracotta pots spilling over with tomatoes, basil, marigolds and nasturtiums. Arranged on old painted tin tables are pots of my favourite succulents, which will retire inside come winter. The seats are old green cricket chairs, some little metal stools from India and a funny old curly metal affair sprayed shocking pink, which a friend was getting rid of.

By the door, old fire buckets perched on top of chimney pots have passion flowers, morning glory and a lemon-scented geranium that releases its scent as you brush past. But my favourite is one of the old fluted metal laundry tubs I found in a junk shop, from which seven *regale* lilies are springing up among dark red, lime and cream tobacco plants, filling the whole garden with their scent. I love to watch the lilies open – their pod-like buds turning from yellowish green to rosy pink to a deep, rich crimson as they swell and lengthen, and then split in the sun to reveal the creamy white insides and quivering anthers.

The drawback of container gardening is all the watering, although, for the earlier part of this damp summer, that hasn't been a problem. In fact, the very day I was out shopping for rainwater butts we suffered a torrential flood that wreaked havoc in our base-ment. So it looks as though the builders will be back. This time they can find somewhere else to put all their junk.

3 *August* 1997 ~ The Allotment

The freak rains earlier in the summer meant that two whole weeks went by when I didn't get to the allotment at all. Every time I thought about indulging in a little light weeding, the heavens opened and I had to think again. When the sun finally came out for more than ten minutes at a time, I was beginning to worry about what I might find.

The site slopes down towards our corner – which in a dry year is a good thing. That was the reason for last summer's twenty foot sun-flowers and forest of sweetcorn, I was told by envious visitors from 'up the top'. But what about after four weeks of more-or-less inces-sant rain? Would our two plots have been transformed into south London's answer to a Louisiana swamp, with a few sad potatoes bobbing on the surface? Or would the contents of the entire site – sixty-three plots complete with bean poles, cold frames and rows of vegetables – have been sent sliding down the slope to land like a muddy avalanche on top of our patch?

In a spirit of apprehension mixed with adventure, my friends and I arrived to survey the scene. No mud avalanches – we were safe on that front. Runner bean poles and cold frames were still in position – good. In fact, the overwhelming initial impression was one of lush, jungly growth. The peas and broad bean plants were heavy with fat bumpy pods – we picked six pounds of peas in less than half an hour. The shallots planted in April were nearly ready to lift, their spiky foliage blown over to reveal eight or ten pinky bulbs to each sett or plant, and the three beds of potatoes were flourishing. Inside the tall glass-walled cold frame, the sweetcorn had germinated and grown six or eight inches, and the aubergines and chilli peppers had three or four flowers apiece. Most satisfying of all, the cauliflowers were beginning to make creamy white hearts. Perhaps things weren't so bad after all.

The only problem seemed to be that the vegetables weren't the only plants to have put on a spurt of growth. The weeds were enormous. Bindweed threatened to engulf the french beans and sunflowers, while spires of fat hen rose high above the heads of spinach and rocket. As for the thistles – there were so many that it looked as if we'd sown them intentionally. We set about with gusto. Wet soil makes weeding easy as the roots come free with the slightest of tugs. There are few gardening tasks as satisfying as pulling up a thistle with its ten-inch tap root intact.

It was then that I saw it – nearly four inches long, and gunmetal grey with frilly orange edges – the biggest, fattest, ugliest slug I have ever encountered. And he had friends. Everywhere I looked, I could see the revolting creatures – and the appalling damage they had wrought. The red oak leaf lettuces and an embryonic crop of the Chinese leaf, Pak Choi had been stripped of their juicy leaves so that only a fan of stark white stalks remained. Some of the runner beans had been attacked so severely they no longer had leaves at all, and the latest young sowings of salad greens and radishes had completely disappeared. How could I have thought there was nothing wrong?

After trying unsuccessfully to interest our dog in the snack potential of slugs, I pulled on my gloves and went mercilessly to work. Fifty or sixty were sent soaring through the air to land on the tarmac of the Territorial Army depot next door, where I hope they were run over by trucks. I am sorry, but I find myself unable to summon up a scrap of sympathy for slugs. And with all the weeding done, they'd have no choice but to come back for the cream of the crop.

10 *August* 1997 ~ Back Gardens in Suburbia

When, as a small child, we moved from a farm in Kent to the London suburbs, I became fascinated by people's back gardens. In the country, borders were defined by fields and hedges; in Bromley a four foot fence separated you from the neighbours. One of my favourite activities was to skulk along the grassy verge of the golf course at the end of our garden and peer into all the back gardens in our street. They were a very mixed bunch — most had been land-scaped to some degree, with the usual curved beds of shrubs cutting into a manicured lawn. My favourite, I'm rather ashamed to say, was a crazy paving paradise belonging to the old man next-door-but-one. It was regimentally tidy and dotted with dwarf conifers, bright red salvias and African marigolds, and I think there were probably a few garden gnomes thrown in for good measure.

Most of our neighbours took an almost obsessive pride in their gardens, and expected others to be of the same mind. Shortly after we moved in, I remember my father being outraged by a note posted through our door, suggesting that the unruly state of our front garden was somehow 'letting the side down'. His response, I am glad to say, was to do nothing at all. But no matter how wild our garden got, it could never compete with that belonging to Mr Pettigrew, an eccentric old bachelor who lived several doors down. To deliver his newspaper on my morning paper round, I had to duck and dive under Sleeping Beauty-like bowers of brambles and get my socks soaked by the dewy, knee-high grass. His back garden was a suburban jungle, where bindweed and ivy hung like Spanish moss from huge oak trees, and foxes and badgers frolicked in almost impenetrable undergrowth. People would moan about the smell of the foxes, the bindweed spreading, or the seed from the thistles playing havoc in their rose beds. But Mr Pettigrew would do nothing to appease them. Occasionally, I would catch a glimpse of him in the early evening sun, just visible above the weeds in an ancient deck chair, a large glass of sherry in one hand and a cloud of butterflies about his head.

These days, of course, Mr Pettigrew could simply have told his busybody neighbours that he was making an environmentally friendly wildlife garden and that would have been the end of that. No one would have had the heart to complain. Gardeners are showing increasing interest in the subject, and advertisements in newspapers following the recent Rio Plus Five Earth Summit in New York urge us all to try to make some space for wildlife in any land we might own, from farms to office compounds to urban back gardens.

I recently attended a course in wildlife gardening held at the London Wildlife Garden Centre in south London (see p. 242) – a fantastic but little-known set-up created in 1987 from a rat-infested derelict council depot at the back of some houses in Southwark. It began as a nursery to propagate native trees to replace those lost in the Great Storm, and has developed into an impressive show garden, with a grass-roofed education centre and a nursery specialising in plants that are indigenous to the Thames Basin. To my great surprise, these include salad burnet, evening primrose, red valerian, marjoram and hops – all of which can be purchased for a voluntary donation to funds. Latterday Mr Pettigrews should be sure to pay a visit.

17 August 1997 ~ Pantelleria, Italy

I recently spent a week on Pantelleria, an island midway between Sicily and Tunisia and known to Italians as the 'island of the winds'. The *levante* from the east brings a much-needed freshness in the height of summer, while the *sirocco* from the south feels like a hairdryer pumping hot air through the already scorching streets. When the *mezzogiorno* blows in from Africa, covering everything in its path with a coating of rusty red dust, the islanders stay inside their domed stone houses and close the doors and windows till it passes. Hardly any rain falls between May and October.

Gardening in such an extreme climate is hard. Surrounded by unpolluted deep blue sea, you'd have thought the Pantescans would be fishermen; however, most try their hand at tilling the fertile volcanic soil. The steep hillsides are terraced with low walls made from lava boulders and planted with olive trees, capers and low-growing vines for the strong local wine. Even town-dwellers have a few small fields to cultivate, supplementing their regular income by selling capers, which they gather at dawn and pickle in tubs of salt.

Plants that grow in Pantelleria have all adapted to the strong winds. Olive trees crouch over the soil like creeping bushes, while the vines are self-supporting, bearing large pale green fruit on sappy side shoots a couple of feet high. Caper plants, low rosettes of white and mauve flowers, look like floral sun hats laid out to dry – it is the buds that are picked, from June to late August, to make into capers, and those from Pantelleria are said to be the best in the world. Many houses also have a *giardino arabo* – a tiny orchard with stone walls ten or twelve feet high – to protect the delicate plum, peach and orange trees from the wind. Most are square, housing four to six trees closely planted, but I saw several triangular enclosures, built for a single tree, and one in the form of a perfect circle, the tips of the branches just visible over the walls. Wooden weights are often tied to the branches to encourage low, compact growth.

Gardens around the houses are vibrant and colourful. Bougainvillaea makes shocking pink splashes against whitewashed walls, often with morning glory scrambling through its branches; and oleander and jasmine release their heady scent into the night air as you brush past. Pots of scarlet hibiscus, faded blue plumbago, pink and white pelargoniums and flowering succulents can survive all year round outside; tomatoes and chilli peppers are dotted among the flowers, with a good stock of herbs for cooking. Some gardens also have a sunken area for eating away from the wind, with tiled bench seats built into the walls and an old bread oven made from lava stone.

Water is the main problem for Pantescan gardeners. Capers and vines need little water while fruiting, but flowers are thirsty, and are watered carefully and sparingly in the evenings. Rainwater is collected in a tiled gutter running round the domed roofs – in older houses this is still channelled into a square tank in the centre of the main room which keeps the interior cool. In all houses, water is a precious resource and not to be wasted – whatever can be recycled is used outside.

We have a lot to learn from this simple, economical way of life, I thought, as I watched the owner of our little rented house carry buckets from the bathroom to water his fine crop of basil. It also struck me that some of the plants that thrive here might do well on our hot, dry, windy roof terrace back home. I took photos of some of the grasses and succulents and santolina-like creeping bushes that seem almost to frill themselves in the heat. Most would have to be brought inside for an English winter, of course, but I rather like the idea of turning our bathroom into a temporary jungle for three or four months of the year.

24 August 1997 ~ The Allotment

The allotment has been full of surprises this summer. An almost total reverse of last year's weather conditions has made for some unexpected successes (a bumper crop of early lettuce and a glut of peas and broad beans) and a few interesting, if disappointing, failures.

As I mentioned three weeks ago, a big problem has been slugs, encouraged by the wet weather and an abundance of damp, shady hiding places in the new plot. Last year we had none, but I keep coming across colonies of the horrible things, ranging from little grey maggots to huge fat Jabba the Hutts, who lie snacking on their sides displaying their frilly orange edges like lurid underclothes. I don't use poisons on the allotment, and even salt (which dehydrates slugs) would leave mounds of sticky bodies which I would have to dispose of. So I'm falling back on the popular 'slug pub', which involves burying glasses of beer in the soil into which the creatures (lured by the smell of a good pint) will tip themselves and drown. My boyfriend has shown considerably more interest in this than in

other allotment projects, and wanders about the plot in the early evening, beer can in hand, 'topping up' glasses and calling on the slugs to roll up at the Last Chance Saloon. Large amounts of beer have been consumed but not, I fear, by the slugs, which are apparently teetotal and thriving.

Slugs devoured many of my lettuces, but at least this was in July, when many of the plants would have wilted or bolted anyway. Luckily, they don't like rocket, Italian chicory or a lovely purple-streaked lettuce, so we are still enjoying good salads, perked up by radishes, raw broad beans and blue borage flowers.

They also munched through a good number of runner and French climbing bean seedlings, but we have more than enough left for a reasonable crop.

The only other disappointment has been the cauliflowers. I had hardly dared hope that the seedlings I planted out in mid-April would develop dense creamy-white hearts – it seems so unlikely in something that looks otherwise exactly like a young cabbage plant. But in a couple of months, there they were – small, but definitely growing. When I went along a few weeks later, however, the hearts had turned into something more like cow parsley flowers. I've since been told that this is what wet weather followed by a hot spell does to cauliflowers. They like their summers cool and constant.

I'm most proud of the peas, broad beans and shallots. Last year's peas did very little – they were planted too late, staked too late and prone to weevils. This year, in spite of the whole lot tumbling down in a storm, we've been picking six pounds per week for the past three months (from two sowings, one in late March, the next on 1 May). The 'sugar snaps' are delicious whole and cooked very lightly, like mangetouts. The broad beans have been similarly delicious, if rather late. Last November's sowing, meant to guarantee an early June crop, failed completely so we had to wait till July for our first tender, milky green beans. I like to eat the first harvest raw, with strips of Parma ham and a little olive oil, as they do in Italy.

The shallots were an experiment, a pink variety from the *Organic Gardening Catalogue*. Twenty setts (single seed bulbs) planted on the surface in April yielded ten to thirteen shallots each by late July. When the leaves yellowed we pulled the roots free of soil and dried

them in the sun. Simon and Clarkey, the friends with whom I share
the new plot in my sister's absence, then wove them into professional-looking plaits with green raffia, which are now hanging
above the kitchen sink. What with the large striped marrows and
baskets of courgettes, our Brixton kitchen looks like an advert for
Country Living. Help!

3 1 August 1997 ~ Home

Late summer evenings, when the sun is already setting noticeably
earlier, are when I most appreciate eating supper in the garden.
Knowing we won't be able to do it for many more weeks makes me
want to linger even longer outside as the traffic dies down and the
stars come out. It has also pushed me into doing something about
our outdoor lighting, till now restricted to a handful of candles and a
security light that throws out a Colditz-like glare the moment
anything goes near it.

Although I know that spectacular effects can be achieved with
electric light systems in gardens, my own preference is for candle-
light, and in a tiny garden such as ours, it hardly seems worth the
expense and effort of laying special cables. Over the years, I have
built up quite a collection of metal and glass candle lanterns. All I
had to do was attach them at strategic points along the walls, either
directly off the trellis or, for the heavier ones, using simple metal
brackets from a hardware store. I saved the prettiest lanterns to hang
around the french windows, where an architect friend is designing a
deck-style terrace, raised a foot above the rest of the garden. This
will have upright supports for climbing plants, and room for
lanterns, bird feeders and wind chimes which can dangle over the
dining table. A string of fairy lights – the small plain white ones –
might be nice to look out on in winter, and could be wired up quite
easily from inside (garden centres sell ones that are specifically for
outdoor use). I would also love a scrolly old iron candelabra hanging
from the branch of a tree in the corner, but we will have to plant the
tree first.

Mirrors can increase the effectiveness of candles outside, as well as
reflecting sunlight into dark corners during the day. I have chipped

out a few of the bricks to make small square recesses in the walls, and have stuck pieces of mirror along the back and a night light or candle in a jar in front. The result is quite magical, creating an illusion of movement as the flickering flames are reflected *ad infinitum*. Small concave mirrors or silver baubles strung from sturdy plants can create a similar effect, and look lovely near water.

For the flower beds, I found some handy round lanterns like glass goldfish bowls suspended from a metal spike which you push down into the soil (from Heals, or try The English Garden Collection, see p. 244 whose new mail order catalogue is out in mid-September). Huge wax flares can even be poked into borders, though they might get out of hand in the wind.

The only drawback with candles is that they need constant surveillance, especially if there is the glimmer of a chance that a flame might come into contact with foliage. Take care. I end with a cautionary tale about one of the many grand eccentric ex-pats who made beautiful gardens on the hillsides outside Tangier in the Forties and Fifties. Wishing to hold a garden party for her arty friends, she hit on what she thought would be a novel idea for the lighting. The party was to begin in natural light, well before sunset. Then, as darkness gathered, hundreds of pet tortoises (which are still two a penny in Morocco) would be released from a hidden trap door, each bearing a single lighted candle stuck on top of its shell. The intention was that the creatures should wander along the pathways among her guests, weaving a constantly moving stream of light through the garden. As it turned out, the tortoises felt like doing nothing of the sort. No sooner let loose, they headed straight for the flower beds which, dried to a cinder by the hot summer sun, shot up in flames and brought the party to a premature close.

7 September 1997 ~ The Allotment

No job at the allotment is half as much fun as harvesting. At this time of the year, bar watering and a little light weeding, the major task for each visit is to fill as many carrier bags as possible full of produce to take home and eat or give to friends.

Some vegetables provide more enjoyment than others. Peas, for instance, I find endlessly absorbing. You need sharp eyes to spot the swelling pods among the tangle of green leaves and tendrils. Standing in front of the plants, I pick as many as I can see at eye level and then bob down on my heels, from which position dozens more come into view. Convinced I've got the lot, I then wander off to another part of the plot only to return to find more have miraculously appeared. The sweet, watery snappiness of a young pea pod is so delicious that a quarter of those I pick doesn't make it to the bag. I never need lunch on allotment days.

Courgettes are also great fun. That moment of deliberation: to pick or not to pick? Do I pluck this little fellow now, while he's fit for Marks & Spencers miniature vegetable section, or run the risk of him becoming an unwieldy torpedo of a marrow by our next meeting? (We've had quite enough marrow for one summer, and friends have started to turn them down.) Harvesting courgettes is wonderful – feeling the weight of the warm, glossy fruit in the hand before a deft twist of the wrist snaps it free.

But for me, nothing can compare with the thrill of lifting potatoes. There are so few clues above ground – the patch looks desolate with the flowers long dead and the stems all withered and brown. But plunge a fork into the soil – well away from the remains of the plant to avoid spiking your spuds – and up it will come, jumbling with a dozen or more egg-sized tubers. 'Pink Fir Apples', which I plant for their superb flavour and texture in salads, are especially exciting. Although the yield is said to be lower than for other varieties, there always seem to be more of the pale red kidney-shaped things than I imagine. They're at their best boiled and mixed with vinaigrette, parsley and sliced spring onions while still warm.

There is also the question of knowing the best moment to harvest. It recently struck me, while admiring my twelve-foot high screen of Jerusalem artichoke plants – which look rather like sunflowers but without the flowers – that I didn't have the slightest idea when they'd be ready. The books say wait until autumn, cut the stalks down to one foot above soil level and dig up the nobbly tubers as required. So only a few weeks to go for artichoke soup.

Sweetcorn is another tricky one. When the silky tassels at the top of the cobs have turned from white to chocolate brown, pull back part of the sheath of leaves and squeeze a couple of grains between thumb and fingernail. If the liquid that comes out is watery, the cob is unripe; if thick and viscous, it's past its best. A creamy liquid means there's no time to lose – carefully snap the ear from the stem, dash home and cook immediately. Or, better still, stick it straight on the barbecue grill – the flavour of corn diminishes rapidly only thirty minutes after picking, as the natural sugars convert to starch.

Aside from vegetables, I've also been harvesting seed this year. The kitchen shelves are crammed with egg-cups labelled 'broccoli', 'rocket', 'poppy', 'love-in-a-mist' – the promise of next year's crop. Will there be a next year at the allotment? I certainly hope so. It's on these early autumn evenings, cycling back across the park in the sun with my bike basket crammed full of produce, that there are no doubts in my mind that the time and effort involved in growing my own vegetables is worth it.

14 September 1997 ~ Compost Lasagne

So far, I have avoided writing about compost-making – for the simple reason that, like many newish gardeners, I didn't really understand it. Despite a rather splendid container, made by my boyfriend from recycled wood, my early attempts looked like the dreaded green slime from childhood episodes of Dr Who and smelt like a stagnant pond. But all this has changed since a visit to the Centre for Alternative Technology (CAT) in Wales (see p. 241), earlier this year. Based in a disused slate quarry in the hills, the Centre exists to encourage a healthier, more sustainable way of living, eschewing hectoring lecturing for working demonstrations that are not only easy to understand, but fun into the bargain.

Alongside the grass-roofed eco-houses, sun-, wind- and water-power projects, geodesic-domed greenhouse and the 'Mole Hole' (an underground mole's-eye view of the soil), a large section of the site is devoted to compost making. All the commonly-used apparatus and methods are on display, from state-of-the-art 'tumblers' that turn the compost in a bin that spins on a central axis, to trendy wormeries and time-worn traditional methods using hay bales and heaps of dead leaves. A neat rack of boxes shows how various different compostable components (woody garden waste, carpentry shavings, dead leaves, waste paper and kitchen scraps), mixed with the right 'activator' (shop-bought products, nettles, worms or the gardener's old favourite, urine), break down to produce almost identical, crumbly dark soil.

'Less slop, more fibre' is CAT's prescription for perfect compost. 'Good compost needs two components – rich, wet waste such as household scraps and grass cuttings, and dry, fibrous matter such as scrunched up paper and cardboard packaging,' says Peter Harper, who has been at CAT since its earliest days in the Seventies. His almost obsessive quest for the perfect compost components is equalled only by his commitment to cutting down the waste that most of us unthinkingly put out for the dustmen every week to be carted off to unecological landfill sites.

'Cardboard lasagne', his recipe to end the soggy composting blues, brings the two together. Of the thirty to forty per cent of our household rubbish that is made up from paper and cardboard, we should recycle newspapers and glossy magazines by taking them to recycling bins, he says. But the rest – cardboard packaging, boxes and cartons, scrunched up paper and tissues – we should add to our compost heaps in layers, to provide a much-needed fibrous element.

'Grass cuttings, weeds and kitchen waste have plenty of nitrogen and water but lack the other vital components, carbon and air,' Peter explains. 'Gardening books tell you to "turn" the heap to aerate it, but it's laborious and, let's face it, most of us never get round to it. Adding paper and card provides the missing ingredients at one stroke, does away with the need for turning, and cuts down on household waste into the bargain.'

If you should have large quantities of grass clippings, Mr Harper has experimented with a *cordon bleu* version of grass layered with cardboard, which apparently gives fine dark compost after just six months. It sounds so easy it made me wonder why our national parks and playgrounds don't do it. His other pet method is peeing on a straw-bale (a traditional trick, apparently), which he swears yields 'beautiful, peaty compost' in under six months.

Being earthy types with little interest in interior design, the CAT chaps don't provide many solutions to the other great conundrum in the composting process: how to store the stuff before it hits the heap. Ikea has recently introduced some nifty sorting systems that fit into drawers or hinge on the back of under-sink cupboards, but I am quite happy with a miniature galvanised dustbin (from Wong Sing Jones, see p. 246). I have yet to empty my compost heap, but when I rooted around recently, the prognosis looked good. This, together with the steady decline in the number of black bin liners we put out for the dustmen, must make the occasional whiff of rotting vegetables in the kitchen worthwhile.

21 *September* 1997 ~ The Allotment

One of the reasons I love gardening is that it is so peaceful. Even living in the city, enveloped by busy roads and a hectic pace of life, it is still possible to find moments of quiet concentration and stillness, when the world fades away in the face of a single flower. I value the tranquillity of the allotment; the quiet companionship with my fellow plot holders, toiling away in silence just a short way from the South Circular.

In recent months, though, the Territorial Army depot next door has begun to be a real threat to this peace and quiet. They have stepped up their manoeuvres to such a point that I've started to wonder whether there might not be a war in the offing. It's not just the revving and reversing of their vehicles a few feet from the dividing fence, nor the constant shouting over loud bursts of Capital Gold. I can do without the intrusion into my privacy – the way they look at me as if to say, 'Sad woman, hasn't she got anything better to do with her time?' when that is *exactly* what I'm thinking about them.

The TA isn't my only gripe with our allotment site at the moment. I've learned to live with the fact that we can't have a shed – despite a good crop of ramshackle huts being an integral part of traditional allotment life. I can even tolerate the fact that we have to water by hand – my consolation, as I trek to and fro with a pair of watering cans, is that Flabby Upper Arm Syndrome, that bane of women of a certain age, might pass me by.

What's annoying me is the rash of rather officious-sounding notices – all nicely laminated on someone's new computer – that has started to spread across the fence near the gate. 'All dogs to be kept on a lead' is fair enough – it's in the rules and our lurcher puppy wasn't the only dog to be caught occasionally romping through someone else's marrow patch. There's another about water conservation – again, fair enough, but slightly galling when this is the only allotment site I know where the hosepipe ban is permanent. The most alarming notice by far is one announcing a new regular inspection patrol with the power to confiscate untidy plots. Looking at the forest of nettles next to our compost heap, I've begun to wonder if we might be in the firing line ourselves.

My grumbles were exacerbated when I paid a visit to a friend who, inspired by our example, has recently taken on a council allotment in Wimbledon. I was jealous of their topsy-turvy shed, with its warm woody smell and potting bench. I was jealous of their view – a river lined with willows and poplars. And I was jealous of the fact that not only hose pipes but automatic watering systems are allowed. Most of all, I was jealous of the total peace and quiet – no traffic, no radios, no revving engines or shouting squaddies – and no clipboarded committee members checking on your every move. The place was a vision of calm contentment, with people sitting in their sheds, enjoying a quiet drink as they listened to the wind in the trees and watched their sprinklers make sparkling arches against the sky.

I was beginning to contemplate a move to Wimbledon. But, as is the way of things, when Jane returned the visit, she saw our site with new eyes. She loved the old oak tree by the hedge, and the birds that come and sing in its branches. She loved our raised beds, and the sunny concrete terrace (made on the foundations of the shed that had to come down) where we sit and have a beer after a long afternoon's work. She even loved the notices – and the fact that people so obviously care about the site and its upkeep. I guess it's no accident that gardening spawned the phrase 'the grass is always greener'.

28 September 1997 ~ Slugs at the Allotment

Not since I wrote about discouraging cats from our garden has my mailbag been so full. When I began my recent tirade against slugs at the allotment (see p. 98), I had no idea of the strength of feeling that these creatures arouse. The majority of the letters are supportive, offering alternatives to my 'slug pubs' – glasses of beer sunk in the soil into which the slugs tip themselves and drown. Elizabeth Lanham of Blandford Forum in Dorset suggests scattering bran around plants.

'Wait till it's dark,' she advises, 'and then you can go and pick them up as they gorge themselves silly. Pop them in a jar of salty water as you go'. Apparently, when she lived in West Wales, she could pick up 400–500 slugs in an evening. Mrs Wilson of Bristol even wrote in support of my most desperate measure – flinging the slugs over the allotment fence to be run over by trucks in the army depot next door. 'With an ancient tennis racquet and smashing forehand drive I toss them over my high garden wall on to the main road,' she writes, adding that 'if you do not throw them far enough they just walk back'.

There has also been another type of letter, however, expressing shock and outrage that such treatment could be dealt out to any living creature. 'Are we to kill whatever we think is ugly or revolting?' writes M. Turpin of Redditch in Worcestershire (like much of my hate mail, the letter is written in capitals, with a Biro pressed so hard it made the lined paper wrinkle – is this a coincidence?). 'Was this action to throw slugs under trucks from a grown woman? Sounds more like a mindless child that has been shown no better.'

One such letter even made it to the letters page of the newspaper. 'Slugs are living, feeling creatures, and are not ugly,' declares Ann Barrass of Sunderland. 'I think it is dreadful that anyone should treat any animal so cruelly.' Instead of killing the slugs, she advised me to take them to a new home in the country – a suggestion greeted with little enthusiasm from my relations in Kent, who say they have quite enough slugs of their own, thank you, without having to cope with deported townies left on their doorstep.

Such was the virulence of the slug-friendly letters, I was beginning to think my name might be on some Slug Protection League hit list, and that I'd come out one morning to find my car covered in slug slime or worse. But it's a difficult and sensitive issue. When I made the decision to garden organically, it wasn't just so that I myself would benefit from vegetables produced without the use of potentially harmful pesticides: I hoped also to contribute positively to the ecology of the area. Pesticides kill animals on whom other creatures, such as birds, feed. Renouncing chemicals protects the food chain – but if I didn't get rid of the slugs somehow I'd have no crops at all.

Other questions start to flood my mind. Is it more painful for a slug or snail to be flung under a truck or drowned in beer than to be pecked by a hungry bird? When I get round to making my pond, will it be OK for the slugs to die in the jaws of a frog or toad? And what about the so-called 'biological controls' where natural predators bred commercially are brought in to do the nasty business for us – slug nematodes apparently devour the creatures from inside, which must make the most agonising death.

Does the fact that it's another creature doing the killing somehow make it all right? All of a turmoil, I rang the Henry Doubleday Research Centre, the National Association for Promoting Organic Gardening. 'Gardening organically doesn't mean preserving every single living creature,' said Maggie Brown, their horticultural advisor, soothingly. 'There are enough slugs in the world to paper the sky. If we didn't kill some of them there would be no gardens.'

So there we are. I now feel at ease with my slug pubs, which seem to be working rather well. And from a bird's eye view, what could be a tastier convenience snack than a freshly killed slug, marinated in beer?

4 October 1997 ~ Written for a Special Fashion Issue of the Magazine

'Gardening is groovy' declared a recent article in Vogue; 'Gardening: the new sex' screamed a Tatler coverline, while the couple entwined on the English Garden Collection's mail order catalogue looks like an advert for trendy Haagen Dazs ice cream. If we are to believe the fashion press, which relies, of course, for its existence on things being 'in', 'out' and 'in' again, then gardening is suddenly, most definitely, 'in'. Ridiculous though some of the claims might seem, they are not a fabrication. The social mix at garden centres has been changing over the last few years. Among the unassuming types in car coats stocking up on hardy perennials, a new breed has sprouted – style-conscious young couples who would probably look more at home in the Conran shop. Suddenly, everyone seems to be gardening – or talking about gardening.

The change has been explained as a 'psycho-spiritual' phenomenon, to do with the Nineties urge to slow down and relish the good things in life. But I suspect it is also a continuation of today's obsession with interior design. For much of the 'new gardening' is actually a sort of 'outdoor decorating' – a World of Exteriors approach that takes the old idea of the garden as an outside room to its fashionable extreme. *Elle Decoration* carried a feature on 'smart garden furniture that looks just as cool indoors' (all wicker, slatted wood and painted bamboo), while Habitat's garden chairs, buckets and watering cans in trendy lime green and orange walked out of the store as fast as the new Gucci stilettos.

Where the trend for 'instant gardening' comes unstuck, of course, is the plants. Plants take time to grow, and stocking even a small roof terrace from scratch is not only expensive but bewildering for a beginner. You see them, those young couples in the garden centres, picking out the potted gerberas they've seen in photographs, but with no idea how to keep them alive; crossing their fingers that those cool new ornamental grasses will be just the thing for that dark, damp corner.

The real problem with instant gardening is that it gives only instant rewards. Surely the pleasure of gardening lies in the slow rhythm of the seasons, from watching the inch and a half gained by this young tree, the flush of new buds on that small shrub. It is not the stuff of fads, to be taken up one weekend and dropped when the trend-spotters deem it's had its day. I really do hope that the new crop of enthusiasts is here to stay. But sadly the chances are that when the Next Big Thing arrives, all those newly potted olive trees will be languishing on the compost heap.

In the meantime, I thought it might be quite fun to come up with what marks out the different sorts of gardener – I'm not sure which of the two I am...

Old-fashioned gardener	Trendy new gardener
Garden News	Gardens Illustrated
Scruffy old shoes	New green wellies
Mossy flowerpot from back of the potting shed	Mossy flowerpot £7.50 from the Conran shop
Bonfires	Barbecues
Liberal doses of Phostrogen	Organic everything
Rickety old bench	Smart new seats from Habitat
Gardeners' Question Time	Garden Doctors
Clay Jones	Dan Pearson
Cabbages	Chinese greens
Round lettuce	Rows of rocket
Spring onions	Organic shallots
Vegetable patch	Ornamental potager
Grass as lawn	Clumps of trendy grasses in the border
White garden at Sissinghurst	Red hot pokers at Great Dixter
Weeds	Wild flowers
Mail order seed catalogues	The English Garden Collection
Aluminium-frame greenhouse	Custom-built conservatory
Slippery terraces	Wooden decking
Old plastic watering can	Vita Sackville West model by the National Trust
Old plastic pot for weeds	New painted trug
Recycled string	Rustic raffia plant ties
D.G. Hessayon's Garden Expert series	Derek Jarman's garden

12 October 1997 ~ Mirabel Osler's Ludlow Garden

'Ooooh, just look at that!' The hairs on the back of my neck stood on end as what looked like a giant Technicolor spider lurched into view, with a body like a blob of mercury and a hundred hairy legs like splinters of spun glass. Next came a creamy white cathedral, its columns carved like underwater coral. And then a flock of tropical birds, their bright orange tail feathers tightly furled against the wind. Reluctantly, I handed back the magnifying glass. Looking at flowers close up through a lens is like a horticultural hallucination, and I was already hooked. My guide to this world, two summers ago in her Shropshire back garden, was the gardening writer Mirabel Osler. What a peculiar sight we must have made, crabbing about her borders with our backs bent double, oohing and aahing over our bee's eye view of roses, eucryphia and honeysuckles.

Being with Mirabel would make any garden fun. In her seventies (though you'd never believe it), her conversation swoops and soars from the passion of the moment to subjects far beyond the garden wall. But her own patch, right beneath the walls of Ludlow Castle, must be one of my favourite urban gardens. Into her seventy by thirty foot plot she has crammed thirty-seven trees, a brick and cobbled path that passes under chunky wooden arches draped with roses, and several very different sitting areas, half-hidden in dense foliage and flowers. Only from the first floor window can you see the whole plan at once. This little garden has all the mystery and surprise of much larger and grander creations – while beyond the pleached limes and trellised fence on either side, the miniature, manicured lawns that are the lot of the average town terrace stretch as far as the eye can see.

'Life should not include a mower, at least not in a small garden,' is one of Mirabel's many passionately argued views. 'Anyone with a small garden, particularly those coping alone, should rid themselves of the tyranny of the lawn.' Her own mutiny occurred within a year of moving to Ludlow, having left behind her the much-loved 'wilderness garden' that was the backdrop to her first and best-known book, *A Gentle Plea for Chaos*. Instead of perpetuating the 'amiable disorder' she had cultivated in the country with her late husband, Michael, she surprised everyone with a new garden full of hard lines, strict structure and dramatic – she would even say obsessive – pruning.

After years exhorting her readers to let nature do its own thing, Mirabel began to 'torture' her trees. A new eucalyptus avenue was decapitated, and the whippy regrowth trained into airy globes. Weeping willows were shorn into giant mushrooms and set on cushions of lavender, while a flowering quince was clipped and snipped into an open-work goblet. Most stunning of all, a pair of Irish yews was corseted into straight, slim verticals, and bound by a coiling white rose – 'the nearest I could get to a cypress in this country,' she says.

In spite of the technical ingenuity all this involves (inspired by a long summer's research for a book on private gardens of France, where they are happy with the secateurs), Mirabel's is still a garden that's more about being than doing. The many seats are for particular times and moods – the bench on the terrace near the house is for morning coffee; the table and chairs, painted different shades of green, are for eating outside with friends (they are reflected *ad infinitum* in mirrored panels on the wall – 'so it makes it look as if I'm more hospitable than I am'). There's the Cat House, like a mini-veranda in slatted wood, with an 'eye' in the wall to see who's coming, and, right at the top, a secret hedgerow seat that catches the late afternoon sun among the roses, ferns and hellebores. Sir Roy Strong, who has become a friend, has taken to referring to the seats in his own garden as 'Mirabels'.

Mirabel is not afraid to make mistakes – to try out the odd hare-brained scheme or plant purple loosestrife for the sheer joy of its name. 'If an idea doesn't work, it leaves space for another to come along,' she says. 'I believe profoundly in a beneficent spirit that lurks in gardens, turning tragedies into celebrations.'

Under her life-enhancing gaze (not to mention her magnifying glass), even plants I've never had time for become objects of bizarre and breathtaking beauty. Gladioli will never be the same again.

2 November 1997 ~ The Allotment

This year, for once, I got round to doing some of those autumn-into-winter gardening tasks while it was still a pleasure to be outside. The splendid September and early October weather certainly helped. My friends and I spent several industrious afternoons tidying up the allotment while the low winter sun lapped like warm water on our backs and lit up the rows of spinach beet and ruby chard like lanterns. You could almost see the pumpkins swelling.

For me, there is always something bittersweet about these fine late autumn days. I have to keep reminding myself to enjoy them for what they are, and not mind that the sun will soon be setting at four o'clock and the central heating pumping out all day. Like the last days of a wonderful holiday, there are also the inevitable slight regrets about the things there wasn't time for, the things that didn't work out. We were late with the sweetcorn this year, and the plants were disappointingly spindly, with few bearing more than one cob. Despite being cosseted in a high-sided glass cold frame, the aubergines and peppers did poorly, too – though if there had been a Smallest Vegetable category at one of the horticultural shows, these perfectly-formed one-inchers would have won hands down. And we never did get round to establishing our cutting garden full of flowers for the house.

There is still a lot to be excited about and grateful for, however. The pumpkins – three large round orange ones and some long yellow squashes rather like rugby balls – will soon be ready to harvest. Tomatoes are still ripening on the bushy low plants, even if

the leaves have turned to brown paper. And the Brussels sprouts are growing away nicely, tucked into the leaf nodes all the way up the stems, like the nobbles on an Arran jersey. I hope some will be ready for Christmas.

We've given up the fight against the brambles that straggle all over the new plot. Instead, we have been training them up and across the metal fences that form two of our boundaries. Not only do they help screen off the army depot next door; they have also been providing us with some delicious blackberry and apple crumbles – a good compensation for the onset of winter if ever there was one. We want to interweave them with some other attractive, fast-growing climbers such as hops, Virginia creeper, a 'Kiftsgate' rose and, on the south-facing side, a passion flower. The prunings can be carried home in armfuls to festoon about the house.

Where the crops have already died over, we have started to prepare the soil for next year, composting spent lettuces and the remains of the runner beans and digging in plenty of organic matter. Half of the new plot is reserved for flowering bulbs and annuals, and I'll be writing about that in the coming weeks. The remaining overgrown areas have been prepared using the method referred to by *Permaculture* magazine (see p. 243) as The Cardboard Revolution. I was introduced to this unlikely technique when I visited Barry Watson at his organic community allotments in Dagenham in the spring (see p. 80). Many readers asked for further information, and as it's such an effective way of clearing and conditioning neglected areas of land, it seems worth repeating in more detail.

First, you need to level the whole area and trample any weeds down flat. Then scatter a generous handful of pelleted chicken manure on top (this will encourage soil bacteria and help break down the weeds). On top of this lay large sheets of cardboard – the thicker the better as it will suppress weed growth – and overlap the edges by six inches or so to prevent weeds from popping up in between. Water the cardboard well and cover with six inches of organic matter – garden compost, manure, mushroom compost or a mixture of the three. As it will have all winter to mature, we used fresh stable sweepings from the local riding stables – the manure element will add nutrients to the soil, while the straw will provide a warm, water-saving and weed-blocking mulch. Water well again and do nothing else till spring, when the whole lot should have broken down into fantastic, rich, crumbly soil – with no weeds and no digging! I can hardly wait.

9 November 1997 ~ Flowers for a Friend

Recently a friend of mine died, tragically young, from breast cancer. Lavender had been particularly important to her in the last months of her illness – the plant itself in her small city garden, its scent in perfumes and essential oils, and the colour of the flowers. It seemed a good idea to try to bring lavender into her memorial service. But lavender in bloom, whether bushes or cut flowers, proved to be impossible to find in October. Someone tracked down supplies of dried stems, but these looked too dreary and too dead on their own. In the end, we decided to have lots of flowers in lavenderish blues and mauves and white, and to mix them with the dried lavender and boughs of fresh rosemary – for remembrance.

It was a sad task, but one I felt very honoured to do, arriving at New Covent Garden Flower Market as an autumn dawn was breaking, and picking out the colours and types of flowers we thought Ruth would have liked. She always hated anything pompous and over-formal, so apart from two large bunches of mauve-y blue delphiniums in a froth of cow parsley, we concentrated on making lots and lots of small bunches, each consisting of one type of flower, placed in plain glass jam jars and crowded together at the front of the hall. There were little fat bunches of dark purply hyacinths, bluey mauve grape hyacinths, white and purple freesias and scabious in both white and that perfect clear lavenderish mauve my friend loved so much. In between the flowers, night lights and scented candles, also in glass jars, lit up the little arrangements and sent flickering shadows up the wall. As the service began, the room was suffused with the smell of dried lavender and rosemary. Afterwards, we made up bunches of the flowers in newspaper for people to take home.

At the eleventh hour, another friend managed to find seven large potted lavender bushes – a large-leaved variety, which looked handsome even though they were not in bloom. These were given to Ruth's closest friends and family, to plant in their gardens in remembrance of her. Many of her other friends, including myself, have decided to do the same. I have planted a pretty French wing-flowered variety, *Lavandula stoechas* 'Papillon', in a large pot which will sit on the new deck in the sun. It will always remind me of her.

Gardens are always rich in such associations – at least, the ones I love are. It doesn't seem remotely morbid – in fact, I would love it if people were to plant something when I die, or take custody of my own plants. There is joy and hope in the idea of something carrying on growing and flowering after you have gone. I used to do a day a week as a gardener in a hospice, and was amazed at the number of patients who found solace in this notion. Gardeners and non-gardeners alike used to love helping plant indoor spring bulbs – whether or not they were likely to be around to enjoy the flowers themselves.

This aspect of gardening is too seldom written about, but is the subject of a new book, *Cultivating Sacred Space: Gardening for the Soul* (see p. 242), by the American writer and photographer Elizabeth Murray. It focuses on various gardens of contemplation and remembrance: the famous Zen moss gardens in Kyoto, Japan; a garden made of rocks from around the world; a Californian garden geared to teaching children about the natural rhythms of life, death and decay into new life. The last chapter tells how the author and her future husband created a special wedding garden in which their marriage ceremony was held, only to have that same garden become his memorial garden within the year, when he died, suddenly, from a brain tumour.

23 November 1997 ~ Home

Creating a garden is a good way to learn the art of patience. I had hoped by now to report that the new deck outside the french windows was stylishly in place, with pots of lilies and other bulbs planted up for next year. Alas, no. Waiting for a small ivy plant to cover a wall is as nothing compared to waiting for builders to get on with the job. The idea is lovely – a square deck running right out into the garden, made from reclaimed timber bleached a silvery driftwood grey. An additional section directly outside the door is to be metal – an industrial-looking open grille that will allow light through to the basement below.

The wooden deck will be solid, but studded with half-inch holes filled with clear plastic dowel-rod so that when there are lights on downstairs, the effect will be that of pinpricks of light scattered all over the floor. I'd imagined us out there by now, dining on the last fruits of the allotment in the late autumn sun, not still gazing at a pile of timber and a gaping six-foot well.

Enough moaning. Digging out photographs of the garden only eighteen months ago, when it was a concrete rubbish tip full of chickweed and cat poo, is enough to cheer me up. At the onset of summer, the white walls looked so bare I dotted them with red and striped pink pelargoniums planted in galvanised metal pots and tied to the trellis with string. This gave the place a jolly, Spanish court-yard feel while different types of jasmine, clematis, honeysuckle and ivy worked their way up the gaps in between.

Lilies, delphiniums, white foxgloves and some silvery clumps of hebe and lavender have all done well in pots and borders, as have the herbs and sweet peas in a sunny patch by the back door. And the tallest plants – hollyhocks, ornamental thistles, teazles and fifteen foot sunflowers – have provided some drama, leaning at crazy angles as the summer wore on. I have left their seed heads for the birds.

We've also had a good crop of tomatoes, interplanted with nasturtiums and tiny purple violas – though the climbing french beans I trained around my study window didn't quite work. Best of all was a large fluted metal laundry tub in which nine or ten *regale* lilies sprang up through a mound of white, cream, wine red and lime tobacco plants just as prettily as last year. The only real disappointment was the nasturtiums. Last year they covered the south-facing wall with flowers right up until the first frost; this year's were sooty with blackfly and devoured by caterpillars. A poor show by the nasturtiums in front of the house put paid to my cunning idea to a sort of horticultural alternative to net curtains. The nasturtiums, sown straight into window boxes at the base of the bay windows, as well as in pots on the roof of the bay, were to climb up and tumble down a series of wires trained across the frame, interwoven with blue morning glory flowers.

They made it half way, but it was by no means the stunning floral screen I'd envisaged, and I've yet to throw out the curtains. I am determined to get it right next year, if someone can please let me in on an effective organic remedy for blackfly. Thank goodness for the morning glories, which flowered away all summer, their beautiful clear blue singing out against peeling black gloss paint. (My indoor morning glories, planted in pots on the bedroom and bathroom window ledges and trained up wires all around the windows, are still putting out flowers.)

Apart from the deck, there are other changes afoot at the back of the house. Contrary to my expectations, the local council seems quite keen on my idea to knock down the single storey warehouse we look out over and turn the site into a quiet community garden. A nice man from the British Trust for Conservation Volunteers spent an hour and a half here last week discussing the proposal and advising me on fund raising and applying for grants. It sounds the sort of thing that will test my newly acquired reserves of patience to the full – but I hope it will be worth it. Watch this space.

30 November 1997 ~ The Allotment

My fingernails were filthy. My hands were numb with cold and I had to book a massage to relieve my poor back. But I was glowing with satisfaction. I must have planted a thousand or more bulbs the other weekend – both in the back garden at home, and in the new cutting garden at the allotment.

The idea to make a cutting garden was inspired by Sarah Raven's book *The Cutting Garden: Growing and Arranging Garden Flowers* (see p. 242), which was published last year. Ms Raven is a doctor-turned-florist, who became frustrated by the scarcity of unusual flowers available in flower shops and markets. When she moved to the country she resolved to grow her own, and is now able to supply weddings, parties and individuals with her wonderfully exuberant arrangements of rudbeckias, ornamental thistles and overblown tulips, all raised in a forty foot by eighty foot plot outside her Sussex farmhouse. The ideas and planting plans in her book can be adapted to create anything from the large decorative cutting garden traditionally found in grand country houses to a small unobtrusive cutting patch at the end of the average town garden. My cutting garden at the allotment will be pitched somewhere between the two.

I have always loved having as many flowers as possible about the house – the intense joy I find in a simple bunch of daffodils can get me through the worst winter gloom. Apart from the satisfaction – and the obvious financial savings – in growing one's own flowers, I can see the other benefits of creating an area where flowers are grown solely for cutting for the house. In a small garden such as mine, it's easy to get possessive about flowers. We made large french windows to bring the view of the garden right into the house, so I hesitate to make too many gaps in the border by picking lots of lilies and delphiniums. At the allotment, instead, it will seem almost wasteful not to pick a flower when it's in bloom. It will also allow me to grow flowers that I have problems with in borders – tulips, for instance. I love tulips as cut flowers – especially the wild, striped and swirling parrot varieties. But their stiff stance and plasticky texture can often seem out of place in a flower bed, and I tend to concentrate them in pots.

Two of the large raised beds on the second allotment and possibly a third are to be devoted to flowers. Following Ms Raven's suggestion, we prepared trenches as wide, and three times as deep as the type of bulb we were planting, using garden twine attached to markers at each end to keep the lines straight. The markers help avoid inadvertent damage to young growth next year, and annual seeds and seedlings can be set out in blocks or rows between the lines of bulbs. We lined the bottom of the trench with sharp sand (to improve drainage) and scattered on pelleted chicken manure. And then it was in with the bulbs. We were less concerned with taste than we would have been in a back garden – cerise parrot tulips are next to orange-trumpeted narcissi; orange crown imperial fritillaries jostle yellow foxtail lilies. They'll be splendidly gaudy all together in the beds, but will really come into their own as they are brought inside the house.

I keep the simplest arrangements for the desk where I work – sometimes just a single stem in a jar. There the flowers can be looked at in a way they never are in a garden. May Sarton expresses it perfectly in her *Journal of a Solitude* (see p. 243): 'When I am alone the flowers are really seen; I can pay attention to them. They are felt as presences... They live and die in a few days; they keep me closely in touch with process, with growth, and also with dying. I am floated on their moments.'

7 December 1997 ~ The Allotment

Visiting the allotment in winter is a bit like entering an empty school during the holidays. The structure is still there – call it the furniture – and all the familiar landmarks. But the usual sense of life is strangely, almost eerily, absent. It happens all of a sudden, with the first heavy frost. Overnight, the sturdy stems and leaves of courgette plants shrink to an insubstantial slime. And nasturtiums, which continue to rampage through the raised beds in a mass of russet, red and golden yellow flowers throughout the early light frosts, are reduced to tangles of sticky green spaghetti. That buzz of life that seems so much a part of the place has gone, replaced by a ringing silence that hangs in the air like morning mist.

A few dependable vegetables soldier on in the cold – leaf beet spinach, which will provide us with salads and pasta sauces all winter long, the few straggly broccoli plants that escaped the birds, and my first proud sprouts, which will soon be ready to harvest. But there is little change in their appearance from week to week. The sense of plants growing all around you – so tangible in summer you can almost feel it in your blood – is no more. It's as if all the energy of the plants has left the air around the leaves and retreated down the stems into the ground. Sitting very still, I really became aware of it. There was something comforting about imagining a slow, but nonetheless important stirring of activity beneath the soil – of the roots of spring bulbs developing, of shoots and tubers burrowing blindly into the dark, like moles.

It's not only the plants that have gone into hibernation. Apart from the Indian gentleman two plots down, who has been sieving and raking his soil into the finest chocolatey brown tilth for spring sowing, I've hardly seen any of my fellow plot holders for weeks. Our own frenetic activity, too, has gone underground for a few months. But, just like the plants beneath the soil, our gardening is still being kept alive in various ways. Some will be browsing through seed catalogues in front of the fire; some will already be sowing next years' annuals in greenhouses or propagators. Others will be visiting hot houses, or even gardens abroad, to glean knowledge and inspiration.

For me, winter means taking myself off to another, quite different garden all together – the garden of my imagination. In his wonderful book *Second Nature: a Gardener's Education*, the American author Michael Pollan makes the distinction between the gardener's actual garden and what he calls, 'the garden of books and memories, that dreamed-of outdoor utopia, gnat-free and ever in bloom, where nature answers to our wishes and we imagine feeling perfectly at home'. The latter is nurtured not by hard manual slog but by reading and dreaming.

The books don't need to have pictures. On the contrary, too many glossy photographs can somehow distract from your vision: they are too specific to place and time and mood. The writing I choose to immerse myself in doesn't rely on visual interpretation to get to the heart of gardens and gardening. Vita Sackville West's opinionated musings are forever good value (*In Your Garden* and *In Your Garden Again* have recently been republished, see p. 243), and I always enjoy Mirabel Osler (see p. 242). She and Michael Pollan are among a crop of excellent old and new authors gathered together under *Bloomsbury Gardening Classics* – beautifully produced, with a stunning photograph of a single flower on the jacket (see p. 242). When it comes to magazines and periodicals, one of the most satisfying for me is *Hortus*, a quarterly journal, bound like an old-fashioned paperback, illustrated mainly with line-drawings and wood-engravings and published privately by David Wheeler from his home in Herefordshire (see p. 243). A couple of copies and a glass of wine is all it takes to transport me to my own outdoor utopia in the comfort of my own armchair.

14 December 1997 ~ Artists' Gardens

About ten years ago, I used to hang out with a group of young artists who squatted a derelict house off Highgate Hill in north London. It was the garden that first lured me to them. 'This Way' read a hand-painted sign that pointed up an overgrown drive between trees. I followed, and was greeted by a giant white bird made from paper, wire and polythene that swung from a cedar tree like a parachute caught in its branches. A herd of other curious creatures were grazing on the lawn, their tin-can snouts and twiggy noses buried in the grass. And all along the roof of the house six life-size models of the artists, hands linked and heads thrown back, were silhouetted against the sky.

You had to cross a sort of moat to enter the house. A shallow recess at the top of the steps had been filled with water in which flowerheads were floating. Inside, the walls bristled and crawled with scraps of paper and coloured cloth. The artists treated the place like a huge canvas for their creations, using anything to hand (which would include what most of us would call rubbish) as materials. Twirling strings of leaves, fragments of broken glass and polythene, yellowed and blistered with age, hung in the doorways, and the ceilings were papered with black and white photographs torn from the National Geographic. The effect was unsettling and bizarre, yet strangely beautiful. Three hours and countless cups of tea later, I was still there, hooked and spellbound, head spinning with tales of the house and its inhabitants.

In the weeks that followed, I was a frequent visitor, and fantasised about throwing in my job and joining the artists in their carefree, yet impressively productive way of life. In the absence of electricity, time was governed by seasonal changes in light and temperature. While there was daylight, each of them worked on their pieces – often outside in the garden. In the evenings they'd sit around the fire in the cluttered kitchen and talk and tell stories and make plans. If they were cold they'd dance or chop wood. Sometimes there were parties in the cavernous sitting room, when we'd sing and play music round a fire that threw strange shadows across the patchwork walls.

I was reminded of all this while looking at *Charleston: A Bloomsbury House and Garden* (see p. 242), a wonderful new book about the Sussex farmhouse inhabited by members of the Bloomsbury Group. Though Vanessa Bell, Duncan Grant and their friends were obviously from a different time, class and artistic inclination than the squatters, there is something of the same spirit behind the two places – in the spontaneity, the fun and the sense of slap-dash, instant artistry. Much has been written about Charleston's interiors – how Duncan Grant decorated a chest of drawers in the morning for a guest due that afternoon, or how Vanessa would repaint the geometric designs on the dining room table whenever they wore faint. But what is often ignored is the way this same spirit flowed out of the house and into the garden, too.

The flowers the artists planted were those they loved to paint – bright, showy blooms such as red-hot pokers, zinnias, dahlias and oriental poppies, as well as the sculptural heads of thistles and globe artichokes. Amid this sea of colour they placed found objects, like an ever-changing Surrealist tableau: plaster-cast statues filched from the local art school and other pieces made specifically for the garden, such as Quentin Bell's brick sphinx and levitating figure, reflected in the pond. Mosaics were made from china smashed during mishaps and arguments – and when a hollow plaster torso was broken by his son, Quentin converted it into a planter.

One of Bloomsbury's most inspiring legacies is this sense of adventure, coupled with a refreshing disregard for perfection. It's something we could all benefit from in our gardens – forget our fears that things might go wrong and just DO it. And if it doesn't work out – well, what else could we turn it into? As for the Highgate artists, when I last saw them, they had built an enormous paper ark in a disused Quaker Chapel, and were holding a candlelit dinner inside it, while, high above the guests, two of their number swung from the rafters on a tinsel trapeze.

21 December 1997 ~ Columbia Road Flower Market

There can be few gardeners living in or around the capital who have not been to Columbia Road Flower Market, held every Sunday morning in Shoreditch, east London. In the summer months, certainly, the place seems almost to have become a victim of its own success. You have to set the alarm early to avoid being crushed by the crowds of horticultural bargain-hunters who push and shove along the narrow terraced street like a herd of cattle. By 8.30a.m. the place is already thronging, and by 1p.m., when the stall-holders pack up, there are near riots over the last lots of cut flowers, which are sold for a song. All morning, the surrounding streets resemble a moving forest as huge yuccas, young fruit trees and trays of pansies or pelargoniums are carried, high over their bearers' heads, to the bus stop or boot of the car. I've done it myself many times, only to crawl back into bed, exhausted, on my return.

But hardly anyone – thank goodness – seems to think of visiting Columbia Road in winter. I spent an extremely pleasant couple of hours there last Sunday, able, for once, to see the plants without any jostling – and to pick up a few unusual Christmas presents on the way. I like to survey the whole street before buying anything – you don't want to commit to £5 for a tray of pansies at the top end when equally good ones are going for half that further down.

First stop is usually Christian Christopher's Rare Plants stall in The Courtyard, a pretty enclosure overlooked by artists' studios on Ezra Street. Quality is sometimes sacrificed to quantity at Columbia Road; the stall-holders sell plants like dodgy pavement goods ('Come on ladies, a fiver for a tray of Busy Lizzies. Who wants a tray of Busy Lizzies for a fiver?') But Mr Christopher's (see p. 244) is the stall to visit if you're after something more than run-of-the-mill bedding plants, ivies and clematis. Plants are meticulously identified with hand-written labels explaining where and how to grow them, and patient verbal advice is readily given. I succumbed to a *Clianthus puniceus* 'Albus' (white claw-like blooms and fine feathered foliage) and a dark blue *Ceanothus* 'Puget blue' for £10 the pair – and a glossy leaved evergreen *Clematis armandii*. In need of pots to put them in, I picked up a nest of three round pots glazed a soft sage green (the largest is almost a metre across) and a taller beaker-shaped one in the most beautiful cobalt blue from Classic Terracotta, also in The Courtyard (see p. 245), who import frost-proof planters in simple, unfussy shapes from Thailand. It's worth inspecting pots carefully before you buy them, as the drainage holes can be poorly placed in some.

Two jumbo bags of potting compost were £6.50 a throw from Jenny's Garden (see p. 244) at the end of the street, and four trays of winter-flowering pansies for £10 completed my morning's transactions. I spent the afternoon planting the huge pots – particularly pleased with the *Ceanothus* in the blue pot surrounded by white 'Mount Tacoma' tulip bulbs and apricot pansies; and the parrot tree in the huge green pot circled by black 'Queen of the Night' tulips and ink-blue pansies.

A planted-up pot would make the most lovely Christmas present, but there's no shortage of ideas both on the plant stalls and in the dozens of little arty shops that line the street – CP Ceramics (see p. 244) and S&B Evans (see p. 244) are good for planters and accessories; Stoney Parsons (see p. 245) has pretty stained glass and crystal drops to string at windows; and Organics on Ravenscroft Street (see p. 245) is packed with trendy wicker plant trainers, galvanised metal buckets and twiggy wreaths from as little as £2.

Even if you live outside London, it's worth making the market part of a weekend visit. A couple of smoked salmon bagels from Brick Lane for breakfast and a browse round the Whitechapel Gallery and you've the makings of a perfect Sunday before it's even lunchtime.

28 December 1997 ~ Plans for a Community Garden

The last few weeks have gone by in a flurry of form-filling, letter-writing and meetings. My idea to turn the derelict warehouse behind our house into a neighbourhood garden, has gone from pipe-dream to paper application and is now in the hands of those who grant funds.

I've been looking out on this building while I work ever since we moved in here eighteen months ago, watching the cats fight and flirt on the asphalt roof and fantasising about doing something with it – laying Astroturf on it, painting a mural of neat rows of vegetables, glazing it over to make a huge tropical greenhouse. Finally my chance came when the building came up for sale a few months ago. It's a large, low, cheaply built structure, the size of about six average town gardens, with access via a locked gate and passageway that passes under the flats on the road that runs at right-angles to ours. The estate agents think it may originally have been an undertaker's. My idea is simply to try to raise enough money to buy it (it's on the market for £75,000), bash in the roof but leave the walls, and turn it into a small enclosed garden. To distinguish it from the crop of 'community' and 'wildlife' gardens springing up everywhere at the moment, I wondered about incorporating fruit and vegetables alongside the flowers and traditional quiet sitting areas. The idea would be to create a modern-day 'kitchen garden' for the next century – including everything from run-of-the-mill beans and tomatoes to River Café-type *cavolo nero* and butternut squash, to Caribbean staples such as maize and 'red peas', which many of the older West Indian residents of this part of London already grow in neighbouring gardens.

The emphasis would be on showing how easy it is to grow vegetables and fruit in relatively small spaces, while still providing a pretty and peaceful garden. We could grow french and runner beans around the entrances; tomatoes in hanging baskets; potatoes in tyre tubs and pumpkins and courgettes in pots. Different types of lettuces could make edgings for the borders, with globe artichokes, sweetcorn and cabbages popping up among the shrubs and flowers. We could train cordon peach and apple trees up the sunnier walls, and have a small fruit cage filled with currant bushes, raspberry canes and strawberries.

To ensure the garden has year-round appeal, we could employ some of the techniques of Permaculture (see p. 118), which originated in Australia but is fast becoming fashionable over here, and replaces traditional rows of crops with perennial varieties, preferring mulch as an alternative to digging. There could be a compost-making demonstration area where people could bring their own kitchen waste to contribute. And perhaps a greenhouse where we could raise tomato plants to sell.

All this might sound a bit pie-in-the-sky, but the local council is very interested, together with the British Trust for Conservation Volunteers (BTCV) (see p. 245), and an organisation called Green Adventure, which can offer advice on similar community-based schemes (see p. 245). Most importantly, we have a good group of locals firmly behind the idea. Last week we all had a meeting at our house, exchanged ideas for the site and decided to register ourselves as a BTCV-affiliated group. This costs £30, but entitles any group with an idea for a similar project an instant start-up grant of £50, together with professional help and support in running your group and applying for funding and insurance cover. I've been working my way through a huge pile of funding forms – but will fall at the first hurdle if we can't think of a name. Anything ending in 'Community Garden' or 'Neighbourhood Park' sounds hopelessly dreary and worthy, and doesn't really get across the idea of growing food. The main contender so far is the 'Mango Garden' – but whether or not we'll ever be able to grow any mangoes there remains to be seen.

1998

4 January 1998 ~ New Year's Resolutions

~ To take the kitchen compost bin to the allotment more frequently so house is not full of rotting vegetables and accompanying odours.

~ Not to say 'all grown at the allotment' smugly when serving up food to dinner guests.

~ To sow rocket little and often, ensuring a constant supply, rather than a glut — enough to feed the River Café seven times over — which immediately goes to seed.

~ To train Rolf the lurcher not to relieve himself on the smart new wooden deck in the back garden.

~ To find or buy some nifty containers for left-over seeds and label them efficiently (like American home/garden and cooking super-woman Martha Stewart) as opposed to my current 'system' which consists of a shoe box filled with dog-eared paper packets with holes in them — nothing in the packets and a pot-pourri of mixed seeds rolling around at the bottom of the box.

~ To plant twenty-five types of lettuces in pretty patterns like Martha Stewart in her book *Martha Stewart's Gardening* (see p. 243), (no use even trying to compete with her twenty varieties of basil).

~ To be more like Martha Stewart in general.

~ To lay proper paths between the raised beds in my allotment rather than slithering about on scraps of decaying carpet.

~ To raise lots of flower seedlings on the sunny bathroom window-sill for planting out into the new allotment cutting garden.

~ To get rid of the layer of mould around my camper van windows – the result of over-enthusiastic watering while using the van as mobile greenhouse in the spring.

~ To make a pond – ideally with some kind of wind-powered paddle to keep the water moving – to encourage frogs and toads which will eat all my slugs.

~ To refrain from flinging slugs over allotment fence into the Territorial Army depot car park next door. The reader who wrote to me some months ago was right. It is not 'appropriate behaviour for a grown woman'.

~ To buy a propagator for cultivating more difficult plants from seed.

~ To not sit about moaning about the state of the allotment while drinking a can of beer with friends, but to get rid of offending weeds/slugs/debris/stacks of old rickety wood forthwith.

~ To sow my own tomatoes from Simpson's Seeds' unusual and old-fashioned varieties (write for a catalogue to 27 Meadow-brook, Old Oxted, Surrey RH8 9LT).

~ To fill in all the tedious grant applications for my scheme to turn the old warehouse behind our back garden into a community garden and really do all I can to make it happen.

~ To clean my tools properly after I've used them.

~ To read right through the beautiful old copy of Gerard's *Herball* that my boyfriend's mother gave me, rather than just looking at the wonderful woodcuts.

~ To think up lots of madly exciting ways of using runner beans so I won't be throwing them back on the compost heap.

~ To not expect *everybody* to be breathless with enthusiasm about my gifts of runner beans and marrows from the allotment.

~ To find a foolproof organic way of eliminating blackfly.

~ To give Michael Pollan's *Second Nature: A Gardener's Education* (see p. 244) – a beautifully written collection of essays on gardening – to all my gardening friends.

~ To persevere with learning Latin plant names.

~ To stop making so many demands on myself and get on with *enjoying* gardening. All the year round.

11 January 1998 ~ Community Gardens in New York

Before my last visit to New York, in December, I'd never associated Manhattan with gardening. Central Park aside, it can seem as if the premium on space has edged out the green to just a few straggly squares between skyscrapers. This is the city of the apartment block; and those lucky enough to have a back yard have to cope with the shade from surrounding tall buildings. The typical British row of houses with their own fenced-off gardens simply doesn't exist.

But just because New Yorkers don't have their own individual patch doesn't mean they don't garden. I discovered this on a walk through the Lower East Side of the city, which is a patchwork of innovative community gardens. Among the scruffy Spanish churches and graffiti-covered shop fronts there are little oases planted with birch and eucalyptus trees, late-flowering tobacco plants and leafy green ferns. Some have ponds, or wooden pergolas grown over with ivy and clematis. In others, old kitchen chairs, painted yellow and blue, are pulled up around low tables. One even had a shrine to the Madonna.

The most extraordinary by far is the plot known as the 6th and B Garden (on 6th Street between Avenues B and C) in Alphabet City, the part of New York east of 1st Avenue, where the numbers run out into letters. Above a painted metal fence towers a forty foot wooden sculpture made from bird houses, old rocking horses, plastic toys and snakes and flags of fabric. This is actually someone's plot – the 6th and B Garden is one of a few gardens where, rather than share the entire area as communal space, each resident presides over his or her own patch (in this case a mere eight by four feet, the size of a small flower border). Such is the demand for space that every scrap of soil is planted up with annuals, herbs or tomato plants and studded with favourite stones, shells and found objects. In the case of the sculpture, the artist who made it decided that, in line with New York's building tradition, the only way to go was up.

Long waiting lists for plots mean that scruffiness simply isn't tolerated. The beds are edged with patterns in pebbles or brick, or neat miniature picket fences, and even on an icy cold day, there were residents at work on their plots. Luckily, one of them saw us with our noses pushed through the railings, and offered to let us in (to avoid vandalism, the gardens are locked up at night and throughout the winter). We were shown the little children's garden, the communal compost bins where people are encouraged to bring their kitchen waste, and the covered stage which the residents use for parties, poetry readings and musical performances in summer. 'The garden is a great focus for the community,' explained Anna, an artist in her early forties. 'In this city, where everybody lives in their own little apartment and rushes from home to work and back again, it's hard for neighbours to get to know each other. I used to live in the Upper West Side, which is supposed to be a much "better" neighbourhood, but there are no gardens like this up there and no-one ever speaks to one another.'

Like many of New York's 750 community gardens, this one was established in the early Eighties, on derelict land overrun by rats, drug addicts and prostitutes, with the help of Operation Green Thumb. The movement to reclaim vacant lots as gardens began in the Seventies, when a Greenwich Village painter called Liz Christy founded the now infamous Green Guerillas [sic]. She and her friends lobbed 'seed bombs' (paper balloons filled with seeds, soil and water) over the fences of derelict sites and sowed sunflowers along the central traffic reservations, as well as planting the city's first community garden in 1974. Eventually realising they were squatters within the lots, and worried about the gardens' future, the Guerillas approached the City authorities for support in 1978. The result was Operation Green Thumb – which now has a budget of $500,000 per year and is pushing for the best gardens to be protected as permanent parks. Many are now in danger from developers, keen to feed the City's ever-growing need for housing.

'It's ironic that making the gardens has helped stabilise previously dangerous areas, making them more desirable to developers,' explains Jane Weissman, Green Thumb's director. 'Many gardens have already been lost – and often in Harlem and Brooklyn, where they had become repositories of lively cultural traditions.'

One of three gardens that have already achieved protected status is New York's first community garden, now named the Liz Christy Garden, on the corner of Bowery and Houston Street. As I explored it in the late afternoon sunshine, the trickle of water and wind in the trees drowning out the screeching traffic, I became inspired about my own little project to turn the derelict warehouse behind my house into a garden. There's a vitality in the air in New York that can make you think anything's possible.

18 January 1998 ~ Gardening for Children

While on holiday in America recently, I was struck by the number of beautifully illustrated gardening books for children that are published there, many of which come with packets of seeds or little tools attached. I have been looking for similar books here, to give my godchildren, but have yet to see anything that quite measures up. Then it occurred to me: special equipment simply isn't necessary to get young kids keen on gardening. They need little or no encouragement to get their hands in the earth on a fine day and – perhaps because they are smaller and thus nearer the ground – their senses can seem particularly attuned to minuscule day-to-day changes such as the greenish tips of spring bulbs nudging through the soil.

Some of this simple enthusiasm stays with gardeners for life – gardening appeals to the side of our nature that still believes in magic and likes to make a mess. The sense of wonder I feel at seeing a sunflower grow from seed to towering giant has changed little since I first sowed one at the age of five. And the excitement of raising cuttings from slices of leaf and stem has never worn off.

One of the books I did buy in America is *The Sense of Wonder* – written by the ecologist Rachel Carson (author of *Silent Spring*) in 1957 (see p. 244). In it she documents the experience of adopting her baby great-nephew, Roger, when her niece died – and in particular, the joy she took in introducing him to the natural world along the stretch of Maine coastline where she spent her summers. Originally published with atmospheric black and white photographs, the book has been out of print for decades, and I'd given up trying to trace a second-hand copy. So it was a joy to find that it has been reissued – on the instigation of Roger himself, now in middle age – with beautiful colour photographs on almost every page.

Carson writes movingly about a child's world, 'fresh and new and beautiful, full of wonder and excitement' and bemoans the fact that for many of us 'that clear-eyed vision, that true instinct for what is beautiful and awe-inspiring', is dimmed and even lost before we reach adulthood. 'If I had influence with the good fairy who is supposed to preside over the christening of children,' she writes, 'I should ask that her gift to each child in the world be a sense of wonder so indestructible that it would last throughout life, as an unfailing antidote against the boredom of later years, the sterile preoccupations with things that are artificial, the alienation from the sources of our strength.'

If today's children are to keep alive their inborn sense of wonder without any such gift from the fairies, they need the companionship of adults who can share it, rediscovering with them the joy, excitement and mystery of the world in which we live. I strongly believe that gardening can help nurture this process. A lucky child will be allowed, as I was, to take over a patch of the family garden. Clear boundaries are a must: if a low tub or small, self-contained bed is not an option, make a low wall or edge the borders with large shells or pebbles.

When considering what to grow, bear in mind that in the early days, instant gratification will ward off boredom and encourage further efforts. Runner beans and sunflowers germinate quickly and on hot summer days you can practically *see* them growing. Anything that can be eaten has an added appeal – try cherry tomatoes in pots, or easy vegetables such as radishes or courgettes that can be harvested young.

Don't be disheartened if the enthusiasm of early years later wears thin. The teenagers who enjoy gardening are few and far between: their world seems to spin at a faster pace. But by then, one would like to think, the good groundwork will have been done and that sense of wonder will be alive beneath the surface. Whether or not they grow up to be gardeners is beside the point.

Encouraging green-fingered children doesn't take much space or money. You don't even need a garden: seeds and a few pots on a sunny balcony will do. And if all you have is a kitchen windowsill, don't despair. Some of the country's keenest gardeners were nurtured on carrot tops in saucers of water, or mustard and cress seeds laid out on damp tissue paper to form their initials.

To quote Rachel Carson once more: 'Wherever you are and whatever your resources, you can still look up at the sky – its dawn and twilight beauties, its moving clouds, its stars by night. You can still listen to the wind, whether it blows with majestic voice through a forest or sings a many-voiced chorus around the eaves of your house or apartment building... You can still feel the rain on your face and think of its long journey, its many transmutations, from sea to air to earth. Even if you are a city dweller, you can find some place, perhaps a park or a golf course, where you can observe the mysterious migrations of the birds and the changing seasons. And with your child you can ponder the mystery of a growing seed, even if it is only one planted in a pot of earth on the kitchen window.'

25 January 1998 ~ The Allotment

Getting to the allotment in winter needs rather more willpower than in summer, when it seems the easiest thing in the world to cycle over for a few hours in the sunshine. Apart from dragging myself away from a good book by the fire, there is the correct footwear to be found and the waterproofs and scarves to be piled on. Since tedious allotment regulations demanded the demise of our shed, there is now nowhere to shelter when the weather turns bad. And even when I'm all togged out and ready to go, it's easy to succumb to delaying tactics.

Not so long ago, my friend Simon and I had scheduled in an afternoon's digging and bulb-planting. Perhaps it was foolhardy to have planned to go on the shortest day with a cold east wind blowing, but we liked the idea of being there at the turning point of the year. We were also keen to sow some garlic (traditional on the solstice) and finish planting the bearded iris roots that had been languishing for far too long in their plastic packets from the mail order company.

My friend had just returned from a gruelling shopping trip, so a quick cup of tea seemed in order before setting off. Then we got embroiled in a discussion about the new deck in the back garden. By then it was half past two. As we were climbing in the van to go, we decided it would be foolish not to replenish our plant label supply and buy a waterproof pen – one of the reasons last year's cutting garden did not come together was the lack of clear, permanent labels to indicate what had been sown where. On the way to the shops, Simon spied a Sixties mohair suit for sale on a second-hand market stall. While he was trying it on, I unearthed some beautiful brown leather hobnailed boots which I fancied might look rather Vita Sackville-Westish with my old cord jodhpurs. By the time we finally arrived at the allotment, it was too dark to see what we were doing.

We made up for lost time the following weekend with a whole day of digging and repairing raised beds. For those not familiar with them, raised beds are one of the most widely used methods in organic gardening. They can either be built up gradually over a number of years, as the natural result of adding a thick mulch of compost or manure to the soil every autumn – or can be constructed within a frame of old floorboards or chunky railway sleepers. The ideal size is no more than four foot across, so you can reach the middle easily from the path on either side, to weed or water or harvest produce.

The advantages of growing in raised beds include improved drainage, deep topsoil with no compaction (as you never tread on it), fast-warming soil for spring planting, and the potential to sustain much more closely-planted crops – and thus, higher yields – than with the traditional system of neat rows. They are particularly useful on waterlogged clay, or where the soil is too poor to use at all (the late Derek Jarman constructed some superb raised vegetable beds from old sleepers behind his house on the shingle at Dungeness).

Our predecessor on our second, newer, plot must have spent ages making his raised beds out of painted planks and timber off-cuts. I would not describe them as objects of beauty, although two have a rather attractive edging of old slate roof tiles. Of the nine he made, we must have used five last year; the rest were still overgrown and dilapidated. One was completely overrun by couch grass and old strawberry plants that had long since ceased to fruit – I spent most of the day sieving the soil for couch grass roots (even a half-inch segment can become a new plant) and runaway runners. Others needed the sides shoring up by driving rough-hewn pegs of wood into the soil to support the plank walls. We even made some new beds, using the remains of the old shed to surround the wilderness area we're trying to reclaim using layers of damp cardboard and compost (see p. 118). Beside all this, the pathways made from scraps of slimy old carpet looked even scruffier than usual. One plan is to replace them with bark chippings, which slowly decay into the soil and keep slugs away into the bargain – they don't like crawling over rough, fragmented surfaces.

By sunset, all of the beds, old and new, had been dug over and given a mulch of stable manure and compost – our forebear had also left an amazingly rich and ancient supply of leafmould, the caviar of top-dressings for soil. For once, we really felt we deserved the beer and hearty supper that followed when we got home. And my lovely new boots got a worthy christening.

1 February 1998 ~ On Cacti

There are very few plants that I do not care for, but cacti are among them. I have tried to love them. In the early days of our courtship – I suspect in an effort to impress me with a sudden enthusiasm for gardening – my boyfriend bought a whole bunch of cacti and installed them in his flat. He arranged the plants – rather endearingly, I thought at the time – as a desert landscape in miniature in a large terracotta trough, and set among them a little toy tin cowboy on a horse. This tableau remained on top of his television for four years, and I have to say that the cacti flourished. They were well looked after – given plenty of light and just enough water – and were fussed over regularly in the way I've grown to recognise that plants love. I even got quite fond of them myself, and was genuinely excited when, once every eight months or so, the 'Mickey Mouse plant' (*Opuntia microdasys*) put out another ear, or the *Echinopsis* seemed to have gained a quarter of an inch in height.

The problems began when my boyfriend and I moved into a

house together. I was reluctant to find a place for the cacti in the sitting room, the kitchen or, indeed, any other room which met their light requirements. Reluctantly, I have put up with them on our bedroom windowsill, but I cannot say that the kitsch little ensemble is a welcome sight every morning. The plants get much less attention now – and, not surprisingly in this climate of hostility and neglect, they are suffering. Mickey Mouse has not produced any offspring in over a year; the new growth on the *Echinocactus* has turned crispy and brown, and the curly, low-growing *Parodia* has sort of shrunk in on itself, like a pile of hairy dog poo. I really don't know what to do with them.

I am surprised by the strength of my dislike for these plants. But, perhaps more than any other plant group, cacti do seem to provoke extreme and opposing passions. For every cactus-hater such as myself there is a clutch of aficionados for whom their graphic shapes and spiny geometry are not ugly dust traps but the very height of beauty. Curiously few people seem to possess just one cactus. They amass huge collections of the things, cluttering every windowsill with their prickly treasures. They become obsessed with growing the things from seed (extremely fiddly and, as you might imagine, extraordinarily *slow*), propagating from slices of leaf or 'pups' (the miniature offsets that cluster off the main stem) and coaxing spectacular blooms from species that take fifty years to flower. Some, like my boyfriend, are tempted to arrange their plants as miniature landscape gardens. One collection I know consists of groups of prickly pear-like *Opuntia burbankii* and hairy Mexican *Cephalocereus senilis* ('old man cactus'), among which have been placed an old 'Dinky Toys' car, upended on its side, and a pair of silver skeleton earrings laid out on a rock. Its owner calls it the 'Thelma and Louise Memorial Garden'.

There is no doubt that the larger cacti can look stunning in the right setting. The soft grey-greens of 'Brazilian Blue' cacti (*Pilosocereus glaucescens*) look particularly good against dark blues and indigo walls, and the earthy tones and textures are natural partners for materials such as stone, wood and terracotta. In a large white loft, a single six-foot *Stenocereus* is the nearest the plant world gets to sculpture. But I think this very stillness is at the root of my dislike. Cacti don't *do* much. I prefer to be surrounded by plants that change from day to day – or at least, from year to year. In January and February, I get huge amounts of pleasure from winter-flowering bulbs – tall terracotta pots of 'Paperwhite' narcissi and amaryllis in particular. I have a bowl of white hyacinths on the desk where I work, and am enjoying watching their tight nubs of flowers shaping up within the glossy green sheath of leaves. Soon their wonderful scent will fill the air. I'm afraid that a cactus can't compete – not even a little slice of Mexico with a toy cowboy riding through it.

But the cowboy's Last Stand may be nigh. A possible solution to the problem presented itself in this morning's post. 'Bio-Light', the press release boasts, is 'a stylish lamp for indoor plants... which even allows plants to flourish in rooms without natural daylight' (see p. 245). Were I to invest in one of those, the cacti could retire to my boyfriend's den in the basement and I would hardly have to look at them again. Hurrah!

8 February 1998 ~ Home

Lack of light is the bane of urban gardeners such as myself – particularly in winter when the sun seems loath to heave itself above the roofs of the surrounding buildings. Our little back garden – a suntrap in summer – is almost permanently shaded for three months of the year by the tall house diagonally opposite. A shaft of late morning light sneaks in through a gap at the end of our row of houses, when it is nice to sit out on the deck with a cup of coffee – but you have to be quick. By the time the coffee's finished the sun has slunk behind the building, only to emerge for another brief hour in the mid-afternoon. No wonder New Yorkers have roof gardens.

To banish wintry blues, I try to make sure that the view of the garden from the house is as pretty as possible. Pots and containers are useful here. I've lugged together some of the most attractive ones and arranged them in a little tableau on the steps that lead out from the french windows in the main room. A winter flowering *Clematis cirrhosa* is doing well in a tall galvanised metal bucket with a tee-pee of canes to climb up – its fragile cream bell-shaped flowers light up like paper lanterns when the sun slants through them. Evergreen shrubs in glazed terracotta tubs are a backdrop for white and blue pansies and the silvery leaves of *Convolvulus cneorum* – which, considering its ideal environment is a sunny Mediterranean roof terrace, is performing quite heroically. I can also keep my eye on the tips of bulbs coming through – daffodils in some pots, and tulips in others – black parrots, inky dark 'Queen of the Night' and 'Spring Green' (a Viridiflora type whose white petals are streaked with green).

One of the virtues of container gardening is that you can move the pots into prime position – even carry them inside the house – when they are looking their best. When that show's over, there will be another pot waiting in the wings. I'm hoping for a good progression of blooms to take me through to spring.

Before moving to this house I was a flat-dweller, and would fill whatever roof or balcony space I had with containers of all shapes and sizes. You can use almost anything – wooden barrels, buckets, boxes and baskets as well as the traditional decorative pots and planters. I have a penchant for lovely old fluted metal laundry tubs, but my latest acquisition is a pair of enormous oval-shaped iron vats – each of them about one foot high and five feet long, with handles at both ends. The market stall-holder who sold them to me said they were for treading grapes in French vineyards. My friends down the road comb the local market for the large round wicker baskets in which fruit is brought over from the West Indies, line them with black bin-liners and fill them with tumbling tomato plants and English marigolds. And nothing is quite so jolly as the rows of geraniums in brightly painted olive tins that you see ranged up outside houses in Spain and Greece.

A new book called *Creative Containers* by Paul Williams (see p. 242) has some other fun ideas such as transforming scrap metal (a copper cistern and heat exchanger) into planters, and making a mini-vegetable garden from an old hip bath. Whatever you use, the crucial factor with containers is drainage. If it's too fast the pots will dry out rapidly in summer and need watering twice a day. Too slow (the most common cause of failure) and the soil will become water-logged and the roots will rot. If the pot or tub you're using does not have at least one good-sized hole in the bottom, make some with a drill. The holes must be covered with a flat stone or shard of ceramic to stop water running straight out when you water. It's also a good idea to fill the base of the pot with gravel so that the roots are never sitting in stagnant water – add a small piece of charcoal to act as a filter and stop the water smelling. Gravel on the surface of the soil can look decorative, and also acts as a mulch to keep weeds down and water in. I've been admiring the coloured gravel sold in the local pet shop for tropical aquariums and imagining purple sage or lime green lettuce sprouting from a bed of indigo gravel in my new grape vats. Just thinking about it makes me long for spring.

15 February 1998 ~ RHS Shows at Vincent Square

On a cold London afternoon, there are few cosier places to be than one of the Royal Horticultural Society's (RHS) winter shows in Greycoat Street just off Vincent Square. It's not just the warm, wel-coming smell of thousands of spring flowers that envelops you on entering – though that is a treat in itself. There's also something infinitely comforting about the slice of Middle England that congregates there. Cool Britannia holds no sway over the throng that moves beneath the cathedral-like glass ceiling of the New Hall; you could almost have stepped into a set from Mrs Miniver or some similar Forties film.

Everywhere you look is a perfect example of middle-class, middle-aged womanhood, calling to her companion in hearty, ringing tones, or reading all the Latin names out loud. My favourites are the many who have obviously made the trip up from the country, each dressed in identical Caroline-goes-to-London outfits of sensible tweed skirt, sensible thick stockings and sensible low brogues. 'D'you think I'll get this camellia on the train, Mary?' shouts one, half-hidden behind an enormous potted pom-pom, while another is complaining that her black hellebore is not as dark as the one her friend has just bought. Apart from some of the exhibitors and a handful of exhausted husbands cowering in the wings with the cheque books, you could be forgiven for thinking that no-one male and/or under the age of forty-five had ever set eyes on a spade.

The RHS is keen to point out that its membership is getting younger every year – the majority of new members are in their thirties and may well go to the shows in the evenings after work. The shows are one of the best places for gardeners of all ages and abilities to find inspiration and education. Some of Britain's greatest gardeners learned about plants here. Rosemary Verey, for one, would not be a household name had her son not given her an RHS membership for her birthday in 1962. 'My daughter gave me a large notebook immaculately covered with Florentine paper and importantly entitled Gardening Book on the opening page,' she remembers in The Making of a Garden (see p. 243). Her study shelves are now full of hundreds of such books, each crammed with ideas and impressions and the names of plants seen at the shows. Her first purchase, she remembers, was a willow, 'a Salix hastata "Wehrhahnii" with silvery-grey catkins'.

I may not have a smart notebook, but I'm one of the many scribblers at the shows. Seeing the plants growing gives a far better impression of how they look than a catalogue illustration – you can appreciate their true colours, as well as the plants they might be combined with. At Foxgrove Plants' display of grasses, for instance, it was interesting to see the different colours set against each other – the grey-blue of Festuca glauca 'Blue Glow' next to the aptly-named 'Golden Toupée'; the black seaweedy fronds of Ophiopogon planiscapus 'Nigrescens' with the acid green Acorus gramineus 'Ogon'.

Sometimes I'm looking for plants for my own garden – this time I replaced a pair of Acanthus mollis that fell prey to the slugs and earmarked the winter-flowering honeysuckle, Lonicera fragrantissima for a spot near the front door, where its scent will greet visitors when there is little else in bloom. I'd also like room one day for a Garrya elliptica, with its wonderful, snaky, articulated catkins that frill out as they open till the tree looks like a giant chandelier.

Other plants take root in my imaginary garden of the future, making me long for when I can spread my wings beyond my little patch in the city. Witch hazels, with their tatters of yellow and deep blood-red blossom, make me want a woodland garden, with young flowering trees underplanted with spring bulbs and, later on, blue-bells. I'd like a rickety old conservatory with gardenias and daturas in pots and a cloud of mauve *Streptocarpus glandulosissimus* – a feathery, ferny variety without the usual felty leaves. And some day, somewhere, I'd like a rough ditch bordering a field, and a little bench to watch the sunset, and a clump of *Anemone japonica*, long since gone to seed, to catch the low winter light through its cotton-wool flower heads.

22 February 1998 ~ The Allotment

The dreaded Allotment Inspection Committee has begun its proces-sion around the plots, clipboards in hand and antennae on the alert for any transgressions of the rules. February is the time when our annual subscriptions are due, and members whose plots are deemed not up to scratch will be given a month to make amends. Neglect to do this, and their plots will be confiscated and given to people on the waiting list.

After all our impressive activity of recent weeks, clearing the over-grown beds and constructing smart new ones from old timber offcuts, my friends and I were confident that our two plots would pass muster. Where it once resembled a giant skip, the new plot is now a network of raised beds and pathways, with the leaves of globe artichokes, Brussels sprouts and a new crop of broad beans thrown into sharp relief against the freshly-dug, dark soil.

We had been envisaging heartfelt congratulations on our efforts – perhaps even an invitation for one of us to join the committee (heaven forbid). Imagine our dismay then, on arriving for work last Saturday, to find the inspection patrol had already passed by, leaving in their wake just a pair of wooden stakes driven into the soil where the boundary of our plot ends and the grass path begins. Our crime, it appeared, was to have stacked our excess wood (albeit in a neat pile) on communal land – the stack had been ransacked and shifted a few feet to one side. The message seemed clear: move it or else.

For some reason, this sent us into paroxysms of rage. The plot felt somehow violated, almost as if we'd been burgled. 'How dare they!' cried Simon. 'This is exactly the sort of petty behaviour one expects from people who sit on committees. A tiny taste of power and it goes straight to their heads.'

'Absolutely,' I agreed. 'And it's so cowardly. Why couldn't they have come and faced us while we were here?'

Our grumbling continued as we began work, and only ceased when I looked up and saw the anorak-clad figure of Barbara, head of the Inspection Committee, coming our way. Bristling slightly, we moved to meet her, leaning on our spades and forks in a manner that we probably meant to be intimidating. But Barbara had a big smile on her face. 'I've come to tell you what a great job we all think you've been doing,' she beamed, handing me a payment slip for the next year's fees.

We'd passed! But we do have to move the wood. Apparently it's too near to the newly layered hedge and may even be endangering the line of young saplings that were planted alongside it. We felt suitably contrite, as Barbara made her way back to her plot up at the top.

There seems to be something of a Great Divide on our allotment site. The committee members and law-abiding 'old-timers' colonise the top end, where neat brick-edged beds and flower borders are the order of the day. As you work your way down towards us, things start to look more chaotic – still well within the rules, but with an anarchic fringe of corrugated iron and old window-frames bashed into makeshift structures. Weeds are more frequent and several plots have become completely overgrown – soon to be clawed back by the committee, no doubt.

Right at the bottom, our predecessor was the Lord of Misrule, presiding over what was really little more than a dumping ground for all the scrap iron and timber he could accumulate. His shed, tacked together from glazed doors and mouldy old wood, was a flagrant breach of the rules. Though he was dethroned a full year ago now, when the committee made his plot over to us, something of his spirit has lingered – in our delay in taking down his shed and in our sulky reluctance to participate in committee meetings, fund-raising events, communal barbecues and the like. Our double plot, which stretches across the entire north border of the site, has felt at times almost like an independent state, secluded, self-contained and removed from prying eyes.

This era may well be over, however. Word of our improvements has spread and we've been receiving a constant stream of visitors from 'up the top', all eager to see how the renegade patch has been redeemed. We're torn between swelling with pride and just wishing they'd go away.

1 March 1998 ~ Spring Greens

The first buds are appearing on the trees. Soon the whole world will be turned my favourite colour – the green of young beech leaves, hanging like tatters of pale silk with the sunlight shining through them. Lime, celadon, chartreuse, acid green – the colour has acquired many names as people attempt to pin it down. The 'greenery yallery' of the Aesthetic Movement comes close – but I think that was a put-down. To me it is a wonderful colour.

Last year acid green – let's call it chartreuse – enjoyed a fleeting flirtation with the fashion world. Suddenly it was everywhere, from T-shirts in The Gap to little skirts by Prada. I thought my hour had come. Sadly, though, lime does little for those with average English colouring, and I left it to the dark haired and olive skinned. This year everyone's in grey.

What a relief that Nature is immune to the whims of fashion and serves up this colour the same every spring. And that all kinds of plants and flowers seem to look good in it. Even before the first crumpled leaves unfurl on the trees, chartreuse is to be found in the milky-pale blooms of the hellebores *Helleborus corsicus* and *H. foetidus*, both of which I have in a tin tub in my garden. *H. viridis* is the most unequivocally green, its cup-shaped blooms the colour of pistachio ice-cream. There is something rather mysterious about green flowers – the common distinction between leaf and petal becomes blurred, making us somehow more aware of the plant's form. Think of the frilly spires of *Moluccella laevis* 'Bells of Ireland' – what appear to be vivid green flowers are actually the calyces surrounding tiny white blossoms inside. There are also the many different types of euphorbia, one of the most plentiful sources of this gorgeous colour in the garden. In my favourite varieties, such as E. *characias wulfenii*, the startling greeny-yellow bracts are accentuated by blood-red 'eyes' in the centre.

True green flowers are somewhat harder to find – but there's a zinnia called 'Envy' that is a pleasing pale green; the snaking spikes of *Eucomis pallidiflora*, like elongated green pineapples – and, of course, the pale creamy lime of tobacco plant trumpets (*Nicotiana alata* 'Lime Green') which I love. The term Viridiflora in a flower's name means it's likely to be green or with green streaks. Viridiflora tulips can have any colour as their base – I've planted lots of 'Spring Green' in tubs, which are mainly white, but look as though an artist has run a brush of pale green paint from the stem to the tips of the petals. The rose 'Paul's Lemon Pillar' also has a greenish tinge to its creamy white petals.

Plants that have leaves of this colour are fantastic for enlivening a dull corner. Our neighbour's golden locust tree (*Robinia pseudoacacia* 'Frisia') lights up like a neon lamp when the sun shines through it. Lady's mantle (*Alchemilla mollis*), has leaves that are lime green to start with and grow gradually darker as the froth of yellow-green flowers appears. Golden grasses, the yellow-green form of the liquorice plant (*Helichrysum petiolare* 'Limelight') and, as groundcover, golden creeping Jenny (*Lysimachia nummularia* 'Aurea') mix well with darker greens and provide a foil for other colours in spring and summer.

Certain colours gain an extra frisson when combined with this particular shade of green. True chartreuse plants, which have rather more yellow than blue, set off colours at the opposite end of the colour spectrum – dark blood reds through crimson and cranberry to reddish-purple. Nature does this to great effect in the red, maroon and lime-green striped leaves of coleus plants, though I'd hesitate to use them in a border. But blackish-purple 'Queen of the Night' tulips and the deep red-black anemones and aquilegias would look dramatic against a lime green ground. The blue-green end of the scale looks best with lavender, violet and indigo – lilac field scabious with alchemilla leaves has become a staple among trendy florists.

Andrew Lawson's book, *A Gardener's Book of Colour* (see p. 243) shows a stunning border which contains all of these colours. Among a mainly blue and violet ground (alliums, anchusas, iris and geraniums) weaves a thread of lime green robinia, philadelphus and golden hops (*Humulus lupulus* 'Aureus'). Later in the summer, the blue-mauve clematis 'Perle d'Azur', deep blue annual cornflowers and the deep smoky red pom-poms of *Knautia macedonica* provide more contrast. Or, for a very simple combination of almost heart-stopping beauty, let blue love-in-a-mist (*Nigella damascena*) self-seed through the vines of the golden hop.

8 March 1998 ~ Rooms with a View

The view from a house is more important, I have always felt, than all the paint effects and furniture money can buy. Given the fact that, in this country anyway, one's principal enjoyment of the garden is going to be from an armchair for at least five months of the year, it seems a wonder more people don't take this into account when buying their homes. The average English terraced house is hopeless when it comes to garden views – the habit of tacking kitchen and bathroom extensions on to the back of older buildings means the principal rooms are situated to the front, with access to the garden through a small door in the kitchen or a dark, dank corridor down one side. I was anxious to avoid this when we chose our own house. For I am among those who gain a disproportionate amount of pleasure from a few objects on a table, bathed in sunlight and framed by an open window, with a backdrop of the garden beyond. This pleasure may be hard to justify or explain, but at least it is shared by some great artists, from Matisse to Mary Fedden – and, of course, Pierre Bonnard.

While at the wonderful Bonnard exhibition at the Tate Gallery the other day, it struck me that in practically all of his paintings, it is the relationship between indoor and outdoor space that gives the work its intense emotional charge. The particularity of the domestic life inside – some fruit in a bowl and some books on a table, perhaps even a shadowy figure arranging flowers – is somehow heightened and made more poignant by the witnessing world through the window, especially when this extends, over the garden gate, to the sea or wild landscape beyond. And our perception of the wider world is, in turn, affected by the transient little tableau in the foreground.

I love being in places which have this progression of settings: happiness, for me, is to sit at the large window of a room overlooking a garden and, beyond it a patchwork of tiled roofs, distant hills or the sea. The room has to be a sunny one – it is the saturating sunlight, as any Bonnard fan knows, turning flowers into lanterns and a bowl of milk into a shining white moon, that seems to capture the transience of the moment, where joy is but a hair's breadth from melancholy. Even in Bonnard's famous bathroom paintings, where there is often no window to be seen, there is something in the quality of the light – dancing, dappled, golden, never still – that suggests it has been filtered through a curtain of moving foliage.

When he does paint them in their own right, Bonnard's gardens are exquisite. The garden at his house 'Le Bosquet', which he allowed to grow wild, was described as 'dense and thick; patterns of trees, shrubs, flowers and bushes intermingled, pierced with window-like openings through which the eye escaped into a panorama of sky, mountains, sea and distant Cannes.' It was planted with wisteria, honeysuckle, mimosa, figs and citrus trees, as well as the almond tree he often painted on its own. But few paintings can compare to *The Dining Room in the Country* – Bonnard's country house, with the back door and windows thrown open on to a garden that seems to stretch all the way down the Seine valley. Inside, two cats eye up the cup cakes on the table; outside, someone gathers flowers. A figure in red leans in across the sill, inhabiting both worlds at once.

I would love to have a long view one day. My present house does not have one – flat old London can't serve up the dazzling townscapes of Paris, Rome or even Bristol. We have to climb up to the roof to see beyond the neighbouring terraces. But I would encourage anyone to do what they can to bring a view of the garden into the house. It's worth even the expense and hassle of major building work. I'm glad I had the conviction to knock a hole for some tall French windows into the back of the house, even if it seemed madness when the view was a pile of builder's rubble. Now we are raising the back flower bed to the height of the new deck and hope to install a little pond on the axis from the window. I can imagine sitting on the steps, listening to the water on a calm summer evening. But just as pleasurable will be the view from inside, when a sudden shaft of winter sun, alighting on a book and a vase of tulips, will seem to me like happiness itself.

I'm still wondering what to do about the 'well' outside the basement below – another common feature in British town houses and a real challenge when it comes to views. My immediate instinct was to paint it white, to capitalise on the sun that does get down there and reflect it into the room, which is used as a study. Perhaps a few potted ferns would look nice, or some trailing plants growing down from troughs on the level of the rest of the garden. Jane Seabrook of The Chelsea Gardener (see p. 244), who has been tackling London gardens for the best part of thirty-five years, and so knows their particular problems better than most, suggests painting a mural on such walls – a Rousseauesque jungle or even (given our basement's proneness to flooding) a Louisiana swamp.

The top two floors of the house look out on to the derelict warehouse which, as I have mentioned before, I hope to turn into a community garden. Several readers have asked for an update and I am sad to report that we have reached something of an impasse. There is no shortage of funding (lottery money, local authorities, private trusts and the like) for transforming the plot into a garden. Apparently it has just the combination that the government's new Local Agenda 21 is looking for – community involvement, environmental improvement, even organic food production. But no one is able to help us buy the site. If this were Notting Hill, we could ask all the neighbours to throw in a few thousand. But few people in Brixton have cash to spare. I am determined not to give up. But until someone can come up with a bright idea (or, indeed, £75,000), or I can win the Lottery, it looks as if my wider view of a wildlife garden with herb spirals and tepees of tomatoes ripening in the sun will have to wait.

15 March 1998 ~ The Allotment

There are some new faces at the allotments in the wake of the Inspection Committee's Great Purge. Eight or nine plots had become so overgrown and ill-tended that they were offered to people on the waiting list, and the spate of warm weather brought the newcomers out in droves. Luckiest among them are the young family who have taken on the plot nearest the gate. Their predecessor was not shoved out; he simply couldn't manage the longer journey when he moved to sheltered housing in Clapham. Harry had held that plot for nearly twenty years and it was always one of the best-kept, with neat runner-bean poles and a row of miniature apple trees underplanted with marigolds. All the new family have to do is some light weeding before they begin to sow and plant – which may be just as well, as the little girl insists on sitting on her mother's shoulders while she's working.

Others are not so lucky. Several of the freed-up plots look as run-down and ramshackle as ours when we took them on. Seeing the keen young couples turning up with their shiny new spades and packets of rocket seed, only to be confronted by a tennis-court-sized rubbish-tip to clear, reminds me of ourselves two years ago. Various people have admitted to thinking we'd give up. But as I watched a pair of newcomers leaving after an hour and a half, having cleared a precise two square yards of their enormous plot, I realised I'd joined the ranks of the cynical 'old-timers' myself as I, too, caught myself thinking, 'Hmmm... I wonder if they'll be back?' Another chap, however, made very impressive progress in just one afternoon. Rather than attempt to clear the thick grass and weeds in his new plot, he simply cut eight square beds into it, lifted the turf, which he stacked in a pile to rot down into compost, and dug six sacks full of manure into the holes. That's the way to do it.

I'll miss some of those who have gone: the Turkish judge who used to sit on his toolbox drinking tea from a Thermos has been replaced by a group of trendy twentysomethings – one of whom seems to be a sculptor, as there's now a block of marble in the centre of the plot which changes shape from time to time. And the unemployed chap with the six children and the husky dog who used to give me his spare seedlings has apparently got a full-time job as a stone-carver. His tribe of children were so well-trained that it's a shame they couldn't have kept the plot on between them. I'm tempted to pull up some of his left-over leeks when committee members aren't looking.

Meanwhile, the mood on plot number 26 is good. Two years of hard work are finally beginning to pay off and the plot is looking – dare I say it – almost smart. In previous years we've had to clear, dig and sow in quick succession; this time, having prepared the soil properly in the autumn, there's been time to sieve and rake it to the 'fine tilth' mentioned in all the books. It's a strangely satisfying process, not unlike kneading bread – repetitive enough to keep the mind occupied but not enough to strain it. And the finished substance is so beautiful – soft, crumbly and a dark, chocolate-brown – that you can see how seeds would prefer it to the stony stuff of previous years.

Last weekend we sowed our first peas (some sugar snaps and 'Onward Early' from the *Organic Gardening Catalogue*) in six inch wide trenches either side of a line of ruby chard that has continued to sprout through the winter, its scarlet stalks almost luminous in the late afternoon sun. Another of the raised beds has alternate rows of pink shallots and red onion setts – the shallots were such a success last year, yielding a cluster of eight to fifteen bulbs for every seed shallot planted, that it seemed foolish not to try again. Cabbages, Brussels sprouts and broccoli and, later on, squashes, corn, courgettes and tomatoes, will all be raised in little soil plugs in an impromptu greenhouse we're rigging up against the south-facing fence – some staggered shelves from the former shed covered with a curtain of heavy-duty clear plastic from the builders' merchants. In the flower garden, a couple of hundred tulip bulbs are surfacing, their leaves tightly furled, together with daffodils, hollyhocks, irises and red hot pokers. We've also sown nasturtiums, love-in-a-mist and old-fashioned marigolds. I fear the slugs may have got the delphiniums, though.

All this activity would not be possible – or, at least, would not be half so much fun – without the band of friends who have become involved. Last weekend there were seven of us at work, including two-year-old Conor, who was digging away with the best of us. I'd strongly recommend to anyone who is thinking of getting an allotment – or, indeed, who already has one – to share it. An average-sized allotment can feed many more people than make up an average-sized family, and it makes sense to share the work and responsibility. It's also a refreshing change to be doing something *useful* with one's friends, rather than just sitting round a dining table, chatting and eating. And, as my sister said last weekend, it's a whole lot more fun than traipsing round Ikea on a Saturday.

5 April 1998 ~ Goldeneye, Jamaica

Little did I suspect, when my love of gardening took root, that it would one day compete with my other great passion, travel. It is a tension that gardeners know well: the urge to head off in pursuit of warmer weather, not to mention exotic gardens to visit, straining against the instinct to remain at home. It's not just the fear that friends and neighbours, no matter how well-meaning, might forget to water the sweet pea seedlings, or let the snails riddle your hostas. From April onwards there are simply too many treats to be missed: flowery ropes of *Clematis montana*, strung about the garden like bunting for a fortnight, bluebells or *regale* lilies in their brief prime, the unfolding of the first peony buds. In her wonderful book, *A Gentle Plea for Chaos*, Mirabel Osler writes of 'the wrench of laying down the trowel and turning our backs on all that early summer activity', and asks: 'How can any gardener turn away from buds in their first year's flowering?'

The answer, of course, is to time a trip carefully, which usually means going away in winter. This year, we managed to get it right, swapping two bleak weeks in late February and early March for the sunshine and warm breezes of Jamaica. My memories of the holiday are all enacted against a backdrop of brilliant flowers – clouds of bougainvillaea (not only the magenta of the Mediterranean but also white, pure scarlet and a rosy, pink-tinged apricot), deep crimson proteas and hibiscus blooms as large and ephemeral as paper plates. Spikes of strelitzia ('Birds of Paradise') line the roadsides, and it's not uncommon to see wild poinsettias the size of small trees.

My previous visit to Jamaica, sixteen years ago, was the first time I'd ever seen tropical plants outside of a hot house at Kew. I remember marvelling at the sheer scale and colour of everything. Even the shrubs – monsteras, codiaeums and caladiums in variegated Technicolor forms – reminded me of Marks & Spencer pot plants with the colour and volume knobs turned right up. I fell in love with daturas, and have been hooked ever since on those enormous trumpet flowers, hanging like white silk nightcaps from the branches, with their indefinable, intoxicating scent. Some of the most incredible plants were at Goldeneye, Ian Fleming's old house on the north-east coast, just outside the small town of Oracabessa. That first summer in Jamaica, I went there every day to use the tiny beach, and had to pick my way through a jungle of trailing leaves and flowers to reach the sea. I remember a curtain of large mauve blooms – like huge streptocarpus flowers – that had to be drawn to one side as you passed, and creamy white hibiscus, opening like twists of crepe paper with a raspberry red blotch in the centre, around which hovered a flurry of humming birds. I made friends with the gardener (only one for the whole fourteen and a half acres), who explained to me how, in a land which is permanently hot and without our distinct seasons, different flowers and fruits still have their appointed times.

On this last visit, we made a trip back to Goldeneye. The entrance, with stone pineapples on the gateposts, was still the same, but inside, all had changed. The flowery jungle had become a lush but trim park, dotted with ritzy little 'cottages' for upmarket tourists, and the house itself, which was almost empty and without electricity when I first came, is packed with bamboo furniture and carved wooden sculptures and rented out to pop stars and royalty. The owner, Chris Blackwell, who founded Island Records, likes his famous guests to plant a tree when they leave, and you can browse around a surreal little orchard of sapling trees, each with a neat, hand-painted placard saying when and by whom it was planted.

I'm in a position to report that Naomi Campbell's cocoa tree, Princess Margaret's tamarind, Marianne Faithful's mango and Johnny Depp's guava are all thriving, while Grace Jones' star apple and Bono's little nutmeg have definitely seen better days. Much to my delight, the gardener, Ramsay, was still working there. He gave us a tour of the place and I got the impression that, like me, he slightly regretted the taming of the Technicolor jungle.

Two weeks later, back in London, the taxi drew up outside a house that had exploded with daffodils along all the windowsills. Dumping my bags on the doorstep, I ran straight through to the back garden to see what else had happened in our absence. The little white courtyard was splashed with colour – not as bright as the Caribbean, it's true, but blazingly welcome on a wet, grey English morning. Tubs full of crocus and narcissi, tiny points of green when we left, were now in full bloom. Wallflowers, ceanothus and a flowering quince were coming into bud and the dark, glossy leaves of *Clematis armandii* were studded with pink-tinged flowers.

Best of all, the builders had been hard at work, constructing a curved raised bed along the back wall which will give me a lot more room for planting. I suppose that's the compensation for the travelling gardener: it may be hard to leave, but it's always exciting to come home.

12 *April* 1998 ~ Outdoor Living

Easter is when the boundaries
between inside and outside begin
to blur and the house starts
spilling out into the garden. Doors
are left open again, curtains billow
in the breeze, furniture is dragged
outside or dusted down from the
shed, and the evening air is heavy with
the smell of a hundred barbecues.
Outdoor living becomes the subject of
endless magazine articles, accompanied
by photographs of tables laid for lunch
with crisp linen cloths, checked napkins and
smart striped awnings. If I come across one
of these on a sunny day, I fantasise about
moving half the house – tables, chairs, sofa,

television, even my writing desk – outside for the summer. But then I remember the British climate and think again.

One of the most elaborate and uncompromising examples of outdoor living must be that at the Italian home of the fashion designer Alberta Ferretti, which was featured in an article in *The Sunday Telegraph Magazine* last August. From March to October, Mrs Ferretti decamps from her house to a large tent-like structure in the middle of her garden. Its decorative cast-iron frame is hung with cream muslin curtains that can be drawn against the wind, and is furnished just like an indoor room, with Persian carpets, a large dining table, palms in ceramic pots and colonial-style rattan furniture piled high with cushions and throws. Glass star lanterns hang from the ceiling, while out in the garden proper, scrolling antique candelabra and white lace hammocks swing from the trees. It is tempting to translate a version of this back home. But even given the British inclination for windswept walks and blustery picnics, it is hard to see it working. With one ear on the weather forecast, we'd be forever racing in and out, trailing chairs and tables in our wake and saving the sofa from a soaking.

What's needed in our unpredictable climate is a much more makeshift approach. Rather than a permanent structure, large cream canvas umbrellas (Habitat have stylish square ones) can be erected in a few seconds to provide shade from the sun or shelter from the rain. Or it's easy to rig up a rough awning which can hang like a large roller blind on the side of the house and be stretched to a tree, fence or sticks stuck in the ground to make a canopy. For furniture, stick to stuff that can stand the odd shower and that won't blow over in the wind. Painted wood or metal, second-hand cricket seats and old kitchen chairs are all good standbys, which can be made more colourful and comfortable by adding bright blankets and cushions. If you have a shed in the garden, these things are always readily at hand (keep them in large plastic sacks with a few sprigs of lavender to keep them fresh and dry).

Even if it rains, there is something rather lovely about being outside in a brief summer downpour, watching paths and leaves become wet and shiny and breathing in the smell of water on sun-baked earth. Hanging mirrors from the walls – even small shards stuck in gaps between bricks – always heightens the atmosphere in a garden, particularly in the evenings, when candles are flickering and plants throw strange shadows. String little tin lanterns around the spot where you eat, or dot night lights in plain glass jars along the walls. A pot of pelargoniums on the table completes the scene.

Small gardens, with their sense of enclosure, really come into their own when creating an outdoor living space. The stronger and more defined the boundaries the better. Stone or brick walls are best, but high hurdle fences or trellis panels that let some light and air through also give the impression of being in a room out of doors. The real challenge is to furnish it.

A good source for simple, down-to-earth ideas for outdoor living is Jane Cumberbatch's new book, *Pure Style Outside* (see p. 244). Some of the most stunning photographs are of the garden of her house in Spain – all cream canvas, whitewashed walls and pale pebble floors against a backdrop of sun-bleached grass and olive trees. But just as tempting are the corners closer to home – a tiny terrace overgrown with tomatoes and trailing nasturtiums, just big enough for a table and chair for morning coffee (a green and white checked plastic cloth looks smart in all weathers); a bower made from coppiced branches lashed together, and a striped cotton deck chair at the shady end of an allotment.

An entire chapter is devoted to food to enjoy outside – from grilled sardines and summer pudding to plates of freshly baked fairy cakes decorated with flower petals. It's true that even the simplest meal takes on an air of festivity when eaten outside. Perhaps it's the knowledge that, in this country at least, it's a pleasure that must be seized with the moment, rather than planned and furnished for in advance.

18 *April* 1998 ~ Exotic plants in Sussex

Holidaying gardeners often return from their travels intent on growing all sorts of plants that are not usually associated with the British climate. On a recent visit to Architectural Plants, the exotic plant specialists near Horsham in West Sussex, (see p. 244), I came across several customers who, like myself, had come in search of plants they'd fallen in love with on holiday. One chap, who told me he was in the music business, was having a new conservatory attached to his house so he could grow the tropical palms and tree ferns he'd so admired in Thailand. Another woman wanted a greenhouse full of plantains and bananas. Luckily, my shopping list did not include such demanding specimens. I was after a bamboo, having been inspired in part by the four mile bamboo tunnel known as Bamboo Avenue near the Black River in Jamaica. These towering specimens were planted nearly 100 years ago and their stems, some the span of a small tree, meet high above the road in a shimmering gothic arch.

Although they are unlikely to achieve such a size, most bamboos grow quite happily in this country – indeed, their main drawback is their (often exaggerated) tendency to spread. In a small garden, they may actually be a more feasible alternative to trees, as they provide instant effect without the problems of dense shade, drying the soil and general domination. I wanted a bamboo for the rear left hand corner of the garden, to help screen the raised deck from neighbouring buildings. Another advantage of bamboo over a tree for this purpose is that the leaf cover remains fairly constant, and is never so dense as to prevent some sun shining through. I also find the movement of the plants, their shifting shadows and the swishing of the wind through the leaves, extremely soothing. After a shower, with their leaves full of raindrops catching the light, they look enchanting.

I had set my heart on a black bamboo (Phyllostachys nigra), as the combination of ebony-black canes and lime-green leaves is so utterly irresistible. However, when I saw the plants – six-feet tall, sadly thin and straggly and with a price tag of £65, I was not so sure. When Angus White, the owner of the nursery, started to explain the rigmarole involved in keeping the canes black (if you feed too much the canes revert to green; too little and the leaves will suffer) I decided against it altogether. For only a few pounds more I came away with a fifteen foot Phyllostachys aurea, which although not exactly golden as the name suggests, does make a luminous impression with the sun in its light green leaves.

Like some of my fellow-visitors at Architectural Plants, I could have got quite carried away had my garden (not to mention wallet) been up to it. The nursery was founded in 1990, driven by Angus White's enthusiasm for evergreen exotic plants with bold, 'architectural' shapes and foliage. A enormous new hot house near Chichester means he is now one of the best sources for seriously large specimens of tree ferns and palms, spiky cordylines and arbutus (strawberry tree) in the country. A former furniture designer, White's interest in these plants is primarily aesthetic – he has no time for what he calls the 'trainspotter approach' – and his strong visual sense has helped to create a quite extraordinary nursery.

From the moment you turn into the drive just outside the village of Nuthurst, it is clear you are a world away from the usual drab expanse of cheap sheds and staging. Rows of huge potted olives and agaves border a cluster of neat greenhouses, while behind them, a compact, colonial-style building, complete with gabled roof and veranda, rises against a backdrop of palm trees and eucalyptus. This is the office, where Angus White is often to be found deep in conversation with more knowledgeable customers. Even the loos, which have been described as 'the most beautiful lavatory in Britain', are in a little white shuttered building on stilts that looks out across a valley planted with Tasmanian tree ferns, New Zealand cabbage trees and the giant rhubarb, *Gunnera manicata*. It looks like the last outpost of the Raj in the Home Counties.

Despite the exotic appearance, Angus White's mission is to educate others as to just how easy a great many exotic plants are to grow in this country. His jolly, well-designed catalogue divides plants into red, amber and green categories to describe their frost-hardiness. Green plants are said to be hardy anywhere in Britain below 1000 foot; amber are hardy if 'sensibly sited' anywhere in the Home Counties, while even some of the red-label specials can be kept outside year-round in favoured sites in the south-west and central London. It's a fantastic vision: urban back yards bristling with exotic evergreens all winter long, while their owners stare at them through steamed-up windows, drunk on dreams of the tropics.

26 April 1998 ~ Yearning for a Greenhouse

Now I understand why retired people spend so much time in green-houses. Before I began raising plants from seed myself, I used to think it was one of those hobbies – an excuse to get out of the house and away from husband/wife/dogs/children etc., for a bit of peace and quiet. Now I know that it's nothing of the sort. It's an all-consuming passion. And if, like me, you don't possess a greenhouse it will consume your house in to the bargain. At this time of the year, every windowsill in our home – indeed, every level surface within reasonable distance of a window – is covered with trays of seedlings, or little terracotta pots of larger plants which are still in the process of being hardened off and have to spend cold nights indoors.

There are two dozen cardoons, beginning to show their distinctive jagged foliage above the first rounded leaves; a tray of black hollyhocks just over two inches high; and serried ranks of Brussels sprouts, red and white cabbage and trendy Tuscan kale (*cavolo nero* to *River Café Cookbook* readers), all showing the distinctive heart-shaped early leaves of the brassica family. There are courgettes and tomatoes, and french and runner beans, all waiting till the threat of frost is past to be taken to the allotment – a few may end up in the back garden. And there are trays full of flower seedlings – zinnias, rudbeckias, white cosmos, morning glory and lovely frilly 'Bells of Ireland' (*Moluccella laevis*), which seem to hold in the cup of their tiny leaves the promise of an abundant, blooming summer.

When I lived in a flat and had less space, I used my ancient purple VW campervan as a mobile greenhouse. There was plenty of room for everything along the interior shelves and on top of the little sink and fridge – and the windows in the roof meant it got plenty of light. I parked it where the sun was, moving it round to the other side of the block in mid-afternoon. The plants grew well on the whole, but I had to be careful not to take corners at speed, and the upholstery got a bit damp and smelly.

This year, I treated myself to three of those little unheated propagators (£5.99 from garden centres) to start my seeds off. But I do find myself wishing we had room in our little garden for a greenhouse. It must be so peaceful, pottering about with a portable radio for company, and not having to worry about getting compost down cracks in the kitchen table. I'd originally intended to raise seedlings at the allotment, where we rigged up a makeshift greenhouse using a roll of heavy-duty polythene and some old shelves against the south-facing fence, but really young plants do need constant care and attention.

Our twenty foot square yard wouldn't have room for much of a greenhouse, but I've begun to wonder whether it might not be possible to shoehorn one in by the back door. In my mind's eye I see a slightly ramshackle – but completely charming of course – construction made from painted wood with coloured glass in the corners. It might even be possible to utilise the heat from the boiler vent, which pumps out puffs of steam into the garden whenever the heating comes on. At the worst, I'd settle for one of those little lean-to greenhouses with sliding doors that are sold in kits by mail order catalogues. They range from ritzy cedar-frame models from the Traditional Garden Supply Co (see p. 245) to £99 for the 'Gro-House' in rather nasty ridged plastic from Home Free (along with orthopaedic cushions, belt tidies, nose hair trimmers and other vital sundries, see p. 246). A large cold frame may be the compromise for this year – even just a few old window-frames leant against a sunny wall can do the trick. But a more decorative (if pricey) option would be a couple of the English Garden Collection's 'Victorian Leaded Glass Cloches', with pointy lids that lift off like lanterns (see p. 244). I also spotted a smart galvanised metal cold frame for £65 in the new Habitat brochure.

While I've been writing this, a rather more exciting option has come to light. It seems that the huge Victorian greenhouses in our local park are to be restored using lottery funding and reopened for community use. They were once used to raise fruit and vegetables for the family who lived in the big Georgian mansion on the hill which now houses the park café. Perhaps one could even rent a small section, like an indoor allotment.

Those huge turn-of-the-century glasshouses really were the business – big enough for peach and fig trees and with elaborate central heating systems and lots of decorative ironwork. When I retire, I'd like to forgo the granny flat in favour of an enormous old greenhouse, with small kitchen and bathroom attached. Then I could live my twilight years in a tropical climate, without having to leave my friends behind, and could garden, sleep, eat and watch the world go by from a jungle of scented and edible plants.

3 May 1998 ~ Home

Whether to builders, bugs or bad luck, I have lost a lot of plants in the eighteen months I've been trying to make a garden in our little concrete yard. So when it came to planting up the new raised bed along the back, I resorted to professional help. David Waters, who had completely redesigned my parents' rather larger garden, turned up promptly at 7.30a.m., apparently unfazed by the diminutive dimensions of this new job. The wooden deck was already bristling with plants I'd accumulated myself, or which had been uprooted into bags when David's men constructed the bed last month. Within minutes, there was hardly space to move, as new material was carted in in plastic crates. Like a general surveying his troops, David moved up and down the ranks, checking off the plants on his clipboard. 'Three *Astrantia major*... yes... three black iris... yes... Now where's that other euphorbia?'

We had drawn up the planting plan earlier in the year, when I'd first got in touch with David. He spent a cold January morning with me, staring out of the open french windows over steaming cups of coffee and looking at pictures of plants and colour combinations I liked. Two weeks later, an immaculately labelled plan arrived, for which I was charged £40 – commissioning a planting plan which you then carry out yourself is a good way of re-vamping your

garden on a tight budget. In the end, though, I asked David to see the job right through; like interior designers with fabric and wall-paper, he gets the plants at trade prices, so to have his help installing them was not so much more expensive than doing the whole thing myself. And, of course, there would be the added peace of mind his experience would provide, particularly with the larger, more expensive plants.

The twelve foot bamboo (*Phyllostachys aurea*, with its light green canes) went in first, into a large hole in one corner filled with water and a liberal sprinkling of bonemeal. It's going to need plenty of food and water to keep it looking healthy, so a good start is vital. In front of it went a six foot *Prunus subhirtella* 'Autumnalis' – the lovely winter-flowering cherry whose tiny white blossoms appear on bare black branches when there's little else in bloom. The rest of the bed – twenty foot wide by four feet deep, curving out to six foot on the left – was planted with a mixture of evergreen shrubs and perennials in shades of white, lime green, bronzy brown and deep inky purple. There are several different euphorbias, including E. *purpurea*, with purply-red stems as a contrast to the acid green foliage; a white climbing rose ('Mme Alfred Carrière'), white foxgloves, acanthus, a pair of cardoons and some purply-black hollyhocks (*Alcea rosea* 'Nigra'). David planted them all in groups of three or five small plants – he says you get a faster and fuller effect than by using a single larger plant. I like the idea of lots of tall plants in a small space, and plan to interplant them with cosmos, cactus dahlias and Californian poppies in shades of ochre and burnt orange. I'm to use an acid foliar spray feed on everything and to look out for cater-pillars – one of the culprits for past losses.

The new bed is too wide to reach all the way back for weeding, so I'd been searching in vain for some large flat stones to stand on. In the end, I found seven old slate roof tiles in a corner which go well with the other colours and textures in the garden – galvanised metal, terracotta, bleached wood and the cobalt blue paint I may use on the deck.

When David left four hours later, I took a cup of coffee out into the sunshine and just sat and stared at it all. For the first time since moving here, I felt I had a real garden, not just a haphazard collection of plants. Though small and somewhat stiff looking now, I could imagine the effect when the new plants take off and the gaps close between them. A light breeze caught the bamboo, sending feathery shadows round the white trellised walls. In that moment, all the mistakes, mysterious deaths and moth-eaten leaves flew out the window and a real excitement was born.

11 May 1998 ~ Home

The freak snows in April sent me scurrying in and out of the garden to check on my new plants. Like a mother hen with a baby chick, I fussed over them obsessively, brushing the snow from the leaves and shaking the bamboo and winter-flowering cherry which had both become bowed under the weight. I'd figured that an inner-city walled garden in London's so-called 'micro-climate' would allow me to get away with some semi-hardy plants, and had included *Holboellia latifolia* (a beautiful evergreen climber with fragrant greenish flowers against glossy dark foliage) and *Cissus striata* (another pretty climber with reddish-green feathery leaves) in my new raised bed. The last thing I wanted was for them to succumb to the cold so soon after planting. Luckily, there were no casualties when the thaw came.

Before acquiring this yard eighteen months ago, I gardened on a sheltered balcony, and was immune to the ravages of extreme weather. I don't have the experience of knowing a certain specimen has survived through much worse in the past. And I can't help but get despondent about losing plants. When a passion flower that had accompanied me across London from one flat to another, blooming and fruiting in profusion every summer, finally gave up the ghost, it was as if an old friend had gone. And I still occasionally yearn for some purple and green auriculas that crisped up one year while I was on holiday.

I'm scared to tot up the number of plants that have disappeared during their short spell in this new garden. A photograph from last summer showing a box full of brown irises, potentillas, astrantias and white geraniums lugged home from a Welsh nursery made me wonder where those plants are now. I suspect that slugs got the irises and I have since replaced them – and I found some chubby caterpillars (too late!) that had been chomping their way through the whole border. This will surely be the year to invest in biological controls (see p. 245).

I've put down my failures to lack of experience – and though that has undoubtedly been a factor, it is consoling to know that even gardeners with a whole lifetime of experience behind them can suffer too. In *Dear Friend and Gardener*, a collection of letters between two of this country's greatest and best-loved gardeners, Beth Chatto and Christopher Lloyd share their losses as well as successes as they compare notes from their two very different gardens (see p. 243). Beth Chatto laments some young French artichokes that were planted without due attention to the roots – 'I was appalled to see them lying flat like dead day-old chicks'. And Christopher Lloyd complains of ravages by badgers and being unable to keep a saltbush (*Atriplex hamilus*) because 'the house sparrows strip it of every leaf' Vita Sackville-West apparently kept a 'graveyard' of metal plant tags in her potting shed at Sissinghurst as proof of all the experiments that had failed.

One of my favourite writers on gardening, the American poet May Sarton, who died five years ago aged eighty-three, wrote this in her memoir, *Plant Dreaming Deep* (see p. 244): 'Gardening gives one back a sense of proportion about everything – except itself... I used to be ashamed of how much waste there was even in my unpretentious garden here. I blamed inexperience, impatience and extravagance. But now I have come to accept that one must not count the losses, they would be too alarming. One must count only the joys, and feel continually blessed in them. There is no unlucky gardener, for each small success outweighs each defeat in his [or her] passionate heart.'

17 May 1998 ~ The Allotment

Gardeners have fine-tuned the art of pottering. Now that some warmer weather has finally arrived, I cycle over to the allotment most mornings, to spend an hour or two while the day still feels fresh. This is not the time for heavyweight jobs involving digging or major construction – they can wait for the weekends, when my sister and friends are there to help. I couldn't say exactly how I pass the time, but I always feel pleasantly, unhurriedly busy as I wander from bed to bed, stopping to tweak a weed here, snap off a dead leaf there, or dive into the tool chest for a spare bamboo stake. There is erratic traffic with watering cans, sudden disappearances into the undergrowth. To a non gardener, these meanderings would no doubt appear meaningless – like a slightly distracted old aunt stopping every now and again to look for her spectacles as she moves about the house.

In fact, looking is exactly what gardeners are doing for most of the time they appear to be pottering. They are looking for trouble – outbreaks of plague or pestilence and hints of hunger or thirst – as well as more promising signs, such as unexpected or forgotten seedlings, renewed vigour in a sulking plant, or the burgeoning of first fruits. This is how at least the first half hour of my morning trips to the allotment are spent – accompanied (usually) by the snufflings of Rolf the lurcher and (often) by a warm croissant from the bakery I find hard to pass on the way. This inspection is what gives rise to the seemingly erratic round of jobs – it's easier to do what needs doing when it's fresh in the mind than to remember it for later. (Rosemary Verey may jot down jobs to be done in a notebook on her dawn patrol of the borders at Barnsley House, but she is of a far more orderly mind-set than most gardeners of my acquaintance, and of course has a team of helpers who need to be told what to do.)

One job gives rise to another – it is while I'm on the way to the water butt that I see the rhubarb could do with mulching, and while weeding around the broad beans that I spot the first sooty clusters of blackfly. And then, in the middle of hoeing between the potatoes, I suddenly remember the new peas need staking. Last year I did this too late, when the seedlings were already three or four inches high, and some of the new growth snapped off in my hands as I tried to train it off the ground.

This week I did do some construction work, but it was hardly back-breaking stuff. I made a net cage, about ten feet by five, to protect the newly transplanted brassicas from the birds. Last year's purple-sprouting broccoli was devoured by birds the second the seeds came up, and I really missed it this spring when there was so little else to harvest. My previous attempts at bird protection have been rather makeshift affairs prone to buffeting by the wind, but this, I'm not ashamed to say, looks rather smart. I used eight six-foot bamboo canes, pushed a foot deep into the earth, and topped each one with a small plastic flowerpot to stop the net from slipping down. The stakes were also lashed together with horizontals near the top to make the structure more secure. It's filled with *cavolo nero* (which can apparently reach five foot fully grown), curly kale and red cabbages, non of which I've grown before. I'll make an extension for the purple sprouting broccoli and the Brussels sprouts, which will be sown in the ground next month to be ready for Christmas. Making the cages considerably higher than the fully-grown plants means it's easier to get in to weed and inspect for pests.

Though simple enough, this task encroached heavily into my pottering time. Leaving the weeding till tomorrow, I headed home, made a cup of coffee and went out into the garden, to poke about there for a bit. My boyfriend can never understand why I don't just sit there in the sunshine.

'What are you *doing?*' he asked as he caught me poised precariously between two slate stepping stones in the flower bed, my nose deep among the leaves of a sprawling jasmine, as my coffee got cold.

'It's sort of hard to explain,' I replied.

24 May 1998 ~ The Allotment

Sometimes I think the world's scientists should stop cloning sheep and re-inventing the computer and turn their talents to breeding a new type of slug: one that eats only weeds. I suppose a silky young lettuce seedling is infinitely more tempting than the snakeshead spires of bindweed that come poking through the soil; but chickweed looks quite juicy, and you're supposed to be able to make salads with dandelions and fat hen. Yet only the best is good enough for the slugs. They polished their way systematically through my first sowing of 'Misticanza' mixed salad leaves, as if the whole bed were laid out like an official tasting of the different varieties. 'Mmmm...the red oak leaf's nice...have you tried the Italian chicory?...Not sure about this rocket stuff, though...' I could imagine them comparing notes as they worked their slimy way from one end of the bed to the other, leaving a mass grave of white leafless stalks behind them.

Last summer, my complaints about slugs gave rise to a healthy correspondence, much of it extremely useful, in which readers commiserated and swapped anti-slug tactics. I was also sent various organic slug remedies to try, in packets bearing slogans such as: 'For gardeners who care about the environment...' or 'who love pets, birds and other wildlife...' It was tempting to scribble on the unspoken addendum 'but who are sick to death of slugs and will do anything to get rid of them NOW'. Many of the organic slug killers contain a substance that inhibits the slug's slime-producing organs and makes them dry up. The drawback is that it has to be reapplied after heavy rain. As this April was little more than a thirty-day rainstorm, it is hardly surprising that the potential effects were washed away. So I was more than ready to try biological control using natural predators or nematodes.

I have been reading about this method of controlling pests for a couple of years but have yet to use it myself. The advantages seem to be many: the remedies are specific to the pest and are harmless to children, pets and wildlife; there is no poisonous residue left on plants and fruits; no build-up of resistance by the pest, and no complicated procedure to follow. Once the beneficial insects or organisms are introduced they apparently just get on with the job, needing only a second application later in the summer. There are different nematodes for vine weevil, aphids, red spider mite, mealy bug and scale insects.

The slug nematode, *Phasmarhabditis hermaphrodita*, occurs naturally in the soil, but its numbers have to be boosted dramatically to be effective. It functions as a parasite, passing through the slug's skin and releasing a bacterium on which it feeds inside the slug's body. The nematodes multiply and within three to five days the slug is supposed to stop eating and burrow underground to die. Another advantage: no smelly, slimy corpses to dispose of. I rang up for my order.

Because the slug nematode is relatively new, and still subject to production difficulties, it can be elusive. Green Gardener (see p. 245), from whom I ordered my supply, had a waiting list and only take orders for it over the phone. I was in luck; a small packet arrived the following day. 'Oh good,' I remarked to my boyfriend over break-fast, 'my nematodes have arrived.'

'Toads?' he replied, looking slightly alarmed. 'Are you getting toads through the post now?'

As we have had several boxes of worms delivered for the wormery, it's not an unreasonable mistake to have made.

The nematodes come in the form of a lumpy brown powder which you mix up with water and pour on to the soil. A medium pack (£10.95) treats fifty square yards. As I patrolled the vegetable beds with my watering can, I had a moment's remorse for the unpleasant, lingering death I was inflicting on the slugs. Only a moment, I'm afraid. If it works, I can live with it. And it is natural, after all.

31 May 1998 ~ Home

Next to my computer, in front of the study window, is a glass jug containing a small branch of horse chestnut. I snapped it from a tree in a friend's garden back in March, when its leaves were still encased in sticky brown buds. Over the past two months I have watched its unfolding – the pinkish scaly calyces followed by crumpled scraps of brightest lime, like stiff little hands at first and now fully grown leaves with the sunlight shining through them. To my great surprise there have even been flowers. Tight, knobbly clusters of buds finally opened, not into the stately 'candles' that deck out the full-grown trees like ballrooms, but a few individual blossoms which, in their sparseness and proximity, have had much more of my attention than they would ever have held on the tree. Witnessing this slow process has given me more pleasure than I can describe. In embarking on it I was echoing, unconsciously at the time, one of the annual rituals of my junior school. As I absorbed and recorded the day-to-day changes, I was suddenly reminded of intricate pencil drawings, done several times a week, of similar branches in a classroom far away.

In front of the horse chestnut there are always other flowers – sometimes just a single bloom – which live out their own cycle of living and dying over days rather than months. I love to watch as tight, green-tinged buds on soldier-straight stems begin to twist and sway as they open, becoming, in their final hours, wondrous, wild and wayward things. Today there is one red parrot tulip in a greenish glass tumbler. Its raggedy petals, furled, grooved, notched and flecked with green, yellow and black, seem to hold all the energy of an artist's brush. Rather than a distraction, its beauty is an aid to concentration. I must spend hours staring into its open face.

Flowers, for me, are vital presences in a house. Walking into a room without them feels like walking into a room without life in it. Since the days when I'd squander my student grant on huge sprays of lilies, flowers have always been an extravagance. The way I finally gave up smoking five years ago was to take my fag money to the flower stall, which meant my tiny flat looked like an opera singer's dressing room.

Although I adore their beauty, flowers, to me, are about much more than aesthetics. Rather than mere objects, they are *processes* – it's the unfolding, blooming and fading, that I crave, and which seems such a lifeline when living in the city. Florists' assurances of a particular flower being 'long-lasting' hold no great allure. Perhaps that's part of the problem with carnations and chrysanthemums – it's not that they are ugly (few flowers are), but they have a stiffness and static quality that makes them seem, somehow, lifeless. Unlike tulip, roses or peonies, which go out in a blowsy blaze of exploding petals, they just go brown and soggy round the edges.

Given my attachment to a profusion of flowers, and that I now have ten rooms to fill instead of two, it is just as well that the allotment cutting garden is finally coming up with the goods. Since the end of February, when the first white narcissi came into bloom, I've scarcely had to look in a florist's. A steady progression of different tulips has been the latest joy – scarlet, yellow and magenta blooms as big as a man's fist as well as the subtler flowers of 'Queen of the Night' (inky black), 'Spring Green' (white star-like blooms tinged with green), 'Mount Tacoma' (creamy, double white like a peony) and 'Merry Widow' (pale violet edged with cream). These and some armfuls of frothy cow parsley from the allotment hedgerow are enough to keep me happy.

Is it an illusion of pride, or do flowers one grows oneself have a deeper radiance than shop-bought blooms? We've had bunches of these tulips around the house for weeks, and their intense colours and luminous glow are a source of constant comment. It may sound fanciful, but I wonder whether flowers grown with love (and with plenty of natural sunlight and space) are actually *happier* than commercially-grown ones, raised in serried ranks in soulless polytunnels, with profit as the only aim in view?

14 June 1998 ~ Review of New Year's Resolutions...

As it is now over half way through the year, I thought I'd review my rather ambitious list of New Year's Resolutions (see p. 135). Among them were:

~ 'To take the kitchen compost bin to the allotment more frequently so house is not full of rotting vegetables and accompanying odours.' Success rate: good – bought a nice old pale green enamel bucket with a lid from a junk shop which has to be emptied every two or three days.

~ 'Not to say "all grown at the allotment" smugly when serving up food to dinner guests.' Success rate: good, as little produce so far and precious few dinner parties either.

~ 'To sow rocket little and often ensuring a constant supply, rather than a glut to feed the River Café seven times over, which then immediately goes to seed.' Success rate: too good – overwintering rocket patch went to seed before new crop matured, so have had to resort to Sainsbury's.

~ 'To train Rolf the lurcher not to relieve himself on the smart new wooden deck in the back garden.' Success rate: 100 per cent!

~ 'To find or buy some nifty containers for left-over seeds and label them efficiently (like American home/garden and cooking super-woman Martha Stewart) as opposed to current "system" which consists of a shoebox filled with dog-eared paper packets with holes in them – nothing in the packets and a pot-pourri of mixed seeds at the bottom.' Success rate: good – a large postcard index file has been purchased and all seed packets are now stored in alphabetical order. Martha Stewart eat your heart out!

~ 'To plant 25 types of lettuce in pretty patterns like Martha Stewart in her book, *Martha Stewart's Gardening'* (see p. 243). Success rate: poor – cheated by using ready mixed 'Saladini' from the Organic Gardening Catalogue (see p. 245) and 'Misticanza' from Suffolk Herbs (see p. 245) – so no pretty patterns.

~ 'To be more like Martha Stewart in general.' Success rate: hopelessly poor – but my allotment friends Simon and Clarkey have threatened to write 'Elspeth Thompson IS Martha Stewart' in bedding plants across the allotment cutting garden.

~ 'To lay proper paths between the raised beds on the allotment rather than slithering about on scraps of decaying carpet.' Success rate: poor – carpet now so decayed that paths are sprouting a healthy crop of ground elder, but plans are afoot to construct proper pathways with a covering of cockle shells (of which more later).

~ 'To raise lots of flower seedlings on the sunny bathroom windowsill for planting out into the new allotment cutting garden.' Success rate: good – pale green zinnias ('Envy'), white and mixed cosmos ('Purity' and 'Bright Lights'), frilly lime 'Bells of Ireland' (*Moluccella laevis*) and teddy-bear brown rudbeckias are thriving in rows between the died-down tulip bulbs, and direct sowings of larkspur ('Blue Cloud'), *Bupleureum*, dill and Californian poppies are coming along nicely.

~ 'To make a pond to encourage frogs and toads who will eat all my slugs.' Success rate: 50/50. Rescued neighbour's hideous orange bath from his front garden, dug enormous hole at the allotment and installed it. Awaiting concrete to block up plug and vital component of water.

~ 'To refrain from flinging slugs over allotment fence into Territorial Army depot next door.' Success rate: good, as I trounced the horrid things with nematodes from Green Gardener (see p. 245).

~ 'To buy a propagator for cultivating more difficult plants from seed.' Success rate: good – two unheated ones @ £5.99 each from garden centre.

~ 'Not to sit about moaning about the state of the allotment while drinking a can of beer with friends, but to get rid of offending weeds/slugs/debris/stacks of rickety wood forthwith.' Success rate: not bad – ground elder a vicious problem, but remaining stacks of wood and debris carted off on communal allotment skip last week.

~ 'To sow my own tomatoes from Simpson's Seeds' unusual and old-fashioned varieties' (see p. 245). Success rate: fail – so blinded by choice in catalogue that I missed the ordering time – had to buy young 'Gardener's Delight' plants from Garden Centre instead.

~ 'To find a foolproof organic way of eliminating blackfly.' Success rate: fail – soap and water ineffective against the sooty clusters now encamped on my broad beans. Help!

There were more – too many, perhaps – but that will do for now. Overall success rate: seven 'goods', four 'so-so's' and four 'fails'. Room for improvement, but no sackcloth and ashes just yet.

21 June 1998 ~ The Allotment

There are times when the state of the allotment becomes an uneasy metaphor for the rest of my life. When all in the garden's rosy, so, somehow, is everything else. But when stuff starts to get on top of me – weeds, work, out-of-control clutter and general late-20th-century urban angst just for starters – life and the allotment seem to hold a messy mirror up to one another, each threatening to drag the other deeper into chaos.

Not so long ago I arrived at the allotment after a short trip away and promptly burst into tears. In what seemed to be a matter of days, knee-high grass and nettles were encroaching on many of the beds, and the bindweed and ground elder we'd tried so hard to banish were back with a vengeance. Stacks of old rubbish were ranged along the fence – debris from the old shed we were asked to take down and about fifty rotting window frames we had thought might come in handy. Like my house, like my desk, like the floor-to-ceiling junk room in our basement – it seemed depressingly messy and I didn't know where to start.

My immediate plan of action demonstrated the willpower of a flea:

1 Weep uncontrollably for ten minutes.

2 File application for substitute allotment on site nearer to home in the hope of inheriting a pristine plot from some dedicated old-timer who has died hoe in hand.

3 Send out SOS to friends to come and play rent-a-skivvy in return for barbecue and beers.

The following Saturday we were out in force (thanks to Kit, Les, Jacque, Steve and two-year-old Conor for heroism far beyond the call of duty). We spent most of the day dragging tarpaulin-loads of rotten wood and rusty metal from our plot to the communal skip by the gate, agreeing with the many observers who saw fit to comment that yes, it was indeed ironic that our plot should be furthest from the skip when we were the ones with most to put in it.

Then it was the turn of the weeds. How could we have been so complacent a few months ago, thinking that by digging over the beds twice and sieving the soil for roots, we had knocked them on the head for good? Still, there is nothing like heavy-duty weeding to banish negative thinking. Forget all that fiddling about with a hoe between the rows – you want handfuls of couch grass, complete with root ball, to fling with a satisfying thud on to a pile several yards away (couch grass needs to be layered with woody prunings to rot down slowly).Or the perverse pleasure of tugging gently on a white snake of bindweed root until seven or eight feet of it unravels from the soil. (We put it in a large metal drum half-filled with water – bindweed must be chockfull of minerals to grow so rampantly, and I've been told that the resulting liquid, drained out after two months or so, makes a good feed.) The best feeling of all, though, is to pull up a large thistle with its long tap root intact.

By the end of the day we had made good headway, but there was still a long way to go. I must at this point confess that the conversation turned – for the first time in two and a half years of gardening without any chemicals at all – to using some kind of weedkiller on the paths. For a moment I was tempted. We simply couldn't face the idea of doing the same thing in two months' time – there are too many other nice things to do with one's Saturdays. But I thought I'd ring the Henry Doubleday Research Association's advice service first.

'No, no, no!' came the nannyish voice down the phone when I

enquired about the temptingly labelled 'organic weed-killers'. Apparently, since these are based on fatty acids which dehydrate the cuticle of the plant, they attack only the top-growth – 'So why not just hoe?' As for the glysophates (the best-known of which, Roundup, claims to do the dirty deed and then depart from the soil within a month), recent research suggests that pernicious effects may linger in the soil, inhibiting the nitrogen-forming activities of leguminous plants, in particular, and possibly damaging insect life. 'Like DDT in the early days, there simply hasn't been enough research to be sure of the effects,' I was told. 'Really, the only way to get rid of persistent weeds is to pull, dig and cultivate,' the school-mistressy tones continued. 'You can't just clear an area and leave it. You have to be persistent, as with teaching things to children. These days, people seem to want quick and easy solutions to every problem in the garden. Well, life ain't like that.'

It certainly ain't, I thought, as I set about those beds and paths once again. Some aspects of gardening are as far removed from the pleasurable side as cleaning out the oven is from cooking. But, as with all these unpleasant jobs, you certainly feel a good deal better when they're done.

28 June 1998 ~ Permaculture in Tottenham

'I try to think of slugs and snails as bird food,' says Judith Hanna. 'It's easier to lose a few lettuces and young plants if you think of it as sharing them with the birds.'

Yes. This is what I need to hear. After losing all my carrots and a row of zinnia seedlings at the allotment to slimy creatures of one sort or another I'm at the end of my tether. It's just a shame the birds can't eat them up faster.

We're standing in Judith's back garden in Tottenham, north London. It's an excellent example of what can be done to make a small urban garden both productive and pretty. There are six small trees – a cherry, three different columnar apples and a 'Minarette' pear, and a couple of large currant bushes. Healthy looking vegetables are planted among the flowers – old-fashioned marigolds sing out against a cloud of bronze fennel; lovage pokes through cranesbill geraniums, while broccoli plants, globe artichokes and alliums make sculptural punctuation marks throughout the borders. A lean-to greenhouse and cold frame produce lettuce all winter – and there's a pond to attract frogs and toads who help keep down the slug population. 'It's all about keeping the balance in your favour,' explains Judith.

Judith Hanna (see p. 246), is a practitioner of Permaculture, a form of gardening that has been popular for centuries, but was given a name and a contemporary boost in the Seventies by Bill Mollison, an Australian. (In certain alternative gardening circles, his book, *Introduction to Permaculture*, is revered as a bible.) Like many good ideas, Permaculture is difficult to explain in a few sentences. *Permaculture* magazine (see p. 243) describes it as 'the design of an ecologically sound way of living – in our households, gardens, communities and businesses. It is created by cooperating with nature and caring for the earth and its people'.

'It's working with nature rather than against it,' is how Judith Hanna puts it. 'When it comes to gardening it means that yield is measured not just in terms of the amount of produce but also factors such as general enjoyment, benefit to the natural environment, effect on the local community and so on.' It is the absolute opposite of working nine to five or far beyond at a job that benefits no one, driving an expensive car to the supermarket and spending a fortune on processed produce that's come half way round the world. So far, Permaculture has tended to appeal most to the alternative fringe in this country. But its ideas seem set to spread.

One of the many very practical aspects of Permaculture is something called Zoning – whereby you split up the various different regular venues that make up your life and try to organise your movements most efficiently around them. When gardening, you want the vegetables you use most and which need the most attention (herbs, salad leaves, tomatoes) to be nearest the house (Zone O) and those you can harvest irregularly and which need minimal care (potatoes, root vegetables, beans and squashes) either at the end of the garden or at an allotment. 'Like most people I can really only get to the allotment once a week, so its role in life is to be neglected,' said Judith – more music to my ears.

Judith's allotment is about ten minutes' walk from her house and is organised to make room for wildlife (a pond, bog garden and wild meadow area) as well as highly cultivated beds filled with colourful combinations of strawberries and lavender, poppies, broccoli and Brussels sprouts, and radishes, onions and leeks alongside the purply leaves of First Early potatoes. The slight air of neglect makes it a relaxing place. 'I'm not terribly strict about weeds,' says Judith, 'Some so-called weeds, like Good King Henry and land cress, one can eat, while others, such as speedwell and scarlet pimpernel, just look pretty.' Spinach, rocket, ruby chard and poppies are allowed to self-seed, and she finds unusual seeds, such as liquorice, through the Permaculture seed exchange.

Involvement in the local community is another important aspect of Permaculture. 'Front gardens are a good way of meeting neighbours and contributing something to the street,' says Judith, who looks after next door's narrow strip as well as her own – both cottage-style jumbles of self-sown foxgloves, columbines, Welsh and California poppies. She has also initiated a project to reclaim the rubbish-filled grounds of the listed Sunday school building at Tottenham High Cross as a nature garden. It is slow, time-consuming work, she says, 'but the rewards come both in seeing the site start to blossom and in the friendships built through people working together'.

5 July 1998 ~ Home

The front of our house is being painted, so for the first time in two years we will no longer be the scruffiest house in the street. Time to reconsider our tiny front garden. We need something that will do credit to the smart new white plaster and indigo-grey paintwork. What's there already is looking pretty good. My friend Clarkey made me the smartest window box in the world – deep enough to put up with infrequent watering (why are manufactured window boxes so titchy?) and painted the same greenish-grey as our hall. I filled it chock-full with a bag of 100 mixed daffodil bulbs last autumn which obligingly came up in sequence, spilling over with blooms from early February (white trumpets of 'Mount Hood' and 'Ice

Follies') right through till May (the lovely pheasant's eye narcissus, 'Actea' followed by white and cream 'Cheerfulness'). The trouble with daffodils in window boxes, though, is that for the bulbs to bloom next year you have to put up with the foliage dying down for weeks. So unless you choose to have your house painted during that time (my original plan) it is better to fish them out and replant in tubs that can be whisked out of sight when no longer required. (Or could I persuade Clarkey to make a matching box that could be rotated from season to season?)

The window box is just coming into its own with a summer planting of climbing nasturtiums (which, contrary to the advice of our house-painter, I shall once more train up wires in front of the wide bay window), nine white cosmos plants (raised from seed in my little plastic propagator) and, bringing up the rear, five of the taller tobacco plant, Nicotiana alata. The last will reach about three feet – not the five foot of its splendid giant cousin, N. sylvestris, which towered over the back garden last summer, but tall enough to give us some privacy in the sitting room. Its white trumpet flowers, pale brownish-violet while in bud, give out the most delicious scent in the evenings.

In the long run, I'd like to establish a permanent arrangement in the window box, which will provide some constant height and interest but can be easily interspersed with spring bulbs and some of the more unusual annuals in summer. One idea, stolen from the clever garden designers Gordon Taylor and Guy Cooper, is somehow to divide off the interior of the box into sections so that smaller containers can be lifted in and out between the longer-term planting. A few of the black hollyhocks I've brought on from seed would look stunning, held in by horizontal wires across the bay.

I have a weakness for those old grey metal council rubbish bins, long since overtaken by the hideous 'Wheelies', and have been collecting them wherever I see them cast out. There is one by the front door sprouting the gorgeous clematis 'Etoile Rose' whose crimson bell-like flowers are climbing round the entrance, and nine regale lilies, just about to burst their purply-pink pods and reveal their fragrant creamy white insides. Round the edge of the bin is a fringe of the regular 'Domino Series' tobacco plants in crimson, lime and cream. The house painter has carefully wrapped the tub in a newspaper collar to avoid snapping the delicate lily stems.

As for the rest of the garden, I want to plant trees in large tubs and shiny new dustbins – anything from the oak and sycamore seedlings that pop up at the allotment to a Japanese acer, some apples for blossom and the corkscrew willow I bought as a flower arrangement but which is sprouting fantastically all over my kitchen. With holes in the bottom and a good three or four inches of gravel for drainage, the tubs will be small enough to keep the trees from getting carried away with themselves but heavy enough to stop people literally carrying them off. For at the end of the day, as a passer-by remarked recently when he heard me complaining about the rubbish outside our local pub, I have to remember that 'This is Brixton, darling, not Maida-bloody-Vale.'

12 July 1998 ~ The Allotment

After a sluggish start to the summer, the allotment has started producing in earnest. New to us this year, and therefore most exciting, are the globe artichokes. Only one of the three young plants I bought last year survived to maturity, and it became a real landmark, dominating its corner of the plot as the silvery serrated leaves grew into huge sculptural scrolls. For a time, it seemed only to be interested in putting out more and more leaves, with no sign of anything edible. And then, one morning back in April, there it was: the first embryonic globe, framed by a rosette of fine-toothed leaves.

Over the following few months the plant was well and truly cosseted. Its base was kept well-weeded, save for a few self-sown nasturtiums; its leaves were sprayed with dilute washing up liquid at the first sooty signs of blackfly; it was fed liquid seaweed every

fortnight. We even found ourselves stroking the leaves – much softer than their jagged appearance might suggest – and taking obsessive photographs of the globes – seven in all – as they grew. A heated debate about harvesting began: whether to cut out the central globe as soon as it was ready and leave the smaller side shoots to grow to full-size; to eat the lateral globes while still small and go for the largest central artichoke obtainable; or (my preferred option) to eat the side globes when mature and leave the central one to form its enormous violet thistle-like flower.

In the end, none of us had our way. I arrived at the allotment after a blustery few days to find the whole plant blown over, like a tree in a storm. The base had all but severed, so there was nothing for it but to get out my pen-knife and cut off all the seven globes at once. We ate them that night, boiled for forty minutes with a little oil and lemon in the water, the leaves dipped in salt, pepper and melted butter. As there were not enough to go round, some local market produce was thrown in too, with the stems left longer so as to identify them. The bought ones may have had slightly more flesh on the leaves, but our own won hands down on flavour. (And, at one pound a throw for organic artichokes at the health food shop, on price, too.)

When the last tender hearts had been devoured, the pile of scale-like chewed leaves in the centre of the table was almost two feet high. It made me jolly pleased we have a compost heap, as it seems particularly wanton to throw away more than the volume of food you have actually eaten. When we had artichokes at a friend's house a few days later, somebody asked me, jokingly, I suspect, whether I'd like the leftover leaves for my compost heap. We were going out later, and I must be the only person in London to arrive at a party in a smart new loft with a carrier bag of old vegetable trimmings on my arm...

Next year's supplies should be more plentiful, with ten or twelve young cardoons growing fast, and a handful of young artichoke plants, too. I even have a couple in the garden, but I fear these may come up blind as the border is crowded and an artichoke needs a good three feet around the stem to grow well. Provided they don't blow down, artichoke plants should crop for many years, but tend to be less productive after year three. New plants can be raised by severing the little 'offsets' that cluster, complete with their own root system, around the bottom of the plant – April is the best time for this. One-year-old plants will produce a single crown, with up to seven or eight globes, but older plants will have multiple crowns. To avoid sacrificing quality to quantity, Christopher Lloyd, in his enjoyable book, *Gardener Cook* (see p. 243), recommends cutting out all the crowns but three on each plant. He also has a fine recipe for artichoke salad – a good way of using up the smallest globes. Cut them into quarters and place straight away in a pan of boiling water (enough just to cover) with six tablespoons of olive oil, salt and roughly-crushed peppercorns. Boil till all the water has evaporated and add the juice of a lemon and lots of chopped parsley. This is a salad I've enjoyed many times in Italy but have never known how to make.

19 July 1998 ~ The 'Mobile' Garden

Get two or three contemporary garden designers in a room together and sooner or later the conversation will turn to one of their favourite collective bugbears: the dearth of patronage for genuinely modern garden design in this country. Why, when the past ten or fifteen years have seen the British public finally embracing modern design in everything from cars to lemon-squeezers, have gardens been left so far behind?

'It's one of the most puzzling aspects of working in this business,' says the garden designer Gordon Taylor, whose book *Paradise Transformed: the Private Garden for the Twenty-First Century* (see p. 243) is packed with stunning, *avant garde* gardens – most of them in America. 'London is full of people who have their smart architect-designed house, bursting with modern art and furniture. But step outside the back door and it's all cottagey borders or repro-Neoclassical nonsense that has absolutely nothing to do with the rest of their taste. We live in 1998, not in some Laura Ashley, Arts & Crafts, National Trust-induced haze!'

I think the explanation lies in the fact that youngish urban dwellers are perpetually on the move. Or if they're not, they think they are about to be. Throw enough money at a house, and you can turn the most down-at-heel Victorian terrace into a temple to *Elle Decoration* in a matter of months. But gardens take time – and a little more nerve. Is it worth spending hundreds on black bamboo when you might not be here to see it when it's fully grown? And while a state-of-the-art kitchen and power shower will do wonders to sell your house when you move on, don't people prefer white roses to white concrete?

Another clever garden designer, George Carter, has come up with a way around this conundrum. He calls it 'the mobile garden'.

'You need four big things,' he says. 'Large plants or small trees in smart, painted pots on wheels, a well-designed bench, a trellis obelisk planter with a climber growing up it – these bring a design element into any garden at a reasonable cost, they can be moved around the garden at will, and can move on with you when you go.' Small urban gardens are particularly suited to this approach: 'It's like putting large furniture in a small room – instead of making it look smaller, as you might think it would, it adds a surreal sense of drama.'

I realise that I have unconsciously been 'mobile gardening' since we moved into our house. It began as a way of foiling the builders, who were using the back yard as their general dumping ground. Then it was a way I could still garden while waiting for the deck and new flower bed to be built. But I'm still doing it now. This is partly because I love container gardening. I find the matching of the right plants with the right pot really satisfying, and love finding new uses for containers that other people throw away. Old galvanised metal makes the perfect partner for grey and silver-leaved plants such as lavender, artemesia and santolina, and looks good beside tall terracotta 'Long Tom' pots of lilies.

I've just made a herb garden in a large oval galvanised urn with handles, which I'm told is an old French wine-treading vat. The silver, green and golden foliage of various different thymes, sages, tarragon, dill, chives, parsley and so on stand out brilliantly against a layer of purple aquarium gravel (fifty pence per pound from pet shops) spread over the surface of the soil. Another vat has been sown with different types of lettuce in what I hope will make a pretty pattern. The next plan is to plant young trees in bins in the front garden. This is where I realise that, like many others in my situation, I am gardening with half an eye to the time (still in my dreams) when 'urban gardener' may one day become 'country gardener', taking her mobile garden with her.

26 July 1998 ~ The Allotment

The allotment is full of flowers – even though they're not all of them ones I intended to grow. Gardening is full of surprises. I'm sad to report that my summer cutting garden – so carefully planned in the spring – has come to very little. In spite of using nematodes and 'slug pubs', and a barrier of eco-friendly slug-pellets round the periphery of each bed, the neat lines of larkspur, zinnias, cosmos, Bupleureum and oriental poppies were all eaten, right down to the last stalk, during a wet spell in June. The disappointment was fierce, but there are some survivors. Californian poppies, their petals like the smoothest, softest, brightest orange silk, seemed to stand out in front of the rest of the garden as if on the 3-D postcards I loved as a child. Perhaps their feathery grey foliage is somehow unappealing to slugs and snails? They look especially stunning next to the drumstick heads of Allium sphaerocephalum, which I planted at the same time as the gorgeous tulips that filled the house all spring. It's a pretty poor outcome from sixteen packets of seeds, but it's made me understand the value of raising seedlings under glass and only planting them out when they're strong enough to withstand some pest damage. I sometimes think slugs and snails have a built-in radar system that tells them when and where succulent young seedlings have emerged.

But it is rare that gardening doesn't offer up some unexpected compensation for losses. We have clouds of lovely love-in-a-mist from seed collected in my grandmother's garden, on the farm where I was born, and passed on by my mother, who also has it in her garden. It has almost completely taken over one bed, where it is interspersed with ochre-yellow daisies and a lime-green wild spurge. The traditional pot marigolds (Calendula officinalis) sewn among the onions and shallots provide a sharp orange ground for the papery minarets of more alliums about to burst into bloom. Next year I'll take some self-sown seedlings to plant among the broad beans as a protection against blackfly.

Some of the best combinations are entirely unexpected. Borage flowers – exquisite stars of the brightest, boldest blue – have self-seeded among the bronzy reds and acid greens of the lettuce patch. A chicory plant, long since bolted in the heat, has burst into lavender cornflower blooms from the top of its towering stalk. Some climbing nasturtiums have studded deep red, orange and ochre blooms among the puckered, deep grey-green leaves of the *cavolo nero* (Tuscan kale), and what could be more beautiful – if you are prepared to look closely – than the off-white, chocolate-veined flowers of rocket, their simple four-petalled blooms as charming and graphic as black-and-white Jacobean embroidery?

The other day, I cut three bouquets – each one as beautiful as any I'd have picked from the cutting garden of my dreams. One was just rocket flowers to display in front of, but not distract from, a huge sepia photograph. One was a mix of love-in-a-mist, lime-green spurge and deep purply-pink spires of marjoram. The last was that simplest and most perfect of high summer bouquets – a circle of small round nasturtium leaves surrounding a posy of the flowers in all their rich palette of colours from blood-red, through orange and saffron to pale blotched lemon. The only way to improve on it would be to trap some raindrops, glistening like pearls, intact on the leaves.

1 *August* 1998 ~ The Allotment

One of the many advantages of having an allotment is the invaluable advice (both solicited and unsolicited) from one's fellow plot-holders. As many of these people have years – even decades – of experience of gardening on the same soil and in the same conditions, their wisdom is often superior to that to be gained from books. Somehow, it also seems to sink in better. Although I was never as green as the friend whose neighbour caught her diligently training bindweed round an arch, much of what I now know about growing vegetables has been picked up by watching, and listening to those who garden alongside me.

It was my next-door neighbour, Mark, who let me in on the secret that allowing some of my rocket plants go to seed would ensure a-year-round supply without buying more seed. Seed sown in August or September will establish itself in time to see you over the winter and self-sown seed will be ready to harvest by the time these plants are over. Collect seed from the dried-out seedheads to fill in gaps between plants and continue staggered sowings over the summer. Mark also taught me the benefits of growing 'green manures' such as buckwheat and clover in unused beds over the winter. As well as providing nutritious organic material that can be dug in prior to sowing in the spring, the root systems of the winter crop improve the soil structure and prevent minerals and nutrients from leaching away in rain. Comparing the soil in one of his beds with mine, which had been dug and manured in the autumn (as most books advise) convinced me to try it – my soil was dry and compacted in comparison, and it seemed as if the stones had somehow risen to the surface.

My Indian neighbour, Mustafa, whose immaculate plot contains the ingredients of a great vegetarian curry, taught me how to ensure a continuous crop of coriander through the summer (it can be slow germinating and tends to go to seed quickly). He makes small sowings of about half a square yard twice a month, wrapping seed in a damp warm flannel overnight for faster germination. The chap with the husky dog, whose name I never did learn and who has since given up his plot, used to put the cigarettes he chain-smoked to good use. As an effective remedy against aphids, he recommended boiling cigarette butts in water for half an hour, straining through an old sock and then spraying the resultant revolting liquid on to plants. (I tried it last time we had a party in the house, and it works.) He also smokes in his greenhouse, which apparently sends off all sorts of pests – non-smokers who don't like cigarette smoke in the house could always encourage guests who smoke to retire to the greenhouse or conservatory after dinner.

There have also been countless useful hints from readers of this column, on everything from slug control (favourite so far: edging raised beds, pots and greenhouse doorways with a strip of coarse sandpaper), to growing great tomatoes (a banana skin placed beneath the young plant provides food and moisture), to storing seed (in cheap, light- and air-tight used film canisters). Thank you all very much indeed.

I have also benefited from a wonderful little book called *Superhints for Gardeners from the Great and Green-Fingered* compiled by the Lady Wardington (see p. 244). Here you can read how the Queen Mother gets rid of slugs ('Gin palaces as opposed to slug pubs?' asked my boyfriend? No – leaving scooped-out grapefruit or orange skins about the garden to attract slugs and snails at night – just gather the skins up in the morning); how Prue Leith uses up her old nylon tights (to tie up roses – 'much gentler than wire and cheaper than rose ties'); and what the Earl of Westmorland uses to train clematis (Blu-Tack). Other useful tips include growing comfrey around your compost heap – the purple and pink flowers make a pretty screen, and can be cut down several times over a summer to add to the heap to aid decomposition (Tom Stuart-Smith, designer of this year's Chanel garden at Chelsea); watering soot into the soil around sweet peas to give the blooms a richer colour (Judith Bannister, Head Gardener at Kiftsgate Court); and, from the late Gervase Jackson-Stops: 'Never go pruning when in a foul temper, or after a row with your spouse.'

8 August 1998 ~ Community Gardens at a Church in Bow

One of the advantages of being nosy is that, occasionally, you can stumble on the trail of a new garden as you stroll from A to B. In Paris or Milan it might be a glimpse into a private courtyard that puts

you on the scent; in New York a rooftop bristling promisingly with plants; in London an unusual strip of front garden or even – I am ashamed to admit – the view right through the front windows and out to the back of a house. I now have the dog trained to sniff about engagingly when I'm in this I-spy mood, to make me look less like a burglar casing the joint.

The other day it was some mosaics on a wall that aroused my curiosity. I was walking through a part of the East End of London in which everything appears to be grey – grey skies, grey pavements and grey, characterless buildings – when I spotted a wall studded with potted plants and portraits made from bright ceramic tiles. The walls belonged to a church and the narrow strip of land between the building and the pavement was overflowing with tulips, daffodils and healthy-looking shrubs. But this was obviously more than just a jolly community enterprise.

Through a gap in the wall I glimpsed a pretty courtyard garden in which children were playing. Just around the corner, an imposing stone arch led into a small cloister garden, where a low modern building in pale stone, slate and wood curved round a lily pond and an intriguing stone sculpture appeared to crawl across the lawn. And a little further along the road, I could see woven willow fencing and a group of people making a path. There was definitely Something Going On.

After making a few phone calls I returned a fortnight later, to meet the Rev Andrew Mawson, the driving force behind all this activity. When he arrived at Bromley-by-Bow in 1984 he found a congregation of twelve old women in a 200-seater church and dereliction and despair in the streets. 'The only sign of nature was a single plane tree,' he recalls. 'This tree was the only obvious connection to the seasons – its leaves came out in spring and fell in autumn – and I found that very sad.' The gardens happened when he began encouraging local people, whatever their religious beliefs, to come and make use of the church buildings. The 'Paradise Gardens' (see p. 242), in front of the church are the creation of a group of Bengali women, while the courtyard was planted with scented climbers to make a pleasant place for young children to play.

The same approach was used when the church bought the local

park – a four-acre haven for ne'er-do-wells – from the council for ninety-nine pence. 'We gave chunks of it away to the local community to look after,' Rev Mawson says. 'If kids are involved with something from the start, they don't trash it.'

Right on cue, we pass Jimmy, a troublemaker-turned gardener who is now seeking a place at horticultural college. He shows me some woven willow fencing, already sprouting with new growth, that encloses a series of curving vegetable beds and a 'storytelling bower'. Most of the beds have been planted with ethnic vegetables by the local Asian community. Another corner has raised beds made from railway sleepers, which can be reached by the wheelchair-bound. The path-layers – a couple of local artists and some members of an art group – are incorporating glazed tiles stamped with fish, snakes and snails (made by a children's craft class) into a gently curving walkway. Vanishing benches were the only teething problem and, as usual, Rev Mawson had a lateral solution. 'I figured that if we were to have ten-ton benches no one would be able to carry them off,' he says. So he commissioned a local artist to make two huge concrete seats in the shape of mythical beasts. You can now snuggle up between the wings of a sleeping bird or on the lap of what looks like a beatific lion.

Most impressive of all is the garden around the new health centre, with its peaceful pond and sculpture. The enormous stone arch – an 18th-century William Kent design from a large local house that was demolished – opens on to buildings of a much more human scale, using natural materials and graceful, curving shapes. 'One of the things I noticed when I first arrived was all the straight lines and boring boxy shapes,' says Rev Mawson. 'In everything we've done here, we've taken our cue from nature – organic shapes and materials and lots of variety.'

It has taken a while to achieve, but the area is now thriving. The café, workshops and other projects bring in an annual income of £1 million and profits are poured back. 'It's another lesson from nature,' beams Rev Mawson. 'Life flies towards a garden, whether its birds, butterflies or people – and then it increases, like plants seeding themselves. All we did here was prepare the ground.'

16 *August* 1998 ~ It's Raining, It's Pouring...

By now, with any luck, the sun will be shining and everyone will have stopped grumbling. But as I write this in mid-July, we are still stuck in the murky, muddy maunderings of The Summer That Never Was. As I look out my window on to yet another spitting sky, I feel a Pollyannaish urge to think of reasons to be cheerful. The most obvious one, of course, is that watering has become an infrequent activity – this time last year my arms were being pulled out of their sockets by the daily round with watering cans at the allotment. (It's important to remember, though, that shrubs beneath trees, closely-planted borders and containers with overhanging foliage do not benefit from the downpours and are prone to drying out. Plants that need liquid feeding, in particular tomatoes, sweet peas and dahlias, will also need watering just the same.)

The second reason for rejoicing in unseasonably cool temperatures is that when it's not raining it is actually very pleasant gardening weather. Hours of hard labour in blistering heat have never been my favourite thing, and I can do without the sun scorching an imprint of my vest straps on my back. It's hard to garden with fingers still slippery from the second application of Factor 25, and sunglasses that slide off your nose when you bend down. This year's beetroot and brassica seedlings are sulking less after transplanting – and we're none of us suffering from wilt.

The other thing is that I rather like gardens in the rain – especially, I have to admit, if I am warm and dry. I've watched many of this summer's showers from our kitchen, with the french windows open – and the garden's tiny size means you get a close and concentrated view. Many of the plants I have chosen seem to respond particularly well to rain. The droplet-forming habit of *Alchemilla mollis* is well-known, and it's easy to understand how medieval alchemists (from whom the plant got its name) believed the dew that gathered, pearl-like, on its fan-ribbed leaves, could assist in attempts to turn base metals into gold. But the plume poppy, *Macleaya cordata*, has similar properties. Its beautiful glaucous leaves, whose intricate indented outlines remind me of the map of some strange island, must have a water-repellent effect, as the raindrops spin and skitter across them like mercury. I also love teazels for the way they collect water in that strange, pouch-like scoop at the base of the leaves. No doubt the plant has its own uses, but it would make the perfect birdbath.

One of the pleasures of rain in the garden is the sound that it makes. In Monty Don's book, *The Sensuous Garden* (see p. 244), beside a beautiful photograph of a garden dripping after a downpour, the author rejoices in the sound of rain on different leaves. 'The brittle slap of raindrops on a shiny leaf like laurel or holly is quite different from the way that yew or box absorbs and muffles the rain, holding the water sponge-like and soaking your clothes as you brush past them after the rain has long since stopped.' He compares the sound of rain on new leaves at the start of summer to that on parched yellow leaves in October. And there are few scents more delicious in a garden than the smell after a light shower on dry, sunbaked soil.

There is magic in watching rain pour down on a garden when you are outside the house, but also under cover. My last flat had a covered balcony overlooking a park, and I used to love standing there as the rain splashed off the leaves of lime trees just a few yards from my face. In a larger garden one could have a potting shed, or a summer house – or, best of all, a sort of tree house high in the branches, from which to enjoy a front-row view of the downpour. At Roche Court (see p. 242), a modern open-air sculpture gallery just outside Salisbury, the owner, Lady Bessborough, has commissioned two contemporary artists to create garden sculptures that will also function as shelters. William Lasdun's resembles the wing of a bird, while Oliver Barratt's, an aluminium and glass piece called *Harbour*, is inspired by an upturned boat.

23 *August* 1998 ~ Home

A war of attrition is being fought in the back garden. Now that the basement well beneath the deck is finally free of rubbish, I had intended to turn it into a potting shed. In a tiny garden such as this, it seems essential to have an area where tools and compost can be stored out of sight, and where messy tasks can be performed. This little space is ideal – partially under cover, but with enough light coming through the metal grid 'bridge' that runs from the french windows above, to be able to see what I'm doing. There's a drain down there already and a hose tap nearby, so any mess can be sloshed away easily. All that's needed are a few shelves and a fold-away work surface. Or that's what I thought. Someone else has rather different ideas.

The other week, when I returned from a work trip abroad, my boyfriend announced he'd been doing a bit of home improvement in my absence. Since this is the man for whom DIY stands for Don't Involve Yourself, I was rather excited, and followed him out into the garden. The well had been painted white, which looked lovely, and would obviously brighten up the basement rooms – not to mention my potting shed. Delighted, I started to tell him about my shelves, but he wasn't listening. 'That's not all,' he said, proudly. 'Look.'

I looked, and at first I couldn't see anything else. Then I noticed that a hook had been screwed into the underside of one of the deck timbers and the garden hose looped over it.

'It's an outdoor shower,' he said.

For the past few weeks, we have tried to coexist. My boyfriend, delighted with his new toy, is cleaner and better scrubbed than I have ever known him, thanks to twice-daily dowsings outside. He's talking of fitting a coloured bead curtain, but till then I can only hope the neighbours are enjoying the show. Every so often, I clear to one side the soap and shampoo that are cluttering the ledges and replace them with my gardening stuff, which then gets wet. There can be few things more revolting than a soaking, smelly packet of bone meal, unless it's a bag of wet manure – which, of course, my boyfriend wants nowhere near his shower.

He teases me by quoting the economical and ecological virtues of showers over baths – which is infuriating because:

a he's right
b neither principle has been a governing influence in his affairs until now
c it takes so long to rig up the hose to the kitchen tap and get it to the right temperature that it's debatable how much water is saved anyway.

The sudden trendiness of outdoor showers is, of course, further grist to his mill. He has taken to leaving copies of *Elle Decoration*, not to mention this month's *Vogue*, open at the pages proclaiming them as 'this summer's style statement'. I begin to feel like an old square for dreaming of my potting shed. Call me old-fashioned, but, in this country at least, I *do* think the place for a shower is in the bathroom.

So – what's to be done? I could get a water-tight chest or cupboard for my gardening things – though part of the appeal of a potting shed is the haphazard display of wonky old pots and tools on hooks. I have investigated the cost of installing a shower in the bathroom – even a solar-powered one with a small tank on the roof. But the sensible option seems to be to bide my time until the novelty wears off and colder temperatures make trudging outside in a skimpy towel less alluring. This would coincide with autumn bulb-planting time, when I could reclaim the space by stealth.

In the meantime, however, I must be careful not to give any ground. Yesterday, feeling somewhat ungracious for not having tried out our new amenity, I braved it myself. It was actually surprisingly pleasant. I have since had visions of the well as a sort of shower-cum-grotto, with shells in pretty patterns and ferns sprouting out of the walls. Not that I'm going to let on, of course.

31 *August* 1998 ~ The Allotment

Like the rest of the country, the allotment seems finally to have settled into itself for a good, relaxed Indian summer. It had got rather overgrown and neglected during the wet weather, and my friends and I had become dispirited by seeing successive sowings sacrificed to slugs and snails. Then, just before the weather broke, I bought myself a new pair of shears and went right round the two plots in a flurry of much-needed activity. By the time I'd finished, and we'd spent a weekend weeding and transplanting some well-grown seedlings that my friends had been raising on their roof terrace, it looked like an entirely different place. We banked up the remaining courgette and squash plants with mounds of well-rotted manure and in the gaps placed new plants and young sunflowers which were soon romping away. Earlier in the summer, four packets-worth of sunflower seedlings had been devoured while only a few inches high, but we're making up for them with a splendid show of Jerusalem artichoke flowers – same family, smaller blooms on top of thickets of twelve-foot stalks.

Free from weeds, and with renewed wooden edging planks, the beds now look most encouraging. In fact, the whole place sort of sparkles, rather like a house after the cleaner has been. And, as is the way of these things, the nicer it looks and feels, the more time we want to spend here. It seemed a long time since I had really looked forward to my visits.

For once, we have arrived at a suitable number of runner bean plants. Every time I turn up there seem to be just enough for a couple of suppers – other summers there have either been none at all or enough to feed a street party. Lush lines of spinach ('Perpetual Leaf Beet') are also doing well – one of my favourite allotment vegetables and obligingly productive all year round. The sweetcorn is swelling nicely, and I have to stop myself prying into the cobs to see if they're ripe. They'll be ready soon enough, when the silky tassels have turned brown (see pp. 106–7).

Cardoons are new to the allotment this year and, after a slow start, are really taking off. Their stalks, crowned by thistle-like flowers of a heart-stopping blue, seem to grow a few inches while we work alongside. It's the flowers and scrolling, silvery leaves I grow them for, rather than to eat. Unlike artichokes, which they otherwise resemble, the stems are the edible part, but only when blanched (by trussing the leaves up around the stems for a few weeks in September), stripped of the outer strings and boiled for thirty minutes.

The brassica bed looks beautiful, if rather tattered by slug damage. Square blocks of *cavolo nero*, calabrese and purple sprouting broccoli are underplanted with a few red and yellow nasturtiums and a lime green spurge which I know to be a weed but rather like. The various shades of bluey-grey and purply-green, with that grapey-grey bloom that cabbages have, look wonderful, even if the calabrese leaves are riddled with holes.

In the long border, teazels, their spiky seed-heads flushed with mauve, are intertwined with the lavender flowers of a towering chicory gone-to-seed. There is also a huge mullein, which a bird must have brought in, rising like a crazy woolly spire nearly twelve feet high. And along the other border, a line of hollyhocks in white, apricot and all shades of pink and red from salmon to shocking to deep purply-black, not only looks stunning but provides a screen (at last!) from the activities of the Territorial Army next door.

All in all, like many people, we've had a difficult year at the allotment, and if I'm totally honest, the best crop (apart from the sweet-corn) looks likely to be the blackberries, into which we have put no effort at all. But on a lazy summer afternoon, with the low sun shining through the bleached long grass and bees swinging heavily through the air, I can't imagine how I'd live in London without it.

6 September 1998 ~ Herbs for Cats and Dogs

Since making my little herb garden in the back yard, I have often noticed Rolf, our young lurcher, sniffing about its edges. He seems to like rolling his head in among the plants, and sometimes nibbles off a leaf or two of parsley or lovage. I thought little of it till an encounter with Abby, one of the dog-walkers in our local park. Abby knows quite a bit about herbs, and is researching their use as natural remedies for pets. 'He'll be looking for something to treat a particular problem – to soothe an itchy coat or calm a digestive upset,' was her opinion. She recommended a book on the subject, Juliette de Bairacli Levy's *Complete Herbal Handbook for the Dog and Cat* (see p. 242) and suggested grating a clove of garlic into Rolf's food as a deterrent against fleas.

Herbal medicine for humans has been undergoing a healthy

revival during the past few years, and it makes sense that similar principles could be applied to animals. Many pet owners will be familiar with the sight of their dog chewing couch grass to aid digestion, or their cat rolling in catnip (*Nepeta*), for its stimulant and tonic qualities, and it makes sense to provide these plants for them in our own gardens (if nothing else, it is a good excuse for having couch grass). But, apparently, the greater the variety of herbs available, the more discrimination the animals will show. Domestic pets can sometimes seem to have had all the wildness bred out of them, particularly the more outlandish-looking breeds, but some memory of their feral past must remain within even the most pampered and elaborately coifed pooch. In the wild, says Levy in her book, they would still seek out exactly the herbs they need, often travelling long distances in the process.

According to both Levy and Diane Stein in her *Natural Remedy Book for Dogs and Cats* (see p. 243) – today's pets need more in the way of fresh greens and herbs than their common tinned or packet diet allows, and relish the chance to nibble at herbs and fresh salad vegetables. Research has shown that animals making a kill – from dingoes in the desert to cats trapping birds in back gardens – go first to the semi-digested plant contents in the stomachs of their prey. They suggest adding a dessert spoon of finely minced fresh greens to the daily meal – the mix can include dandelion, clover, parsley, mint, watercress, nasturtium, mustard greens, lovage or young mallow leaves, as well as lettuce and the tops of turnips and celery.

Back in our local park, Abby has convinced Green Adventure, an environmental charity which has secured lottery money to create a community garden around some derelict greenhouses there, to include a herb garden with special provision for pets. The idea is that the dog-walkers, in particular, could drop in on the garden with their dogs and look up specific ailments on a wall chart. There would be large beds of lavender – good for rolling in to relieve an itchy coat; alfalfa (for general vitamins and minerals and for cleansing the digestive tract); chamomile (a natural sedative); comfrey (a general healer and good for applying direct to skin wounds, bites and itching); golden seal (a laxative and diuretic); parsley (for vitamin C and healthy digestion); and slippery elm (good for very young and very old or convalescing cats and dogs, also for coughing and vomiting). It sounds a lovely idea, but whether the reality would be flattened lavender bushes and dog-fights among the dandelions remains to be seen. In the meantime, I shall continue observing and experimenting with plants in my own garden.

Some herbs can be fed to pets raw, but many need to be made up into infusions, by boiling up in water for a few minutes and steeping for four hours. (Follow instructions from a book before attempting all but the simplest remedies.) I can't say I have noticed any marked improvement in young Rolf's health since adding raw greens to his diet, but he eats them readily enough, and the garlic does seem to deter the fleas. As for the other remedies, I haven't tried any yet. The argument that it's the way dogs would heal themselves in the wild does seem to pale beside the image of Rolf in a pinny, boiling up his fresh alfalfa in a saucepan in the forest.

13 September 1998 ~ The Allotment

After all the leafy turmoil and extravagance of high summer, it is something of a relief to see some bare soil again at the allotment. We've been tidying up, pulling up blackened broad bean stalks and rows of bolted chicory and spinach, and taking time to rake and hoe the empty beds. The other weekend, my friend Simon spent two whole hours tending and tilling a patch of ground that can't have been more than about a metre square. By the end of the afternoon he was completely in love with it, and I can sort of understand why.

There is something lovely about bare soil. It has to be the right sort of bare soil — and in the right place. A tatty, leaf-strewn gap, left behind when a neglected crop has rotted away, will not do at all — no virus-flecked courgette leaves, broken stalks or old plant labels. Nor will the barren, crusted earth around the shrubs and plants of over-zealous gardeners — the result, more often than not, of regular doses of weedkiller, which can destroy the soil's subtle natural eco-system along with the weeds. No, I'm talking about the 'rich, even tilth' beloved of old-fashioned gardening books. I never used to know exactly what that lovely word 'tilth' meant, but once you've seen it, you can't forget – earth as soft and brown and crumbly as if it had been rubbed between the fingers, like flour and butter when making pastry. Even the word itself seems onomatopoeic. Perhaps it feels so precious partly because you know it will not last for long. In a few days, a patch of bare soil will either have dried out to a cakey crust or be showing the first green pinpricks of weeds. Or, like the good organic gardener I am trying to be, I will be filling it with a follow-up crop such as Chinese brassicas or winter cabbage or salad or, even better, a green manure. If soil is left bare over the winter, it can lose a lot of its vital nutrients through leaching, and a green manure crop, which covers the surface fast, can help prevent this, while also improving soil structure. In spring, and well before flowering, it can be dug into the top six inches of soil in preparation for new crops. Green manures are suitable for any area of ground that would otherwise be left free for six weeks or more, and many are of particular value through the winter. Field beans are very hardy, and help fix nitrogen in the soil for next year's leafy crops; fodder radish has a deep tap root capable of bringing up nutrients from the subsoil, while mustard and the exotic sounding Hungarian grazing rye are fast-growing and effective. All can be sown up until October, and are available from The Organic Gardening Catalogue (see p. 245), along with a leaflet called Gardening with Green Manures for seventy-five pence.

About half of our plot is still cropping away – with giant marrows, courgettes and runner beans reappearing as fast as we can eat them. This year's sweetcorn has been particularly successful, which I can only put down to lots of rain at the right time in the growing season, followed by a good recent dose of sunshine. It's really a very undemanding crop – the rewards of utterly fresh corn, before all its sugars turn to starch, far outweigh the effort involved in growing it, which certainly can't be said for all vegetables. For the past month or so, I've been cycling over to do the watering, pulling off a couple of cobs just before leaving and rushing straight home to plunge them straight into a pan of boiling water. Then all that's needed is plenty of butter and ground pepper.

Pretty soon, it will be time for these beds to be cleared too, and all the undiseased debris returned to the compost heap to make next year's soil. All that will remain will be the Brussels sprouts, growing away nicely in time for Christmas, various winter greens and salad stuffs, a lifetime's supply of Jerusalem artichokes and my pride-and-joy, cardoons, which look all the more splendid and sculptural against the newly dug dark soil. The rest will go over to green manures.

But not quite yet. We'll leave some of that lovely bare soil for a while – if only as a symbol of the need for both ourselves and the soil to take a breather. Because, otherwise, nothing ever really ends in gardening. The cycles just keep on going round, and it can seem that no sooner has one job been finished than it's time to start on another – or even the same one all over again. Simon's little patch remains a small piece of perfection, fragile and temporary – an illusion of the control that gardeners crave all year and a promise of what's to come.

20 September 1998 ~ Home

Urban front gardens are sociable places. Unlike back gardens, which look inwards, aiming to provide stressed-out city-dwellers with the peace and privacy they so crave, the front garden has its face to the street. It interacts with other people as well as its owner. Besides the personal pleasure of stepping out and returning home to flowers round your front door, there is also the satisfaction of creating something which others – friends, neighbours, passers-by and postmen included – can enjoy. Having always lived in flats before, this aspect of our new home has come as a surprise to me, and a real joy.

Since we moved here two years ago, and even when the rest of the house was a building site, I have always had flowers along the front window ledges and piled up in pots on the roof of the bay – purely because I liked to. The first summer it was just scarlet pelargoniums – lots and lots of them – which flowered away right through the winter. Somehow those perky red blooms helped cheer me up when the builders were getting me down. But I slowly realised they were doing more than that. The flowers were helping us, too, take root in our new neighbourhood. It was while I was out dead-heading that people who are now friends first stopped for a chat – and it was nice to get compliments from passers by on their daily trip to the tube. The window box, spilling over all summer with a mixture of tall white and lime tobacco plants, white cosmos and trailing and climbing nasturtiums, has had many admirers this year, as has the tub of *regale* lilies, whose scent almost overpowered people coming up the path. The greatest honour, though, was when Mrs Mills, a larger-than-life character who has lived in the house opposite since arriving from Jamaica in the Fifties, asked if she could take a few of my daffodils to her church on Easter Sunday.

It may be the Afro-Caribbean influence, but in our street, in particular, people really make use of those few square yards between house and pavement – the young sit on the walls chatting and listening to music, while older people lean over their gates in the sunshine and greet you as you walk past. It has made me wonder whether, in this country's tradition of concentrating our gardening efforts behind the house, we haven't got it all back to front. Rare is the urban back garden that isn't noisy and overlooked. We aim for a peaceful patch of solitude in the city, but often, the reality means sunbathing in full view of all the neighbours, while suffering the cacophony of their combined output of hip-hop music, child mayhem and marital rows. A front garden gives something back to the street.

Like many London terraces, we have a front garden space about twenty by seven foot, currently paved in concrete with a three foot rendered wall. Originally, according to Linda Osband's book, *Victorian House Style* (see p. 244), there would have been flagstones and a smart black and white tiled path, enclosed by cast iron railings. During World War II, these railings would have been requisitioned to be melted down to make weapons, leaving the owners of such houses to replace the boundary as they chose – hence the typical mismatch of picket fences, painted breeze blocks and privet hedges to be found along the average urban street. Only the posher Georgian terraces retain their railings – is that because the poorer streets were first to be plundered, or because the rich could afford to replace them?

We shall probably keep our wall, though the garden would get a lot more sun if we lowered it. So far, all I've done is to plant up more large galvanised bins (ex-council dustbins and shiny new ones) with different types of lavender – the violet French lavender *Lavandula stoechas* 'Papillon', with its charming butterfly 'ears' and a darker blue one with silvery blue leaves which I think may be L. *officinalis* 'Munstead' are my favourites. The plants have bushed out well and release their scent as you brush past them to the front door. Their smoky mauve colours, along with the clematis 'Elsa Spath', which has clear violet-blue blooms in May and June, look well with the new mauvey-grey paintwork.

I'm not quite sure what else I shall do. My sister has transformed her front garden by laying down lots of gravel and edging the little flower beds with pebbles. A friend has clipped his privet hedge into star-like spikes and is threatening to paint the wall below it bright purple. I'd be happy turning our entire patch over to different types of lavender. But perhaps I'd better ask my neighbours first. After all, they'll be looking at it even more than I will.

27 *September* 1998 ~ The Woman Who Married a Tree

Our local newspaper recently carried a story about a woman who is so fed up with men that she has decided to marry a tree. A vicar in Wales has apparently agreed to carry out a ceremony in which Dee Brophy, a twenty-three-year-old office administrator from South London, will marry a silver birch tree on Streatham Common, South London. 'Compared to some men I've been out with, my tree is a far better option,' she is quoted as saying. 'At least I can expect it to be completely loyal and faithful to me.'

Though I can't imagine ever taking things to such extremes, I can understand how people can develop an almost unreasonable attachment to particular trees. There are a few in our nearby park – an ancient oak, a huge billowing lime and a pair of graceful holm oaks – that have become almost like friends over two years of daily dog walking. And when the tree over the road from our house showed signs of disease a few months back, I was full of concern. It's a purple-leaved maple, not the most remarkable tree in itself, perhaps, but when, by mid-summer, it was still showing only a few small leaves on the tips of its branches, I realised how much I value the shade it provides, and its splash of colour in an otherwise drab and treeless section of street.

My first move was to phone our local Tree Warden, who advertises his services on the side of a scruffy transit van that is often parked nearby. The Tree Warden scheme, set up by The Tree Council (see p. 246) six years ago, aims to create and train volunteer Tree Wardens throughout the country to help monitor, plant, care for and promote awareness of local trees. When my calls went unanswered, I tried the local Council, but by the time they got round to replying, the tree had already died. I was told, however, that the Council has plans to plant 2000 new trees in Lambeth by the year 2000, and that our street might be eligible to be included in the scheme.

Peter Smith, Monitoring Officer for trees in the Borough, offered to come round and look at the street and see whether, at the very least, our maple could be replaced. He diagnosed damage caused by trench digging for cable television last summer as the culprit for the tree's decline. Apparently, though the contractors are specifically ordered not to cut through tree roots, they often do when a job is proving time-consuming and difficult. Other common causes of death are residents taking to the hacksaw and lopping off branches ineptly in an effort to reduce shade, and even trying to poison trees by dumping road salt round the roots.

Mr Smith was reasonably hopeful about the dead tree being replaced, and promised to put our street down on the list of those to be considered for more trees. He was also able to throw light on the Tree Warden's reticence. Apparently he's a rogue who had slipped through the net and was exploiting the title for his own ends. He was knocking on people's doors, informing them that under Council orders their hedge would have to be cut/tree pruned/Virginia Creeper cut back, and offering his services for a knockdown fifty quid.

Should the Council fail to come up with the goods, Trees for London (see p. 246), which was launched on Friday is an interesting new venture, aiming to plant 20,000 new trees throughout all the London Boroughs over the next three years. Sponsored by London Electricity, the focus here is on community projects – research has shown that if local people are involved in planning, planting and caring for new trees, the usual statistic of twenty-five per cent of new trees succumbing to vandalism in the first five years can be significantly reduced.

At the risk of setting myself up as the Linda Snell (the busybody character from *The Archers*) of my corner of Brixton (the Community Garden scheme had to be shelved due to the high price of the site), I am contemplating trying to get another group together. Perhaps Dee Brophy, soon to be Mrs Birch, might be interested in joining – provided her new husband isn't jealous.

4 October 1998 ~ Designing for Children

Design-conscious parents often bemoan the fact that, with the arrival of young children, their stylish homes are turned into giant toy boxes full of moulded plastic and appliquéd elephants. The same fate often befalls their gardens. People who might otherwise be inclined to try something more adventurous – cobbles and gravel, for instance, a deck or a pebble mosaic – tend to assume that children cannot survive without huge expanses of lawn. It's easy to see why – from the earliest ages, what could be safer, softer and more inviting than a patch of mown grass in the sunshine? – and it's nice for adults, too. Frequently, though, that lawn is strewn with bats, balls, bikes and tyre skidmarks. Given the fact that the average urban garden rarely receives enough sun for turf to establish itself successfully, many city lawns are a muddy mossy mess for half the year and a parched desert for much of the remainder. So what's the alternative in a small city garden?

'If children can't have space, the next best thing is adventure,' says

Karena Batstone, one half of an innovative new landscape design company with offices in London and Bristol (see p. 245). As mothers of young children, both she and her partner, Helen Tindale, who trained at the Chelsea Physic Garden and then in the States, understand the requirements of clients who want to accommodate their children's needs into a garden design, rather than allow them to dominate.

'A small garden mostly taken up by lawn is not adventurous – nor does it allow much scope for bikes and games,' she says. 'If you don't have large expanses, it's best to concentrate on mystery and originality – creating features that look good in themselves but can also play a part in children's games.'

They have recently completed a garden in Barnes, where the lawn has been divided into squares, each large enough for a couple of people to lie on comfortably, with paths made from large beach pebbles in between. Around the edge runs a decking boardwalk bordered by purply-leaved shrubs, bamboo and grasses. 'The board-walk has become a bit of a trademark of ours,' says Helen Tindale. 'It looks good, kids love it – and you don't get bike marks on the lawn.'

Water features are another favourite – even though they are often avoided by parents due to fears over safety. 'For us, water is a vital component in garden design,' Helen says. 'There's absolutely no reason why it can't co-exist with children – you just have to handle it sensibly.'

For a family in Bristol they designed a very shallow rectilinear pool with large square stepping stones, while the Barnes garden has a pebble-lined paddling pool whose water level can be determined by a flick of a parentally controlled switch, just like emptying a bath. Other smart, geometric pools are covered with industrial-looking galvanised metal gridwork. 'It looks very modern, is utterly safe, and children enjoy the illusion of walking on the water,' says Helen.

In her own garden in Bristol, Karena Batstone has hit on perhaps the ultimate solution for accommodating children, adults and good design in a smallish town garden. At the furthest end of the garden from the house is a sunken den where her children, aged seven, five and three, can play with their friends – just within sight and earshot of the adults, who sit on the sunny terrace at the top. York stone steps with wide grassy treads lead down to a sunken trampoline (surrounded by bark to ensure soft landings), a sand pit and a shed which doubles as a play house, with window boxes full of early bulbs and ivy. 'It's a very shady area, so it's an area where the children play rather than grow things,' explains Karena, 'But that's what they tend to be interested in at that age. What they like about it is that it's a secret place just for them. They can hide down there and have their parties, and I let them paint the shed whatever garish colours they choose and scrawl graffiti on the wall. And what I like about it is that I can't see it.'

11 October 1998 ~ Maye E Bruce and her Common Sense Compost

The last column about compost making generated a lot of post – particularly from readers interested in the Centre for Alternative Technology's 'Compost Lasagne' using layers of fresh grass clippings interspersed with cardboard (see p. 107). But I can't compete with an article published in the *News Chronicle* in 1938, which gave rise to 4000 inquiries. The subject was a Miss Maye E Bruce and her *Common Sense Compost Making by the Quick Return Method* (see p. 242).

I was given Miss Bruce's book of that title by my friend Clarkey the other week, not long after we had inspected our allotment compost heap for the first time in several months. There was an encouraging amount of crumbly dark compost, which I immediately used as a mulch around the base of cropping bean, courgette and pumpkin plants, but the rest was either a smelly, slimy mess, or not broken down at all. So I was delighted to learn of Miss Bruce's apparently foolproof instructions for creating 'rich, sweet, friable compost' in only four to six weeks. The secret is a herb-based activator which, added to the compost heap in small but carefully controlled amounts, speeds up the decomposition process and produces compost of exceptionally high quality.

The book makes fascinating reading. Miss Bruce was one of the generation whose pioneering concern about chemicals in food production, and almost mystical belief that 'the health of plant, animal and man depends on a living soil', led to the formation of The Soil

Association in 1946. Interested in Rudolph Steiner's Biodynamic soil preparations (still used by many organic farmers), but put off by the secret esoteric rituals involved in their production, she set out to develop a similar compost activator that would be simpler to make and more accessible.

She began with the long list of herbs used by Steiner but narrowed them down to just yarrow and stinging nettle which, between them, supply all the vital minerals (iron, lime, potash, ammonia, nitrates, etc) for healthy plant growth. She made a powder from dried leaves mixed with honey and experimented with various different strength solutions before discovering that the weakest (1:10,000, as in homeopathy) had the most dramatic effect on the compost heap. Her findings were verified by baffled experts.

Miss Bruce was not only interested in producing large amounts of compost quickly. She was also convinced that the speedy breakdown of organic matter makes for better compost, as more of the plants' vital energy is retained. When building the heap, she recommends alternate four inch layers of tough matter and soft green stuff, with a dusting of lime and a few spades of soil every foot or so, an occasional two inch layer of manure and a final four inch covering of soil. The heap must be evenly, but not too tightly packed (air is vital), and must be kept covered at all times, to preserve the heat generated by the breaking down process. Weeds and vegetable matter must be added as fresh as possible – don't let it dry out in the sun. If new matter is added little and often, she says, the heat generated will be enough to kill even seeding weeds and bindweed.

The book includes lengthy instructions for making the herbal activator. Thankfully, I do not need to pass them on here, as 'QR Compost Activator' is still available. In old age, worried lest her life's work should die with her, Miss Bruce handed on distribution of the formula to Mr Chase of Chase Organics and The Organic Gardening Catalogue (01932 253 666 – prices start at £1.20 per sachet). A spokesperson said it still sells to a 'small and devoted' following, 'but the main problem is convincing people you need so little. It's easier to sell a nice big bottle'.

I have just received my first supply of QR and can't wait to use it. Compost doesn't disintegrate much over winter, but, according to

Miss Bruce, layering the contents of a winter pile with fresh grass clippings in the spring, when you also add the activator, will produce a large volume of ready-to-use compost in just one month. I shall report back.

Common Sense Compost Making went out of print in 1986, but it is worth tracking down. The ending has an almost mystical tone as Miss Bruce ponders: 'What is Life? Do we not find the answer in the words of the Eastern sage as he writes of: "The divinity that sleeps in the stones, stirs in the plants, wakes in the animals, is conscious alone in man". The breath of God in all there is. That is Life.' They certainly don't write gardening books like that any more.

24 October 1998 ~ The Allotment

My sister – the non-gardening one – has a look on her face when she visits the allotment which I know means one thing: 'Why go to all this trouble when you can buy it at Sainsbury's?' This year, I might concede she has a point. Every year is different with gardening – I have learned that much by now – and this year was most definitely not a good one for vegetables. I'm by no means the only one to have suffered: the constant wet and cold throughout much of the growing season meant gardeners up and down the country were grumbling – and losing much of their young produce to a bumper crop of slugs. If this had been my first year at the allotment I might have assumed it was always this way and thrown in the trowel.

The peas were the worst. Last year we were picking more than we could use, even leaving pods to turn crisp and yellow like parchment on the plant. This year the first sowing vanished as soon as it had sprouted, prey to our slimy friends, no doubt, and the second yielded scarcely enough peas to scrape together for a risotto. I missed them, as they're one of my favourite allotment crops and nothing beats their watery crispness for snacking on while working.

Our salad crops also suffered. Early sowings were snapped up by slugs while less than an inch high, and relentless rain washed away the (bio-friendly) slug pellets and watered down my beer traps. In the end I resorted to growing salad greens at home where I could keep an eye on them in a large metal vat (once used for treading grapes) with a lip too sharp for slugs to circumnavigate. This at least meant we had a constant crop of 'cut-and-come-again' salad leaves: red oakleaf, 'Salad Bowl', lamb's lettuce, cos and endive from June to mid-September when we went away on holiday. I hope to keep them cropping into winter in our largely frost-free walled garden. Rocket, by the way, seems to disagree with slugs. Indeed, it seems almost impossible not to grow and at £1.79 for a tiny bagful at the supermarket, it makes sound financial sense, too. There have been times when setting up a rocket stall at the bus-stop outside the allotment has seemed like a viable career sideline.

The best way to extend crop production into winter, and one I'm keen to try, is by using a polytunnel – not one of the low, plastic cloche-like things but a proper tunnel high enough to stand in. I'm too late to do it this autumn (crops need to be sown in late summer) but I may try to get hold of one for an early start next spring. I've read that you can heat them by storing horse manure below the growing bed (for details, call BUG – Biological Urban Gardening – magazine: see p. 242).

To continue my Annual Allotment Review, the rest of the crop did as follows:

Potatoes 'Pink Fir Apples' were delicious as usual, though the yield was slightly smaller. I would like to grow some earlies (ready in June) next year, to help break up the new ground we are clearing.

Onions Good crops of red onions and pink shallots which are hard to buy organic in the shops.

Broad beans Excellent, and well worth sowing in November, as the earlier rows were much less prone to blackfly.

Runner beans 'Painted Lady' and yellow 'Marvel of Venice' the best yet, which I can only attribute to well-prepared trenches full of compost and plenty of moisture.

Courgettes Sadly poor, as early seedlings were devoured by slugs; my summer cooking suffered.

Marrows Good enough for me to yearn for a cookbook on 'Winning Ways with Marrows'.

Squashes Great fun and definitely decorative – but does anyone have a recipe for thirty small, elliptical golden squashes?

Sweetcorn Best of all. In fact, I'm in danger of becoming a sweetcorn bore. Even my sister, when presented with a newly picked corn-on-the-cob – totally organic, freshly boiled and dripping with butter – had to agree that there is nothing quite like it.

1 November 1998 ~ Home

I have often thought of doing something to encourage birds into our little town garden. I realised that the time had come when I mentioned the idea to my boyfriend over breakfast. 'Birds?' he mused. 'I did see one of them in there once. It landed on the trellis briefly and then cleared off.'

This is a terrible state of affairs. Thinking about it, I can't remember seeing a *single* bird in our garden. The neighbourhood cats may have something to do with it – they patrol the tops of the walls and occasionally, when the dog is not around, drop down for a rummage in the flower beds. But I have to confess I have done little – apart from add plants – that would make a bird want to linger here. The lovely little nesting house my father made me as a present has yet to be positioned outside my study window – partly because of the logistics involved in securing it to the wall two floors up – and the seedcake I made them last winter out of leftover fat and nuts sat at the back of the fridge for so long it went off. Must try harder. And autumn seems like a good time to start.

It's vital that any bird tables, hanging treats or houses be positioned well out of the way of cats and other predators. This calls for a little ingenuity. I'd planned to make free-standing tables – like platforms at the top of tall totem-poles made from lengths of painted skip wood or scaffolding posts – placed at random in the flower bed. The urban aesthetic would sit well in this garden, I thought, and might even add a vaguely sculptural interest when foliage dies down. The first one – an old painted tray nailed on top of a broomstick – has just gone in, and a couple more will follow. Ideally, a bird table should have a roof, as shelter from the rain, a slightly sloping floor for drainage, and a perch on which shy birds can queue.

The man who is painting the windows at the back of the house has agreed to fix the bird house where I can see it when I'm writing. Of course, it'll be spring before it's used for nesting, but I thought I'd get the birds used to it by suspending a bundle of millet from the perch. And the window box outside my study has been turned into a sort of 'bird smorgasbord' for the winter. The surface is now covered with wholemeal breadcrumbs, seeds, nuts, fats and berries. I was thrilled to see some blue tits arrive yesterday.

Birds also need water – even in winter, which can be just as dry as high summer. Many need water for cleaning their feathers, and to keep themselves fluffed up for warmth. An old casserole dish has been wedged into the window box, while in the garden itself I've propped up an old dustbin lid on three bricks. A simple but beautiful birdbath, which I saw in a garden in the States, is a circle of copper sheeting, hammered into a shallow recess and suspended by three wires from the branch of a tree.

Of course, the most natural way to encourage birds into a garden is to plant trees and shrubs that provide food during winter. Sue Stickland's book, The Ecological Small Garden (see p. 243) suggests Cotoneaster horizontalis, which we already have scrambling over a low wall; types of crab-apple and sorbus (my favourite is Sorbus cashmiriana, with its milk-white berries and bronzy leaves); honeysuckle, berberis, hawthorn and the guelder rose, Viburnum opulus, as well as the more obvious holly, ivy, skimmia and pyracanthus.

Some flower seedheads are also popular with birds. If you've cut down your sunflowers, the English Garden Collection (see p. 244) has air-dried sunflower heads with a hole through the middle, which would look stylish hanging from a branch. Or, as a special treat, I might even splash out on the ultimate bird extravagance – a dear little log cabin made entirely from natural grains and seeds, with a wire chimneystack crammed full of sunflower seeds. At £42, if that doesn't encourage a few birds to pay us a visit, I don't know what will.

15 November 1998 ~ Home

When I went away for a month in mid-September, it was on the assumption that this wet, cold summer had already done its worst and that both garden and allotment could get along fine without any further help from me. This has proved only too well the case – but in the most delightful way. I returned to find the garden more full of flowers than it has been all summer.

The front window box was cascading with orange, red and yellow nasturtiums, whose tendrils had twisted right down to the ground and begun to snake along the floor. The lavender in the metal dust-bins had come into a late second bloom and is still throwing out its wonderful scent.

I'd expected the back garden to look rather bedraggled but, largely thanks to the friend who came to water occasionally, it was full of pleasant surprises. The tomato plants in pots against the sunny south wall were studded with ripe fruit – I picked a good two or three pounds of the tiny, sweet fruit straight away. Cardoons were still in flower, their fluffy violet thistle-heads contrasting well with the glossy green leaves of acanthus, which has bushed out a lot this first summer and will, I hope, flower next year. My young winter-flowering cherry tree (Prunus subhirtella 'Autumnalis') had shed most of its leaves but was sporting tiny, star-like white blossoms on some of the bare branches.

Finally, I could see the point of the rather dull-looking shrub at the back of the big border. For most of the year Cimicifuga simplex is unremarkable, putting out long spikes of green-tinged nobbly buds towards the end of summer. Now, when the clematis behind it has long since ceased to bloom, its bottle-brush spires of fragrant white flowers can come into their own. The purple-stemmed variety,

'Elmstead' might have been a more interesting choice, particularly with the bronzy fronds of Phormium tenax 'Purpureum' immediately in front of it and the dark wine-red 'eyes' of Euphorbia x martinii to one side. Next year, the combination will be further set off by chocolate-maroon hollyhocks (Alcea rosea 'Nigra') which I raised from seed and planted in that corner. I think I shall feel the need for a shock of deep orange – a blazing crocosmia, perhaps, sprayed like a firework across the foreground.

The longer I looked and explored on that first potter round, the more pleasant surprises I found. On the walls, white stars of Solanum jasminoides shone out against the backdrop of ivy, jasmine and clematis leaves, while the foliage of the 'Crimson Glory Vine' (Vitis coignetiae), was just beginning to turn purple, red and yellow. Potted pelargoniums on the round metal table and in metal buckets tied to the trellis up and down the walls are still in full, frothy white bloom. And one of the auriculas I raised from tiny 'plug' plants in lovely old salvaged clay pots is covered in perfect violet flowers, splashed with lemon in the centre, and with every petal outlined in lilac as if an artist had run a deft brush around the edge.

By far the biggest thrill, however, was the discovery of a single huge trumpet flower on my little datura bush – the shape, shade and texture of a peach silk nightcap. I have been in love with daturas since I first saw a huge tree in the tropics many years ago, covered with ghostly white blooms in the early evening, so I was delighted to be given two tiny cuttings earlier this summer. If I'd planted them in bigger pots they'd have grown faster, but somehow I never got round to it. I certainly never expected to see a flower nearly half the size of the plant itself. In this country, daturas usually have to be brought inside over winter, so people often prune them down to a manageable size and keep the cuttings in water on a sunny windowsill, to be raised as new plants the next year. I'm wondering, though, whether this little walled London garden might provide enough shelter for one to survive outside all year. One plant I shall bring inside. The other might almost be worth risking, just for the joy of a tree-full of those marvellous mad flowers in the border.

22 November 1998 ~ Home

In the city, features in a close neighbour's garden can become almost a part of your own. In a latter-day, scaled-down version of Humphrey Repton's principle of 'visual appropriation', we 'borrow' trees, plants and architectural elements that are way beyond the confines of our own property and incorporate them in our own designs. Subconsciously, I'd done this with a beautiful golden locust tree (*Robinia pseudoacacia* 'Frisia') behind one of our neighbours' houses. Its feathery foliage formed a striking lime green backdrop to our own little garden – and, although I would have chosen euphorbias anyway, I particularly enjoyed the way their leaves and flower bracts echoed the colour of the tree. The decision to include a golden hop (*Humulus lupulus* 'Aurea') in the opposite corner this summer definitely took the Robinia into the equation. It was a terrible shock to wake up last Sunday to find the tree had gone.

I still can't quite believe it. On Saturday I was in the kitchen with a friend, admiring the way the leaves were beginning to turn from acid green to yellow as we got further into autumn. When I looked out the bathroom window the following morning there was no tree – just a small pile of sawdust on the flat roof it once overhung. Instead of the graceful branches and luminous lime green leaves, I now beheld bare brick walls and our opposite neighbours' faulty plumbing. 'Something terrible has happened!' I cried, hurtling down the stairs on the verge of tears. My boyfriend, relieved to hear I had not just discovered some dreadful and disfiguring disease, said he'd heard a chainsaw while I was walking the dog.

Three days have elapsed and I still can't accept the change. Just as when I've made some stupid mistake or hideous *faux pas* I sometimes wish it were possible to press the rewind button on my life, I yearn to turn back the clock. But it's not as if I could have saved the tree. Explaining how much we loved it, and that Robinias are naturally slim trees which seldom grow very large would have done nothing if the owners of the house – or most likely, their insurance company – had concerns about root damage or lack of light. Like many trees over this terrible wet summer, the Robinia *had* gained several feet in height since last year and must have completely dominated their little garden.

These things do happen. Provided they are not in a Conservation Area or protected by a Tree Preservation Order, trees on private property can be felled without permission from anyone. (It's worth noting, however, that the penalty for damaging a protected tree can be up to £20,000, and that in a Conservation Area the local Council should be advised of any alteration to existing trees, including basic pruning.) I do wonder, though, whether our neighbours aren't having some doubts themselves as to the wisdom of their action. If they had thought that by felling the tree they'd be bringing more direct sunlight into their lives they were certainly mistaken – it stood due north of their tall house and the garden would always have been shady. Surely, like me, they must now be contemplating a world that seems relentlessly grey and man-made without that softening frame of foliage.

Enough already. The good news is that, following my meeting with the Council about the dying tree in our street (see p. 205), I returned from holiday to find a note saying that five new trees have been allocated to our stretch of street under the Borough's '2000 new trees for the year 2000' scheme. There are already white marks on the pavement denoting the proposed positions of the trees, which will be planted early next year. Leaflets will soon be sent to residents to check if there are objections. Here I must confess to a slight sense of relief when I saw there was no mark directly outside our own house. After all, it would have been the ultimate irony were I to have got hot under the collar over the felling of a tree outside my neighbour's house, only to be ringing up the Council with concerns about one closer to home.

29 November 1998 ~ The Hydroponicum, Summer Isles, Scotland

On our recent holiday in Scotland, it was a great surprise to be eating bananas grown in an unheated greenhouse on the far north-west coast. The small town of Achiltibuie, just north of Ullapool and overlooking the beautiful Summer Isles, is a challenging place for any gardener, let alone a lover of exotics. Further north than Moscow, it is home to plants and animals that are also found in the Arctic and is visited by salt-drenched hurricanes and cold easterly gales as late as May and June. Many gardeners give up and move. Robert Irvine met the challenges head on by building The Hydroponicum (see p. 241).

You see it as you round the bend from the road through the mountains – a sprawling structure built from polythene and corrugated plastic, as if a slightly scruffy space-ship has touched down on the boggy shoreline. Mr Irvine must have had good friends on the local planning committee. Inside, though, is a lush flowery jungle of hibiscus, bougainvillaea, orchids, olive and citrus trees. Strawberries ripen in April and peaches and grapes are picked in June. Not only is all this achieved with no extra heating, there is no soil either. Plants are grown in pyramid-shaped containers using hydroponics – from the Greek for 'the water does the work'.

Robert Irvine was never

a gardener by profession. A film director in the Sixties, he turned Highland hotelier in 1970 on buying The Summer Isles Hotel in Achiltibuie. Before long its restaurant was winning top awards, though the transportation of fresh produce to the remote spot posed problems. For meat and dairy produce he bought his own livestock, but early fruit and vegetables continued to defeat him. Even using polytunnels, the soil was too wet and cold to raise many crops in time for the hotel's seasonal opening in Easter.

The idea to garden hydroponically came to Mr Irvine on a walk up the hill behind his hotel. As he lay in the heather, gazing out over the islands, he contemplated the requirements for healthy plant growth. Sunlight he had in plenty, particularly during the long summer days, with the sea acting as a huge reflector bouncing additional light back. Heat could be provided by a plastic or glass cover. When it came to nutrients, he realised that if he could supply the plants with exactly the elements they needed, he could do without soil, which under cover, and in that area, is particularly prone to pests and diseases. He ran back down the hill and designed the first hydroponicum on the back of a menu. It was built in 1985.

There are now three adjoining growing houses which provide a range of climactic zones from those found in Hampshire and Bordeaux to the Canaries. (As cool air enters the lower 'Hampshire' greenhouse it is heated by solar energy through the polycarbonate roof before it enters the next house, where it is heated again till it rises into the upstairs 'Canaries' climate, where the bananas are grown.) Instead of soil, plants grow in a perlite and vermiculite mix enriched with an initial supply of all essential plant nutrients. When moistened by capillary action, this mixture apparently holds exactly the right balance of air and water for optimum root growth. Regular doses of a specially formulated liquid feed provide the plants with all the subsequent nutrients they need – at The Hydroponicum this is done by an automatic watering system.

The system is easily adapted for amateur gardeners, and is especially suited to troughs and hanging baskets. The shop and mail order service sells growing kits that range from mini-propagating kits at £1.50 to self-watering greenhouse units at £99. It has spawned several related schemes nearby – the Flower Tunnel café in

Applecross, where you eat beneath a bower of hydroponically grown flowers, and a private indoor swimming pool near Inverness surrounded by strawberries, grapes and figs. In 1994 Mr Irvine sold The Summer Isles Hotel to his son and the Hydroponicum to Viscount Gough, and retired to (usually) sunnier Surrey.

6 December 1998 ~ Home

I was later than usual in tidying up the garden this year. The non-existent summer was partly to blame – my seed-sown annuals got off to such a late start that some were blooming for the first time in October, and the tomatoes and nasturtiums were putting on a fine show until only a few weeks ago. Perhaps my reluctance also sprang from the fact that this is the first year that our little back yard has actually *felt* like a garden. There's still a lot I'd like to do, but, finally, the climbers and main border plants have grown big enough to create an enclosing sense of privacy, and to interact with one another, rather than look like a collection of plants in bare soil. And I'm a sucker for late autumn sun shining through leaves – is it my imagination, or do nasturtiums have a sense of recklessness, saving their greenest, most luscious leaves for the weeks and days before the frost will catch them?

A difference in temperaments among gardeners seems to come to the fore in autumn. Some seem almost indecently eager to get out there with the secateurs, pulling out annuals and cutting down perennials while they still have life left in them. Others, like me, will put the job off – as reluctant as the flowers to admit that winter's

upon us, especially when the sun comes over the neighbour's roofs
and persuades us it's still – sort of – summer. The truth is, I rather like
the late autumn garden. True – the last late flowers of cosmos and
rudbeckia may be raggedy, tattered things beside the fat perfect
blooms of summer, but there's an almost decadent beauty in them –
like the crumpled clothes, tumble-down hair and danced-out glow
of those in the 'survivors' photographs they used to take at dawn
after May Balls. If my flowers want to keep on dancing, who am I to
call time? By the time you read this, the frost will have claimed
them, anyway, turning the festive swags of nasturiums into slimy
green spaghetti overnight and reducing the astrantias to a limp mass
that has to be prised off the ground. But I'll cope with winter when
winter comes to me and not before.

I came across one of the stricter school of gardeners last month
while I was staying in Scotland. A group of us had been asked to
'tidy up' a long herbaceous border in the garden of the house where
we were staying. There was a lot to do – and I set about clearing
dead leaves and cutting out the dead growth around the mounds of
cranesbill geraniums. But when it came to dead-heading and cutting
down plants, my heart just wasn't in it.

'Come on!' cried the woman working next to me, whose tidy
front garden is the toast of her village. 'You want to take that right
down to the ground,' she said, brandishing her secateurs at an
echinops thistle whose leaves, it is true, waved like scraps of burnt
black paper in the wind.

'But it seems such a shame,' I began feebly. 'The seedheads look
so lovely in the frost.' 'That's all very well,' she replied grumpily,
'But someone left them last year in my garden and I've never seen
the back of them since. They self-seed like crazy.'

Perhaps, as a novice gardener, I shall pay for my naive sense of
romance next summer. But I shall always leave some of the seedheads
– for the birds, who so enjoy pecking at sunflowers and teazels and
asters – and also for the sheer good looks of them. The thistly blue
blooms on my cardoons are fast fading, but the spiky brown heads
have a strong sculptural quality; teazels and eryngiums are given a
second lease of life by a white outline of frost. Some plants towards
which I feel at best indifferent – asters, achilleas, bergenias and some

of the sedums – to my mind are actually enhanced by a tracery of frost around the leaves and seedheads. Grasses, grouped in graceful arcs where the late sun can slant through them, come into their own in autumn and winter. And there can be few sights more beautiful than the paper discs of honesty, sugary with frost and shot golden in a shaft of winter sun.

13 December 1998 ~ The Allotment

The onset of winter usually means a slackening in attendance at the allotment. The lures of paper gardening – seed catalogues, coffee table garden books and sketching fantasy potagers on the backs of old envelopes – seem suddenly much more appealing than the real thing. Visits to the plot creep down to one or two per fortnight – to deposit smelly accumulations of kitchen compost and check on the progress of the Christmas Brussels sprouts. Not so this year. The allotment is getting a makeover.

'Before' photographs from nearly three years ago – featuring wall-to-wall brambles and a thick mulch of litter – show how far we have come since we first took possession of Plot 26. But there is still a lot to do. Twice annual mulchings with compost and horse manure have raised the soil levels so much that the beds are bursting their wooden surrounds – time to replace them with taller skip timbers. Also, our normally friable soil has caked into clay over the wet summer, and is particularly compacted in the parts we've had to walk over. We aim to get all the remaining open areas converted to raised beds before spring – keeping them just over a metre wide means all parts of each bed are accessible from the paths. If we fill the empty beds with manure now, the worms can draw the organic matter down into the soil to improve the structure over winter.

This is also the time to put down proper paths. I've been offered large quantities of cockle shells – apparently the cockle farmers near Southend in Essex now have to pay for the shells to be taken to land-fill sites once the cockles have been extracted, so they are promoting them as a gardening material. The white shells would make an attractive alternative to gravel, so we are removing the worst weeds in the paths and putting down cardboard and carpet to stop them reoccurring, in preparation for a four inch layer of the shells on top. I'll report on their effectiveness – and whether the initial rather fishy smell fades (as I'm assured it will) after a few rainfalls.

We are also in the process of making a pond. The hideous orange bath rescued from our neighbour's front garden is to become a bog garden full of irises, and we have dug a shallow cavity for a larger wildlife pond ready to line with a three-ply butyl liner. The idea is to attract frogs and toads to help us solve our slug and snail problem. To function properly, a wildlife pond needs at least five hours of sun a day – we've sited ours towards one end of the plot, where the excavated soil could be thrown up to cover last year's 'long-term' woody compost pile and make a large raised bed for summer squashes next year.

The most exciting project by far is the shed. I have dreamed of a shed for years but, like many allotments, ours forbids permanent structures over four feet tall. So the only way to go is down – to build a 'sunken' greenhouse with its floor a couple of feet below soil level. I saw one recently at another London allotment, and was immediately green with envy. Rather than excavate the whole area, we'd only need to dig out steps and a narrow 'trench' to stand in – the soil level would remain the same, but would function as 'raised beds' once you're inside. We've saved some smartish metal-frame windows and will start work soon. Thank goodness for friends and helpers who are keen on the construction side of gardening.

'You need vision to be a gardener,' I declared to my sister as we packed up to leave the plot on Sunday. 'You have to be able to look at a patch of ground in the dead of winter, when all your plans are still in your head, and imagine how it'll feel when it's finished.' We stood there for a few minutes, holding in our minds' eye a criss-cross of cockleshell paths, a pond with swaying reeds and hopping frogs and a neat little greenhouse full of peppers and tomatoes, until Sarah, shivering, tugged at my jacket and we walked to the gate.

20 December 1998 ~ Festive Ideas from the Flower Market

New Covent Garden Flower Market is a cheerful place on a frosty morning in the run-up to Christmas. When you drive in at dawn it's still dark outside and the ice is still crunchy round the windscreen. An hour or so later, when you emerge like a walking tree bristling with flowers and foliage, the sun is just heaving itself over the houses. The winter sunrise and the warm banter of the stallholders inside – not to mention the satisfaction of securing a good bargain or two when others are still sleeping – seem to set you aglow. It's a real tonic if your festive feelings have yet to materialise.

It's also a great place to pick up last-minute Christmas presents or decorations for the house. We're not having a traditional tree this year – after three Christmases of putting out old trees to graze at the allotment, the place looks like a mini Pension Fund forest, and it seems a shame to uproot the trees for such a brief sojourn inside. We've decorated them – with hanging treats and ribbons of bacon fat for the birds – but they're staying put. Instead, I splashed out on a pyramid bay tree, which we have covered with tiny white star lights. Quality Plants (see p. 245) have all sorts of smart clipped evergreen trees and bushes for a fraction of the price of the garden centres. My bay tree, which is about four and a half feet tall, cost £35 – comparable with an average spruce or fir, but with post-Christmas potential in the garden. Seven-foot bay standards were £85, large box obelisks £35 plus, and the small fruiting orange trees at around £27 would look good on the Christmas table. Most dashing was a ten foot fir for £85 trimmed into a spiral – swathed in white lights it would throw wonderful shadows round the walls.

Flowers are obviously the greatest temptation at the market – you can usually pick up ten bunches for the price you'd pay for two or three in the shops. I came away with an armful of white anemones (some that lovely milky green, others with a scarlet splash in the centre) and dark wine-red ranunculus, their blooms like soft fat coils of tissue paper. The foliage merchants along the outside of the market are the place for huge boughs of dogwood, pine and corkscrew willow, as well as mossy logs and the inevitable holly and ivy.

Some of the best and most unusual bargains can be found at the sundries shops around the perimeter, such as Something Special (see p. 245) and C Best (see p. 244). It was here that I found hyacinth forcing glasses for just £1.20 each – growing the bulbs in water takes me back to my childhood. I love to watch them growing while so little goes on outside – five white ones are ranged along my study windowsill. For last-minute presents to last into new year, I bought large shallow glass bowls (£7.95), filled them with coarse pea shingle (£1.60 per sack from our local builder's merchant) and planted them with lots of 'Paperwhite' narcissi. These are my favourite winter bulbs and also the fastest, growing from green-spiked bulb to a froth of fragrant white blossom in four to five weeks. They look best crammed in tightly – keep the bulb bases just in contact with the water and add a piece of charcoal beneath the stones to keep it all fresh. Galvanised containers from eighty pence also look clean and modern.

Another idea (which also takes me back a few years) is to make an 'indoor garden' to run along a chimneypiece or down the centre of a table. Trays of budding narcissi, grape hyacinths or tiny white cyclamen can cost as little as £7, and look good in a long low container with moss and lots of pale grey pebbles. Keep the shapes graphic and simple, or it will look like Dingly Dell – and place a border of plain white night lights a few inches away, all around the edge.

27 December 1998 ~ Gardens to Visit in Winter

Winter is actually a great time of year to go garden visiting – provided you match the place and the weather with care. Not only do you avoid the picnicking crowds of summer; you can also enjoy the bones of a good garden with no more adornment than frost on the branches and a haze of icy mist. Even if the weather's too wet for doing much exploring out of doors, there's always the heated option: the palm houses and large greenhouses of our finest Botanical gardens. Here are a few of my favourite winter haunts that are open almost all year.

Wyld Court Rainforest Gardens

With the cries of monkeys and rolling thunder overhead, and the smell of frangipani and ginger flowers all around, you can almost believe you're in a real rainforest in this glasshouse garden just off the M4. Many of the plants, grown from seeds or cuttings taken on expeditions, are now extinct in the wild, but thrive here in three connected greenhouses that simulate different rainforest habitats. The place manages to be educational and extremely beautiful at the same time, with lots of interest for children and adults, gardeners and non-gardeners alike (see p. 242).

Stourhead, Stourton

The classic landscape garden for still, wintry days – and a real treat if you can have it almost to yourself. Follow an anti-clockwise route around the lake for slowly orchestrated glimpses of classical temples across the water and distant follies in the mist. Highlights include the boat house, Temples of Flora and Apollo, the Pantheon and rustic cottage, and the surprise of the secret rock bridge and cascades. Afterwards, warm up with a pint by the fire in the Spread Eagle Inn by the entrance (see p. 242).

Glasgow Botanic Gardens

The glasshouses of any Botanic garden are a cosy place to head for on a cold afternoon, but Glasgow's Victorian Kibble Palace is among the smartest, with its palms and temperate plants interspersed with white marble statuary. Other attractions include a splendid orchid collection, featuring Dendrobium heterocarpum, a rare type from Thailand with fragrant winter blooms, and the new 'Arid Adaptations' house which features some of the world's most outlandish plants. Check out the curious Doryanthes palmeri, which has recently produced its first huge flower spike after forty years – the flowers will open gradually over several weeks (see p. 241).

Roche Court Sculpture Park and Gallery

Swing off the A30 in to a surreal new world peopled by huge Matisse-like cut-outs doing back-flips across the fields, Anthony Gormley figures floating tip-toe above the grass and a crouching beast that seems straight out of Picasso's *Guernica*. All the pieces in the ever-changing display are for sale – ranging from Lynn Chadwick's *Beast Alerted* (£350,000) to sculptural benches and simple graphic pieces by lesser-known artists that would be perfect for small gardens (from £1000). Great care has been taken in the siting of the work, and it's a real thrill to 'discover' a new piece behind a section of wall or hedge (see p. 242).

The National Gardens Scheme

This also has a clutch of private gardens open through the winter, such as Brady Mount House in Alresford, Hampshire on 6 February (an informal plantsman's garden full of unusual snowdrops, hellebores, daphnes and woodland plants); Cinderdene Cottage in Dymock, Gloucestershire on 9, 11, 14 and 16 February (excellent snowdrop collection and other spring flowers) and Little Court in Crawley, Hampshire (one and a half acres with spring bulbs, a Victorian kitchen garden, bantams and geese and views over the Downs (21,22,23 February) (see p. 242).

1999

17 January 1999 ~ The Allotment

Of all the new projects underway at the allotment, the pond has provided most fun. We certainly seem to have picked the right place for
it. This naturally wet corner of the plot just got wetter and wetter as
we dug, until we hit what appears to be the water table about eighteen inches down: a layer of sticky ochre-yellow clay. (I say 'we', but
the bulk of the digging was done by Clarkey, one of the friends with
whom I share the plot, on a day when I'm sure he would rather have
been pursuing his major new passion: fly fishing. Still, making a
pond is probably as near as you get to fishing on the allotment,
unless you go on to stock it with trout.) When we left that first day
the hole was six inches deep in water; five days later, when I
returned to harvest sprouts for Christmas dinner, it was full.

The water level remained high over the following weeks, regardless
of the rainfall. The rest of the plot wasn't waterlogged. I consulted my
books – The Natural Garden Book by Peter Harper (see page 243) and Sue
Stickland's The Small Ecological Garden (see page 244) are the most helpful
on ponds, telling you how to create shallow steps around the edges so
that plants of different heights can grow and animals hop in and out.
Normally you need a plastic liner to make a pond, which must be laid
over two inches of damp builders' sand and a further layer of old
carpet or pond underlay to prevent the liner being pierced by roots or
stones, but in very clayey soils, a liner may not be necessary. The
natural clay retains the water; and it does this more efficiently if you
tread the clay down well and spread an even layer up the sides – a
process known as 'puddling'. So, the other Sunday we spent a pleasant,
if muddy, afternoon 'puddling', the water coming dangerously close
to the tops of our wellies and making us all wish we had thigh-high

fishermen's waders. At one point the dog jumped in, too, only to leap out immediately and shake mud all over us. When we finished we looked like soldiers in old photographs from the Somme.

Surveying our work, we suddenly noticed bubbles coming up to the surface. At first, we thought they were just air pockets emptying. But when we looked again, after an hour or so tidying and weeding, the bubbles were still there. 'It's a spring!' cried Simon, jumping up and down. 'We've struck mineral water!' and immediately we began fantasising about syphoning it into trendy bottles, marketing it as 'Dulwich Woods Spring Water' for £1.20 a throw and making our fortunes. (This may seem far-fetched, but a spring recently unearthed in Tower Hamlets in the grimy East End of London, has been certified as pure water.)

At this point, I remembered having seen springs at the top end of the site just after I'd first arrived. In wet weather, water runs freely down narrow brick-lined channels constructed by the plot-holders 'up-top' to prevent it swamping their crops. Could we have tapped into the same source? We trooped up to investigate, and were excited to note that the flow was in direct line with our pond at the foot of the hill. 'This could be the answer to everything,' said Simon. 'All we have to do is build an irrigation system like the ancient Egyptians and we'll never have to water again!'

Before we get too excited though, we'll have to see if the pond remains full all year. The water level may well drop in summer, necessitating a plastic liner after all. We could always dig out the clay and start a pottery – anyone for Dulwich Woods Ware? But one thing's for certain... My plan to beat the allotment committee's height regulations for buildings by constructing a sunken shed may not be quite so clever after all.

23 January 1999 ~ Old Garden Books

These long winter evenings, when it's too dark and cold to garden, have been perfect for getting stuck into my ever-growing pile of old gardening books. I've collected them on and off for years, but the shelves are now groaning after several extravagances at the RHS Shows in Westminster. I go to these shows with the intention of building up my knowledge of plants – to enjoy the displays, note down varieties I'd like to use one day and maybe buy some plants for the garden. Time and again, however, it is not plants I come away with, but heavy carrier bags of books. Last time it was a first edition of Georgina Masson's classic, *Italian Gardens* and a beautiful, embossed leather book of *Flower Lore* subtitled 'the teachings of flowers – historical, legendary, poetical and symbolical' and packed with poems, old sayings and superstitions involving plants (both extremely beautiful, but costing the best part of £100 the pair). The time before that it was *The Shaker's Garden* as a present for my mother, *Tales My Father Taught Me* by Osbert Sitwell – 'an evocation of extravagant episodes' with several amusing chapters on gardening and a snip at £5 – and *Grounds for Change*, a stunning collection of modern gardens all over the world that has only been published in America. There is always something.

The most frequent source is Ivelet Books (see p. 244), who specialise in classic and antiquarian garden titles; but I've also been tempted by Jill Hedges (see p. 244) and Mike Park (see p. 244) at the shows. Bookshops such as Garden Books in Notting Hill (see p. 244) and Lloyds of Kew (see p. 244) are also wonderful places which specialise in new and old gardening books and can trace particular titles for you. But any old bookshop in a sleepy town will do for me – the thrill of stumbling upon Christopher Tunnard's *Gardens in the Modern Landscape* (1938) is all the greater when it's surrounded by stacks of car manuals and Jeffrey Archer.

Second-hand gardening books include several categories. Newly-published books, often cast-off presents or review copies, can be bought at reduced prices while the titles are still relatively hot off the press. 'Gardening classics' in their original bindings and sometimes long out of print are very much sought after. Vita Sackville-West is a hot favourite of course – Alan Aherne of Ivelet Books says a first edition set of her four *In the Garden* books in reasonable condition could fetch up to £250 and E. A. Bowles, early Christopher Lloyd and classic post-war horticultural monographs such as F. C. Stearn's *Snowdrops*, the last now exceedingly rare, are sold as soon as they appear.

Popular antiquarian books include good early editions of Gerard's *Herball* and 18th century writers and designers such as J. C. Loudon and Humphrey Repton – Repton's *Observations*, which includes some of his famous overlays showing 'before and after' drawings, can go for up to £4500. I'm also a sucker for Victorian books with gold-embossed covers and intricate illustrations – one of my favourites is *The Plant World* by Elizabeth Twining, published in 1866, with watercolours of exotic palm trees and people picking tea and cotton interleaved with tissue paper.

Part of the appeal of older books is their design – in spite of the modern advances in photography, few books are as charmingly presented as Anne Scott James' *The Pleasure Garden* and *Down to Earth* with the original quirky illustrations by her husband, Osbert Lancaster. And no recent title can rival David Hicks' classic *Garden Design* (long out of print) for its rigorous layout, bold use of black-and-white photographs and clever scribbled overlays showing how Hicks, that great aesthete, would attempt to transform a boxy modern estate house with rose-clad trellis ('square not diamond'), squares of box and gravel, and gothick windows on the garage.

The dealers mentioned will also, of course, receive your unwanted books for a fee. Looking at the state of my study – book-shelves already crammed and stacks of books on the floor – I'm thinking of paying a visit. True, there will always be the temptation to exchange them for something else. But if it's one lovely old title for ten neglected new ones, who's complaining?

31 January 1999 ~ Home

As I write this, my friend Clarkey is out in the wind and the rain, knocking down and rebuilding a brick wall in our garden. He's been at it for four days now, bashing at the old concrete footings with a crowbar and dragging bags of cement and rubble in and out of the house. So far, this little project is in danger of costing him his health (he is sneezing a lot and complaining of backache) and me several hundred pounds (I am too embarrassed to admit how many). And all because I *changed my mind*.

Almost a year ago, I cheerfully reported the completion of a new raised flowerbed in the garden. The construction work was done while we were away on holiday, so it was exciting to come home and find the garden transformed. I remember feeling slightly bothered by the way the curve in the wall of the bed jutted out towards the steps, but the relief at having some sort of order restored in the garden put paid to my doubts. As time wore on, however, it began to annoy me. The curve had created a strange sunken area that couldn't really be used for anything; the entire space seemed somehow awkward and unresolved. I felt unable to get on with making my pebble mosaic and finishing off the garden.

I tried to compromise. I placed a tub of flowers on top of the offending corner to draw the eye away from it. I invested in trailing plants to shroud it in foliage. But, rather like slapping make-up over a spot, my efforts only served to draw attention to the problem. I asked visiting friends for advice. A landscape designer was keen to revamp the whole garden, reshaping the wall and treating it and all other surfaces with a steel blue render (very smart, but so it should be at £2000). Simon from the allotment wanted to knock out a few bricks and go for a more rustic effect, with water running down shallow steps that would link the wall with the rest of the garden (full marks for innovation but it would be easier to rebuild the wall). The wild-card idea was to turn the area into an outdoor jacuzzi complete with floating bar.

Eventually, Clarkey agreed to rebuild the wall for me – probably just to stop me going on about it. We drew up a plan that retained as much of the old wall as possible, but replaced the curve and jutting out corner with a simple inverted right angle. As work began, I realised I had said little about it to my boyfriend who has never really understood my dislike of the wall and, unlike me, is blessed with the sort of temperament that would rather live with it than go through all the hassle and expense of change. I had hoped that by keeping the kitchen curtains closed, he might not notice what was happening outside. But a hundred salvaged bricks, four sacks of cement, three sacks of sand and one of aggregate being lugged down the hall are pretty hard to miss – particularly when, as penance for my indecision, I insisted on carrying half the stuff myself.

But everyone agrees it was worth it now the job is finished. The bed is a smart 'L'-shape, its angles echoing the other squares and straight lines in the garden – the deck, the chunky trellis on the walls, the galvanised metal grid of the 'bridge'. And the area below it is now large enough to make a square sunken terrace – a secret place to sit, out of sight of the surrounding houses, with white roses all around and bamboo swishing gently above. We're going to deck it over and then the garden will feel finished.

I'm half-ashamed of my fussiness, but at least I'm in good gardening company. When visiting gardens, I'm often struck by the obsessive indecision of their creators. All gardeners move plants around, change colour schemes, make new paths and seats. But I've also seen avenues of fully-grown trees transplanted; greenhouses shunted halfway across the garden; yards of York stone (newly laid) torn up and moved elsewhere. The grander the garden and the more money involved, the worse it seems to be. I'm told that a famous pop star who spent millions on his garden changed his mind so many times that the designers themselves would forget their way around. Perhaps it's just as well my garden is so small. There's a limit to how many times you can change your mind in a space only twenty feet square.

7 February 1999 ~ Spring coming

I do not usually like this time of year. The short grey days and lack of change outside get me down; it's as if nature is somehow stuck in the groove of winter and can't move on into spring. My way of coping with February is to try and get away – ideally somewhere hot where the flowers are out. This year, however, feels different. There seems to be an awful lot going on. It may be my attitude, or it may be the mild weather, but everywhere I look there are signs that spring is coming.

The allotment, which is usually quiet as the grave in January, has been buzzing with new life. Dark red nubs of rhubarb are nudging through the soil, accompanied by the first crinkly lime leaves. Garlic and broad beans are surfacing; the purple sprouting broccoli has started to sprout. Over by our fence there's a spray of forsythia in full flower, and the tulips are showing spiky folded leaves. Alongside these new arrivals, the cabbages, sprouts and rows of spinach that have made it right through winter look like tired old soldiers. This strange juxtaposition of old and new is even more marked at home – the lack of a severe frost means last summer's nasturtiums were still flowering in the window-box while the daffodils came into bud.

People are out and about, too. The warm weather has brought more allotment folk down in pursuit of winter jobs: mending raised beds, turning their compost; spreading manure. The plots belonging to these winter visitors are pictures of neatness, with fringed lines of green showing up against the bare dark soil. Beside them, the stretches of neglected land look shockingly, but splendidly wild – waist-high in grass and weeds and dotted with Brussels sprout plants whose tight green buttons have exploded into ragged rosettes. Abandoned runner bean teepees are shrouded in the ghosts of last year's produce – black pods hanging heavy on rustling raffia stems. Tangles of rose briars, bare save for the hips, are silhouetted against the sky like an illustration from Arthur Rackham's *Sleeping Beauty*. Tools lie rusting where they were last used. But even here, new life is breaking through. A rosemary bush is flushed with blue flowers; self-seeded rocket has peppered a patch of bare ground with seedlings. If I know our strict allotment committee, it won't be long before some of these plots are requisitioned and new owners will be arriving to weed and plant and sow.

Our back garden, too, is full of exciting changes. My favourite flowers, the milky green and dirty red blooms of hellebores, have been appearing over the past few weeks, and the ceanothus, its glossy dark leaves studded with lime-green buds, already has a few blue splashes. Bulbs are beginning to show – I must have put in about a hundred tulips in large tubs, and the beds are chock-a-block with different kinds of allium and foxtail lilies coming up. Drinking my coffee out there first thing in the morning, I can almost feel them all growing.

Indoors, pots of white amaryllis and hyacinths in glass forcing jars have been coming into flower since Christmas. There are several in front of me on the desk where I work and I love to watch their daily – sometimes hourly – changes. I swear the amaryllis stems stretch a good half inch on a warm day. Everywhere, there are huge glass vases of pussy willow and catkins brought up from the country. Last week I was down on my uncle's farm in Kent with friends, thinning out his hedgerows to decorate a barn for a party: we found armfuls of alder catkins, witch hazel and whorls of old man's beard to twist into ropes of ivy and hang from the rafters, and wove white fairy lights in among them.

And here I have a confession to make. This party was not just any old party; it was my wedding. By the time you read this, the person referred to in this column for all these years as 'my boyfriend' will have become 'my husband'. Perhaps that helps explain why this February I am full of the joys of spring.

SOURCES

Places to visit

The *Achiltibuie Hydroponicum* Achiltibuie, Ullapool, Ross-shire IV26 2YG (01854 622 202). The Hydroponicum and Lilypond Café are open to the public daily from Easter to 30 September, 10 a.m.–6 p.m., with guided tours on the hour.

Brady Mount House Alresford, Hampshire. See National Gardens Scheme (NGS) Yellow Book, p. 242.

The *Centre for Alternative Technology* is open to visitors every day and runs regular courses, For further information send an sae to CAT, Machynlleth, Powys, SY20 9AZ (01654 702 400).

Charleston house and gardens, which are sign-posted off the A27 between Brighton and Eastbourne, are open from April to October, Wed–Sun 2–5p.m. (01323 811 265).

Cinderdene Cottage Dymock, Gloucestershire. See NGS Yellow Book, p. 242.

The *courtyard gardens of Cordoba* are open from mid-May. Contact Asociación de Amigos de los Patios, 50 Calle San Basilio, Cordoba, Spain (00 34 57 29 29 89).

Garden Sculpture is every summer at Wolseley Fine Arts, 12 Needham Road, London W11 2RP (020 7792 2788).

Glasgow Botanic Gardens 730 Great Western Road, Glasgow G12 OUE (0141-334 2422). Gardens open all year daily a.m.–dusk. Kibble Palace Glasshouse open 10 a.m.–4.15 p.m. in winter, admission free.

Little Court in Crawley, Hampshire. See NGS Yellow Book, below.

The London Wildlife Garden Centre, 28 Marsden Road, London SE15 4EE (020 7252 9186).

The National Gardens Scheme, Hatchlands Park, East Clandon, Guildford, Surrey GU4 7RT (01483 211 535) or buy the Yellow Book of gardens open to the public through the scheme, £4.50 from bookshops.

Paradise Gardens at the Bromley-by-Bow Church and Community Centre, Bruce Road, London E3 (020 8980 4618).

Roche Court Sculpture Park and Gallery East Winterslow, Salisbury SP5 1EG (01980 862 244). Open daily 11 a.m.–4 p.m., admission free, large groups must telephone first.

Stourhead, Stourton, Warminster BA12 6QD (01747 841 152). Gardens open all year daily, a.m. till dusk or 7 p.m. (whichever is sooner), admission £4.50 (concession £2.50); free to National Trust members.

Wyld Court Rainforest Gardens Hampstead Norreys, Thatcham, Newbury RG16 0TN (01635 200 221). Open daily except 25 and 26 December, 10 a.m.–4.45p.m., admission £4 (£3 concession).

Books and publications

Bloomsbury Gardening Classics, £10.99 hardback, £7.99 paperback.

A Breath From Elsewhere by Mirabel Osler, Bloomsbury, £15.99.

BUG magazine, PO Box 206, Worcester WR1 1YS (01905 22179).

Charleston: A Bloomsbury House and Garden, Frances Lincoln, £25.

Common Sense Compost Making by the Quick Return Method by Miss Maye E. Bruce (out of print).

Complete Herbal Handbook for the Dog and Cat by Juliette de Bairacli Levy, Faber & Faber, £9.99.

Creative Containers by Paul Williams, Conran Octopus, £12.99.

Cultivating Sacred Space: Gardening for the Soul by Elizabeth Murray, Pomegranate, £19.95.

Cut Flowers, a Photographic Essay by Elspeth Thompson and Tricia Guild, Quadrille, £15.

The Cutting Garden: Growing and Arranging Garden Flowers by Sarah Raven, Frances Lincoln, £25.

Dear Friend and Gardener by Beth Chatto and Christopher Lloyd, Frances Lincoln, £14.99.

The Ecological Small Garden by Sue Stickland, HDRA, £5.95.

Gardener Cook by Christopher Lloyd, Frances Lincoln, £20.

A Gardener's Book of Colour by Andrew Lawson, Frances Lincoln, £25.

Gardens of England and Wales Open for Charity by National Gardens Scheme, £4.50 (also known as the Yellow Book), ISBN 0 900558 318

Gerard's Herball (out of print – facsimile editions may exist, try a specialist bookshop).

Hortus: an annual subscription costs £30. Send a cheque to The Bryansground Press, Bryans Ground, Stapleton, nr Presteigne, Herefordshire LD8 2LP (01544 260 001).

In Your Garden by Vita Sackville-West, Oxenwood Press, £13.99.

In Your Garden Again by Vita Sackville-West, Oxenwood Press, £13.99.

Journal of a Solitude by May Sarton, Women's Press, £7.99.

The London Gardener is sent free to members of The London Parks and Gardens Trust, who also receive information about Trust activities and events. To become a member, send £12 to the Trust at Duck Island Cottage, c/o The Store Yard, St James's Park, London SW1A 2BJ. For a copies of issues one or two of the journal only, send a cheque or postal order for £4 per copy (inc p&p) payable to The London Historic Parks and Gardens Trust c/o Todd Longstaffe Gowan, Malplaquet House, 137 Mile End Road, London E1.

The Making of a Garden by Rosemary Verey, Frances Lincoln, £25.

Martha Stewart's Gardening, Ebury Press, £19.99.

The Natural Garden Book by Peter Harper, Gaia, £14.99.

Natural Remedy Book for Dogs and Cats by Diane Stein, The Crossing Press, £13.99.

The New Vegetable Garden by Anna Pavord, Dorling Kindersley, £16.99.

Organic Gardening with Love by Thelma Barlow, Robson Books, £7.99.

Paradise Transformed: The Private Garden for the Twenty-First Century by Gordon Taylor and Guy Cooper, Monacelli Press, £35.

Permaculture magazine (01730 823 311 for subscriptions). *Permaculture* magazine is full of articles and book reviews that help explain the principles of Permaculture and its application in both urban and rural situations. For a free copy, together with the Earth Repair catalogue featuring 200 book titles on ecological gardening and sustainable living, send £1 in stamps and an SAE to Permanent Publications, Hyden House, The Sustainability Centre, East Meon, Hampshire GU32 1HR.

Plant Dreaming Deep by May Sarton, The Women's Press, £8.99.

Pure Style Outside by Jane Cumberbatch, Ryland Peters & Small, £18.99.

Second Nature: A Gardener's Education by Michael Pollan, Bloomsbury £17.99.

The Sense of Wonder by Rachel Carson, The Nature Company, $15.

The Sensuous Garden By Monty Don, Conran Octopus, £20.

Silent Spring by Rachel Carson, Penguin Books, £4.95.

The Small Ecological Garden by Sue Stickland, Search Press/HDRA, £5.95.

Superhints for Gardeners from the Great and Green-Fingered compiled by the Lady Wardington, Michael Joseph, £9.99 (all royalties to the Katherine House Hospice in Banbury).

Terence Conran's Garden DIY, Conran Octopus, £9.99.

Victorian House Style by Linda Osband, David & Charles, £20.

Many specialist garden bookshops or dealers can track down out-of-print titles. Try:

Garden Books, 11 Blenheim Crescent, London W11 (020 7792 1991).

Jill Hedges (01873 860 236).

Ivelet Books, 18 Fairlawn Drive, Redhill, Surrey (Tel: 01737 764 520; Fax 01737 760 140; E-mail ivelet@mcmail.com).

Lloyds of Kew (020 8940 2512).

Mike Park (020 8641 7796).

Plants and seeds

Architectural Plants, Cooks Farm, Nuthurst, Horsham, W Sussex RH13 6LH (01403 891 772).

The Chelsea Gardener (020 7352 5656).

Mr Christopher's (0958 299 914).

CP Ceramics (020 7247 4223).

Sarah Raven's *Cutting Garden Seed Catalogue* (01424 838 181).

C Best (020 7720 2306).

The English Garden Collection (0800 203 0000).

S&B Evans (020 7729 6635).

Jenny's Garden (020 7613 4607).

New Covent Garden Market, Nine Elms, London SW8 is open Mon–Sat,

3 a.m.–10 a.m., parking £3 for non-permit holders. As the market is wholesale, prices are exclusive of VAT.

Peter Nyssen Ltd at 124 Flixton Road, Urmston, Manchester M41 5BG (0161-748 6666) is a great source for bulk-buying bulbs etc. (minimum order of each variety is usually 50, which keeps prices low). Their spring list, containing many varieties of lilies, gladioli, begonias, dahlias and perennials, is available from January.

The Organic Gardening Catalogue, Riverdene Business Park, Molesey Road, Hersham, Surrey KT12 4RG (01932 253 666).

Organics on Ravenscroft Street, London E1 (020 7739 7103).

Quality Plants (020 7720 6943).

Something Special (020 7720 3466).

Simpson's Seeds (01883 715 242).

Stoney Parsons (020 7729 6389).

Suffolk Herbs (01376 572 456).

Traditional Garden Supply Co (01483 273 366).

Miscellaneous

For information on urban agriculture contact Sustain, The Alliance for Better Food and Farming, 94 White Lion Street, London N1 9PF (020 7837 1228).

Karena Batstone and Helen Tindale (020 7944 1004 or 020 7794 1065).

Bio-Light can be ordered for £27.50 plus p&p (01494 771 541).

To find out more about BOG write to Barry Watson, c/o 44 Gale Street, Dagenham, Essex RM9 4NH.

British Trust for Conservation Volunteers (01491 839 766).

Classic Terracotta, The Courtyard, Columbia Road, London, E2.

Earth acupuncture workshops are organised by the Feng Shui Network International (020 7935 8535).

The Feng Shui Company (020 8293 4471).

Green Adventure (020 7277 2529).

Green Gardener offers a telephone advice service on 01603 715 096 as well as mail order packs of nematodes to prey on slugs, vine weevil, aphids, caterpillars, mealy bug and red spider mite among others. Send two first-class stamps to Green Gardener, 41 Strumpshaw Road,

Brundall, Norfolk NR13 5PG for a catalogue showing scary close-up pictures of pests and predators and information on how nematodes work.

Judith Hanna can be contacted for Permaculture advice and garden design (020 8211 0159).

Home Free (0990 748 494).

The Land is Ours, 82 Percy Street, Oxford OX4 3AD is a non-membership, non-hierarchical campaign for the fairer use and distribution of land.

National Association of Allotment and Leisure Gardeners (01536 266 576).

National Gardens Scheme, Hatchlands Park, East Clandon, Guildford, Surrey, GU4 7RT (Tel: 01483 211535, Fax: 01483 211537).

Anthony Noel (020 8693 5002).

A free leaflet with further information on Esso National Tree Week is available from The Tree Council, Titlemore, Unit 3, Deptford Trading Estate, Blackhorse Road, London SE8 5HY or telephone the Esso National Tree Week hotline (020 7828 9928).

Trees for London (020 7287 5407). For further information about the Tree Wardens Scheme contact The Tree Council, 51 Catherine Place, London SW1E 6DY (020 7287 5407).

John Pitt, 44 Marsala Road, London SE13 7AD (020 8690 2245).

Wong Sing Jones, Portobello Road (020 7792 2001).

The Original Wormery is available from The Traditional Garden Supply Company (01483 273 366 for brochure); a DIY kit for adapting a dustbin yourself costs £14.90, plus £6.90 for an additional pack of worms (£6.90) from Original Organics in Devon (01884 841 515).

My body is heavy, but my spirit is light!